"With the same grace and gene...
Meyer's instructive how-we-di...
entrepreneurs in any industry"

"Filled with insights and advice ... ...ror people
running other businesses. . . . Anyone in the hospitality industry would
do well to consult *Setting the Table.*"   —*Wall Street Journal*

"Thought-provoking . . . engrossing."   —*Washington Post Book World*

"This may well be required reading for anyone even remotely interested
in the restaurant biz."   —*Buffalo News*

"Award-winning restaurateur Danny Meyer, cofounder of Union Square
Cafe, Gramercy Tavern, and nine other New York establishments,
delivers instruction in 'enlightened hospitality,' a novel approach that
turns the conventional wisdom about the hospitality business upside
down."   —*Fort Worth Star-Telegram*

"The principles [Meyer] has embraced . . . are as applicable to airlines,
dry cleaners, and cable operators as they are to restaurateurs."
    —*Fast Company*

"While . . . chapter headings . . . evoke . . . common themes of most
leadership books, this book is really . . . more . . . It is . . . the story of
Meyer's restaurant empire and how he got to where he is today, overlaid
with his own views on management and what has worked for him. A
fun and enjoyable read, it provides a good behind-the-scenes view of the
restaurant business"   —*Library Journal*

"Danny Meyer, restaurateur nonpareil, shares his never-fail recipe for
business success."   —*Vanity Fair*

"Danny Meyer builds great restaurants through an old-fashioned mix of
good food and personal service. He's an innovator who has mastered
the art of marketing. He's a leader who has developed world-class
teams. He's a trendsetter who is always one step ahead of the times.
And he's a competitor who partnered with an entire industry to bring
new meaning to the concept of community service."
    —Kenneth I. Chenault, CEO of American Express

"In *Setting the Table*, Danny Meyer outlines the principles of, and the experiences behind, his philosophy of enlightened hospitality, principles that have elevated him to his current position as one of the world's most successful and admired restaurateurs. It is essential reading for anyone interested in restaurants and the importance of the hospitality industry to the economy of the twenty-first century."
—Nicholas Lander, restaurant correspondent
for the *Financial Times*

"Danny Meyer's marvelous book is not just about restaurants, but about how to really learn a business, create a distinctive strategy, engage a team in continually improving that strategy, and integrate the success of a business and the success of its community. This book is full of wisdom for entrepreneurs and for every manager."
—Michael Porter, Bishop William Lawrence
University Professor, Harvard Business School

"Rightly renowned entrepreneur-restaurateur Danny Meyer dazzlingly demonstrates here that he can nourish our minds as well as please our palates. A feast for action-oriented executives, entrepreneurs, and investors."   —Steve Forbes, President and CEO of Forbes

"A rich menu of business tips."   —*Time*

"A memoir–cum–business manual that mixes commonsense object lessons in hospitality with . . . bits of autobiography. . . . [Meyer is] persuasive and interesting, both as a storyteller and as a business adviser."
—*New York Times Book Review*

"Danny Meyer knows something about hospitality. His New York restaurants—Union Square Cafe, Gramercy Tavern, The Modern (in the Museum of Modern Art), among others—all receive high marks, and not just for their food and ambience. One of the keys to his restaurants' great success is their great service. Read how Meyer has accomplished it in his new book"   —*Town & Country*

"Meyer candidly reveals the personal journey and hard-won truths that have made him successful not only at his restaurants (New York's Gramercy Tavern, Union Square Cafe, The Modern) but with the people who work there, too."   —*Newsweek*

"*Setting the Table* is far more than an engaging book about establishing and running restaurants: it is studded with reflections that have wider application to business and management. By basing his enterprise on a cheerful, optimistic vision of human nature, Meyer sets up a direct challenge to the dominant game theorists, transaction-cost economists, and management scholars who put economic man, the rational utility-maximizer, at the heart of their desiccated equations."
—*Observer* (UK)

SETTING THE TABLE

SETTING THE TABLE

The Transforming Power of Hospitality in Business

DANNY MEYER

HARPER

NEW YORK · LONDON · TORONTO · SYDNEY

HARPER

FIRST HARPER PAPERBACK PUBLISHED 2008.

Designed by Helene Berinsky

The Library of Congress has catalogued the hardcover edition as follows:
    Meyer, Danny.
    Setting the table: the transforming power of hospitality in business / Danny Meyer.
      p. cm.
    ISBN-10: 0-06-074275-5
    ISBN-13: 978-0-06-074275-1
    1. Restaurant management. 2. Meyer, Danny. I. Title.
TX911.3.M27M49 2006
647.95068—dc22   2006043529

ISBN: 978-0-06-074276-8 (pbk.)

08 09 10 11 12 ID/RRD 10 9 8 7 6 5 4 3 2 1

For Audrey, Hallie, Charles,
Gretchen, and Peyton
and
For Mary Smith

CONTENTS

SETTING THE TABLE

INTRODUCTION

Over the course of the past twenty-one years I've opened and operated five white-tablecloth restaurants; an urban barbecue joint; a feel-good jazz club; a neo-roadside stand selling frozen custard, burgers, and hot dogs; three modern museum cafés; and an off-premises, restaurant-quality catering company. So far, I haven't had the experience of closing any of them, and I pray I never will.

My business is very much in the public eye; it's highly scrutinized, and it invites passionate opinions from experts and amateurs alike. A debate between people about their favorite restaurant can take on the heat of a political or religious discourse. And if you want to persist and thrive, you'd better not rest on your laurels. Every time you look up, there's another new, eager competitor trying to attract the attention and affection of the public and the media, each hell-bent on tasting and weighing in on the newest thing.

But there's nothing I'd rather be doing. I was born to go into business for myself—and I was destined to find a business that would allow me to share with others my enthusiasm for things I find plea-surable. My craving for the adventures of travel, food, and wine is what first compelled me to do what I do. In fact, like so many other entrepreneurs I've met, I'm not even sure I had much of a choice: a career in the restaurant business was going to tap me on the shoulder even if I hadn't found it first.

All these years later, the delights of the table continue to stimulate me as I pursue my career. But what really challenges me to get up and go to work every day, and has also motivated me to write this book, is my deep conviction about the intense human drive to provide and receive hospitality—well beyond the world of restaurants. Within moments of being born, most babies find themselves receiving the first four gifts of life: eye contact, a smile, a hug, and some food. We receive many other gifts in a lifetime, but few can ever surpass those first four. That first time may be the purest "hospitality transaction" we'll ever have, and it's not much of a surprise that we'll crave those gifts for the rest of our lives. I know I do.

My appreciation of the power of hospitality and my desire to harness it have been the greatest contributors to whatever success my restaurants and businesses have had. I've learned how crucially impor-tant it is to put hospitality to work, first for the people who work for me and subsequently for all the other people and stakeholders who are in any way affected by our business—in descending order, our guests, community, suppliers, and investors. I call this way of setting priorities "enlightened hospitality." It stands some more traditional business approaches on their head, but it's the foundation of every business decision and every success we've had.

Since the beginning, people have told me that in going into the restaurant business, I chose one of the hardest businesses in the world. True, a restaurant has all kinds of moving parts that make it particu-larly challenging. In order to succeed, you need to apply—simultane-ously—exceptional skills in selecting real estate, negotiating, hiring, training, motivating, purchasing, budgeting, designing, manufacturing, cooking, tasting, pricing, selling, servicing, marketing, and hosting. And the purpose of all this is a product that provides pleasure and that people trust is safe to ingest into their bodies. Also, unlike almost any other manufacturer, you are actually present while the goods are being consumed and experienced, so that you can gauge your customers' reactions in real time. That's pretty complex, emotional stuff.

This is not a typical business book, and it's certainly not a how-to book. I don't enjoy being told how—or *that*—I ought to do something; and I'm equally uncomfortable doling out advice without having been asked for it. What follows is a series of life experiences that led to a career in restaurants, which has, in turn, taught me volumes about business and life. Along the way, I've learned powerful lessons and language that have allowed me to lead with intention rather than by intuition. In the process of writing the book, I've done no research, gathered no evidence, and interviewed no one else. But I hope that admission won't stop you from enjoying it.

You may think, as I once did, that I'm primarily in the business of serving good food. Actually, though, food is secondary to something that matters even more. In the end, what's most meaningful is creating positive, uplifting outcomes for human experiences and human relationships. Business, like life, is all about how you make people feel. It's that simple, and it's that hard.

CHAPTER I

The First Course

I'VE LEARNED MORE OF what I know about life from people than from books, and I've learned much of what I know about people from the food they eat. I'm on the road a number of days each year, solo, or with my family, buddies, or colleagues—and when I travel, the first thing I do in my first free moments in a town is visit its food markets, pastry shops, butchers, and grocery stores. I read menus posted outside restaurants. I watch the residents argue back and forth with the merchants over the virtues of their wares. When I meet people who look like locals, I ask them where they'd eat if they had only one or two days in town, as I do. Cultures that care deeply about food often care about life, history, and tradition. I'm constantly on the lookout for local idiosyncrasies, ways of eating that exist nowhere else. And I'm always energized by a hunt for the best version of any local specialty.

In towns throughout Italy's Piedmont I've tasted a meringue-hazelnut cookie called *brutti ma buoni* ("ugly but good"). In Siena I've searched for the supreme *panforte,* a sweet cake. In New York's

Chinatown I walk into butcher shops—not necessarily to buy, but to observe how people select their cuts of meat and and sausage. In Maine, of course, I cherish tiny wild blueberries. In northern Wisconsin I'm unable to resist perch, bass, pike, and Native American fry bread. In Miami, I look for Cuban counter restaurants. In Texas, there isn't time enough to visit all the Mexican taquerias for breakfast. And the barbecue—within a thirty-five-mile radius of Austin in the Texas Hill Country lie five towns I revere, each with a distinctly different style of barbecue. The elements of barbecue are limited—ribs, brisket, pulled pork, chopped pork, minced pork, sausage, chicken, cole slaw, beans, and a handful of side dishes—but it has become an American culinary language with thousands of dialects and accents. I try to understand each variation. During one thirty-six-hour road trip through North Carolina, I tasted fourteen variations on chopped pork, each defined by subtle and dramatic differences in texture, the degree and type of smoke used, the amount of tomato or vinegar in the sauce, how much heat was applied to the meat, as well as how much or how little crackling got chopped up and tossed in. And that's in addition to checking out the many styles of fried chicken, Brunswick stew, and hush puppies on offer.

From as far back as I can remember, I've been eating with my eyes, nose, and mouth. When I was four I fell in love with stone crab at the Lagoon restaurant in Miami Beach. I couldn't stop eating it (and apparently I couldn't stop talking to anyone who would listen about the "cwacked cwab"). Over the next years I remember savoring variations of key lime pie in Key West; eating my first roadside cheeseburger somewhere in the hills outside Santa Barbara; trying Dungeness crab and saline abalone at San Francisco's Fisherman's Wharf; and having a lobster roll in Ogunquit, Maine. I devoured my first custardy quiche lorraine as a seven-year-old when my parents took us to the city of Nancy in France. I tasted bottled water (Evian and Vittel) for the first time in the town of Talloires, and I can also remember exactly how the water of Lake Annecy tasted as I swam in it. I discovered *fraises des bois* (wild strawberries) and crème fraîche at La Colombe d'Or in Saint-Paul de Vence; I tasted a baguette with *saucisson* and pungent *moutarde* in Paris's Jardin des Tuilieries. My writing improved because my mother insisted that I keep a diary of our trip. At the time, I hated doing this. But the diary turned out to be one of the greatest gifts she ever gave me. I wasn't writing about the museums and churches we'd seen. Instead I chose to write about food.

Back in my hometown, St. Louis, I was no less curious about what people ate. When I brought my lunch from home to elementary school, I swapped and shared sandwiches, not because the other kids' lunches were better, but because this was the best way I knew of to learn about another family. I had never heard of Miracle Whip until I traded my braunschweiger on rye with another kid for his baloney sandwich (one slice of Oscar Mayer and Miracle Whip on Tastee white bread). It tasted nothing like the Hellmann's mayonnaise we used at home, and I began to understand something about families, solely on the basis of their preference for Hellmann's or Miracle Whip. I was fascinated to discover that the household across the street used Maull's, the thin, tangy classic St. Louis barbecue sauce, whereas my family was in the more mainstream Open Pit camp, using it as a base to be doctored with other ingredients. I learned that various brands of peanut butter tasted better with certain brands of jelly. I observed that some families chose Heinz ketchup, while others used Hunt's or Brooks. I got to know and cared about the differences in the flavors of these ketchups.

These explorations of food not only taught me about myself and others but were central factors in how and why I chose to go into the restaurant business, and perhaps even in why the restaurants have fared so well. My discoveries have also convinced me that there's always someone out there who has figured out how to make something taste just a little bit better. And I am inspired by both the search and the discovery. The restaurants and other businesses I have opened in New York City—Union Square Cafe, Gramercy Tavern,

Eleven Madison Park, Tabla, Blue Smoke, Jazz Standard, Shake Shack, The Modern, Cafe 2, and Terrace 5 (our cafés for visitors within the Museum of Modern Art), plus Hudson Yards Catering—were all conceived and are all driven by a passion to add something new and compelling to what I call a dialogue between what already exists and what could be. When I decided to create Tabla, our Indian-inspired restaurant, I wrote a list of ten things that one could ordinarily expect of an Indian restaurant in New York—they included a predictable menu; ornate décor with background sitar music; and austere service and hospitality. Then I asked myself what Tabla might add to these expectations—what it could perhaps add to the dialogue New Yorkers already had with Indian restaurants. Although its earliest years were rather rocky—perhaps because we were trying to learn and educate at the same time—Tabla has more than exceeded my goals for it, pioneering "new Indian" cooking in America and building a solid foundation of loyal customers. Perhaps the surest sign of its success is that it has inspired derivative restaurants in New York and beyond.

Whether the subject is Indian spices, new American cuisine, the neighborhood bistro, barbecue, luxe dining, a big-league jazz club, the traditional museum cafeteria, or hamburgers and milk shakes, my passion is always to explore the object of my interest in depth, and then to combine the best of what I've found with something unexpected to create a fresh context. I then look at the result and ask myself and my colleagues what it would take to do this even better. Creating restaurants or even recipes is like composing music: there are only so many notes in the scale from which all melodies and harmonies are created. The trick is to put those notes together in a way not heard before. For us, the ongoing challenge has been to combine the best elements of fine dining with accessibility—in other words, with open arms. This was once a radical concept in my business, where excellent cuisine was almost always paired with stiff arm's-length service. Sometimes, we've moved in the other direction, beginning with the casual atmosphere of a barbecue joint or a shakes-and-burgers stand,

and then attempting to exceed expectations by employing a caring staff and using the finest ingredients. Our formula is a lot tougher to achieve than it sounds, but it can be applied successfully to virtually any business you can name.

WHERE DOES MY HUNGER for good food served with thoughtful care and consistency come from? Why am I so energized by seeking to uncover the best? The answer is my family, though its various influences on me have often been at odds. My three most important male role models were businessmen with profoundly different business philosophies, personalities, and styles.

My parents, Roxanne and Morton Louis Meyer, had spent the first two years of their youthful marriage in the early 1950s living in the city of Nancy, capital of the French province of Lorraine, where my dad was posted as an army intelligence officer. He was the son of Morton Meyer, a St. Louis businessman who had been educated at Princeton and ran a chemical company called Thompson-Hayward. Grandpa Morton was a visionary civic leader and a die-hard Republican—but one who understood the importance of working effectively with Democrats. For instance, he collaborated with Senator Stuart Symington to raise the funds and forge the coalitions necessary to build the St. Louis flood wall. He was a stoic member of the city's establishment, and rarely talked to his family about his work, though he often talked to me about baseball and horse racing. There were no surprises with Grandpa Morton, and I loved him for that. He was in many ways the opposite of his flamboyant, entrepreneurial son, my dad, who also attended Princeton, where he demonstrated a flair for languages, having mastered French, Italian, and Latin (and, as the managing editor of the *Daily Princetonian,* English).

My mother too was the child of a privileged midwestern family. Her father, Irving B. Harris, was a singular man whose combining of social consciousness with business acumen was an enormous influence on me as a human being, and ultimately as a restaurateur. He graduated from Yale, and he made his first fortune before he was forty years old, having cofounded the Toni Home Permanent Company with his brother Neison. They sold it to the Gillette Safety Razor Company in 1948 for what was then an enormous sum: $20 million.

Grandpa Irving's piercing analytical business mind was radically different from my father's intuitive entrepreneurialism. Morty, as my dad was known, always had an abundance of new, imaginative ideas for companies that he would run—or try to run—by himself. Irving, on the other hand, invested in or acquired other peoples' businesses, especially when the ideas that defined these companies were compelling to him. His passion wasn't to operate the companies, but rather to bet on the quality of their senior leadership. Evaluating human potential was every bit as important to him as any business idea.

I adored Grandpa Irving, and I was awed by his otherworldly business success. Through him I became aware of my own competitive zeal and began to believe in my own potential for winning. But for many years I suppressed my love for him and also muffled my own self-actualization, out of misguided deference to my father. Irving and Morty may have once loved each other, but as the years went by they grew to dislike each other intensely. If pressed for his true opinion, Irving would have described Morty as an unpredictable, irresponsible riverboat gambler. For his part, my dad considered his father-in-law an overbearing tyrant who couldn't loosen his all-controlling grip on his daughter, or for that matter on anyone else in the family. Morty called Irving "the boss." Their adversarial relationship turned out to be detrimental to my parents' marriage, which would end twenty-five years after it began.

In 1955, at the conclusion of my dad's overseas military service, my parents were still very much in love with each other and with Europe. Their knowledge of and fondness for France in particular was a powerful bond between them. From a very young age I was lucky to be taken abroad on family vacations, and it was on those trips that

I was first immersed in the unaffected, timeless culture of gracious hospitality represented by European restaurateurs and innkeepers. In France we usually stayed in low-key, family-run inns where the welcome felt loving and the gastronomy was exceptional. Those trips left a lasting impression. The hug that came with the food made it taste even better! That realization would gradually evolve into my own well-defined business strategy—the core of which is hospitality, or being on the guests' side.

Hospitality is the foundation of my business philosophy. Virtually nothing else is as important as how one is made to feel in any business transaction. Hospitality exists when you believe the other person is on your side. The converse is just as true. Hospitality is present when something happens *for* you. It is absent when something happens *to* you. Those two simple prepositions—*for* and *to*—express it all.

In St. Louis my father parlayed his love of all things French into a career as an innovative and successful travel agent. Among his prized collections were what must have been every back issue of *Gourmet, Holiday,* and later *Travel and Leisure;* he also built on a wide range of friendships he and my mother had established with French innkeepers. His agency, Open Road Tours, packaged customized driving trips, often in conjunction with *Relais de Campagne,* a network of lovely family-operated inns around France. (*Relais de Campagne* later evolved into *Relais et Châteaux,* now a prestigious international network of small luxury hotels. My dad remained active with *Relais et Châteaux* for years; he was enormously proud when his own small hotel in St. Louis, the Seven Gables Inn, became affiliated with *Relais et Châ-*

teaux in the late 1980s.) This was long before such excursions off the beaten path became common in the travel industry. Dad exulted in planning these driving tours of the countryside; he'd note exactly where travelers would stumble upon a certain vineyard, a worthwhile museum, or a particularly good bistro. His clients loved his attention to detail, his business thrived and I was bursting with pride when I told people my dad had become president of the American Society of Travel Agents (ASTA), an important trade organization.

At home, too, he and my mom were Eurocentric: They often hosted cocktail parties and dinner parties for friends and business colleagues from France, Italy, and Denmark, who either were in town on business or had made a detour to St. Louis just to see us. For several years our house was home to the grown children of French innkeepers. By day these young people would help out in Dad's office with translations and administrative tasks, and by night they would act as au pairs for my sister, Nancy; my brother, Tommy; and me. They became, for me, informal cultural ambassadors from a wondrous place called France. French was always being spoken around the house, either by our guests or by my parents (who used it at the dinner table especially when they wanted to discuss something not meant for our ears). Our neurotic, inbred French poodle, Ratatouille, was named after my dad's favorite Provençal dish. To this day the pungent smell and sound of garlic, olive oil, and eggplant sizzling in a skillet will evoke powerful memories in me. There was always a bottle of Beaujolais-Villages on the table, and when dad and I cooked a chateaubriand on the grill and the fat-induced flames shot too high, he brought them under control in his own idiosyncratic fashion—by dousing the steaks with whatever bottle of red wine he happened to be drinking at that moment. Which, of course, caused more flames.

My father was unquestionably my childhood hero: a hedonist, a gastronome, and a man who cherished and passionately savored life. He loved the excitement and risk of the racetrack and gave me a taste for it, even when I was too young to place bets legally. Going to the track was a Meyer family tradition of long standing; my dad's parents spent most of every August in Saratoga, New York, going to the track six days a week for nearly a month. Dad also took risks as a businessman. He was always coming up with exciting new ideas based on his love of travel and food, and on his constant drive to share his finds with others. At one point Open Road Tours had offices and staffs in Chicago, Los Angeles, New York, and Paris. Later, it opened offices all over Europe; and I'll never forget the day he proudly showed off an Open Road stock certificate bearing the name of Ava Gardner as an investor. He had a publicist in New York named Ethel Aaron who promoted his business in fascinating ways, like having my dad cast as an imposter on *To Tell the Truth*. As an eight-year-old I was proud to boast to my friends that my dad was an imposter on television.

I never fully understood how or why, but sometime in the late 1960s, when I was still a young boy, Open Road Tours went bankrupt. I remember abundant tears and shame, but few details. I heard comments like, "We expanded too quickly"; and I had thoughts like, "My hero failed." My paternal grandparents were torn apart too: their only two sons had been in business together—my father as president and his younger brother, my uncle "Bo," as vice president. Whatever events had led to the bankruptcy had also driven a sharp wedge between the two brothers. I was crushed when my Aunt Lois, my Uncle Bo, and my first cousins—whom I loved dearly—moved from St. Louis to rebuild their lives in Washington, D.C. This was another confusing and painful consequence of the failed business. My mother was anguished, and her disappointment and disapproval were apparent. Business details were not openly discussed, but the family's bruises were deeply felt.

In 1970, when I was twelve, my father leaped into the hotel business, in Italy. Despite the pleas of my mother and with Irving's begrudging help in the form of a $1 million loan, he committed himself to long leases on one hotel in Rome and another in Milan. He was certain that becoming a hotelier would be his ticket to fortune.

My mom—correctly—maintained that it promised nothing more than protracted absences from home. There was always some reason my dad had to go to Italy. Each time the hotel workers went on strike, he flew to Rome or Milan to help make beds. Business flagged and lagged, and although he was spending half a month at a time away from his family to address problems, it inevitably proved impossible for him to operate a hotel business across two continents. At an enormous financial cost and an even greater emotional cost, my father finally found a buyer for his two leases. He then went on to his next idea.

In 1972, still irrepressibly optimistic, my father created another new business, called Caesar Associates. This new company would sell packaged group tours at a deep discount for a very narrow niche of travelers known as "interliners"—airline employees and their families. As members of the International Air Transport Association (IATA)—an industry trade group—interliners could fly standby at unbelievably low rates. Dad's business model was simple but original. He aggregated all the discounts to which members of IATA were entitled and packaged trips lasting up to two weeks. In addition to low airfares, he negotiated rock-bottom rates for hotels, ground transport, sightseeing, shopping, and dining. The value he added was to offer highly imaginative itineraries and use the underlying buying power of group travel to create an extraordinary rapport between price and quality. He hired sparkling young tour guides at each destination, and he kept his clients informed of travel opportunities by writing an endless stream of marketing collaterals. He was a terrific writer and editor, and his direct mailings inspired me—years later—to create my own newsletter as a way to reach out to and widen our base at Union Square Cafe. He was always after me to correct every grammatical mistake I made or delete every superfluous word I used in the USC Newsletter. (Doubtless he'd have some editorial comments about this book as well!)

Caesar Associates actually thrived for many years, with outposts in London, Paris, Copenhagen, Madrid, and Rome. But this success wasn't enough for my father. Having failed to learn some critical lessons from his earlier business failures in the 1960s and 1970s, he gambled the fortunes of his entire business on another new one, involving risky and questionable real estate and hotel deals back in St. Louis. He eventually owned two hotels in St. Louis, one of which—the Seven Gables Inn, with its French restaurant, Chez Louis—met with critical acclaim. But the other hotel—the Daniele Hilton, with its mediocre London Grill—was a failure on every count. My father had leveraged his entire company to purchase these hotels, and also to purchase a medical building in Clayton, Missouri, which he planned to reimagine and redevelop into something big. However, by the time he had emptied the building of its existing rent-paying tenants, the bottom had fallen out of the economy. His funders dropped out, but not before suing him. Although Dad may have been an inventive entrepreneur, he did not have the necessary emotional skills or discipline, and he failed to surround himself with enough competent, loyal, trustworthy colleagues whose skills and strengths would have compensated for his own weaknesses. By 1990, shortly before he died of lung cancer at the age of fifty-nine, he was once again bankrupt. Once again, he had to inform his family—his second wife, Vivian, and his three children and their spouses—about a failure. We all had a painful sense of déjà vu.

LOOKING BACK, I REALIZE that gambling is a metaphor for how my father ran his businesses, and my deep fear of repeating his mistakes has always colored the way I run mine. Because each of his doomed experiences was marked by overly rapid expansion, I have always been afraid to expand my business too quickly. I'm not risk-averse, but I have tight self-control, and I am not ordinarily a gambler. I go to Saratoga one weekend a year, and losing even a $10 bet at the track there bothers me enormously. Still, I've been willing to make a $1 million bet on a new restaurant. I'm far more inclined to take risks when I'm essentially betting on myself, but I can do that only because

I've surrounded myself with highly talented people of solid integrity. I'm also far more confident in my ability to handicap humans than horses. My father, on the other hand, never felt compelled to surround himself with people who were better or smarter at anything than he believed he was. He had a greater need to feel important, to be agreed with, to be the king. It was no coincidence that he named his company after Caesar. While I, too, love sitting in the captain's chair, my greatest joy comes not from going it alone, but from leading an ensemble. Hospitality is a team sport.

There were, it must be said, many aspects of my parents' marriage that kept them together for a quarter of a century, including shared interests that left a lasting impression on me and would later inform many of my own business choices. Both of my parents loved modern art, and each had a keen eye for collecting. Thanks to their wise selection and prescient purchases, I had the privilege of growing up amid works by Joseph Albers, Morris Louis, Jasper Johns, Alexander Calder, Man Ray, Henry Moore, Joel Shapiro, Cy Twombly, Helen Frankenthaler, Pierre Alechinsky, and Gerhard Richter. In 1968 Mom, along with a close family friend, Joan Loeb, opened Forsyth Gallery, a gallery of contemporary art that, for St. Louis, was groundbreaking. My older sister, Nancy; my younger brother, Tommy; and I were exposed to fine art through this gallery and through museumgoing and family conversation. Each one of us developed exceptional fluency in and appreciation for the world of fine art—and learned to share our enthusiasm with others.

My mother and father also brought to our home a shared joy and love for music. It's difficult for me to remember sitting in our den at any time when the hi-fi was not playing the original-cast album for a show by, say, Rodgers and Hammerstein, Hart, Loesser, Lerner and Loewe, Newley and Bricuse, McDermott, Kander and Ebb, Sondheim, Bernstein, or Gershwin. And when those records weren't spinning, we were being treated to Frank Sinatra, Barbra Streisand, Peggy Lee, the Modern Jazz Quartet, or Oscar Peterson. Each hot and humid summer in St. Louis brought trips to see musicals at the outdoor Muny Opera (the highlight for me was drinking a refreshing half-pint carton of Pevely lemonade during intermission). During the winter, my parents would take us downtown to the American Theater for road versions of Broadway shows. A point of contention between them was that my father—who knew all the lyrics to all the songs—could not come close to carrying a tune. Whenever he had had too much to drink, he would sing off-key and with increasing drama and volume. This was occasionally amusing, but only for a while, and he rarely stopped when he should have.

And then there was travel. My parents took vacations alone together at least twice each year, and with us in tow another three times a year. The Christmas and Easter vacations were often spent in Florida (in or around Miami, where my dad could be within striking distance of Hialeah or Gulfstream Park so that he could bet on the daily double). Every summer meant a family vacation of up to three weeks. We went to California when I was six (Pea Soup Andersen's in Solvang and sourdough bread and abalone at Fisherman's Wharf made an indelible impression). We went to France when I was seven (*everything* made an impression: the hot chocolate at breakfast, so bitter that it needed two cubes of sugar; the yeasty baguettes; the sour crème fraîche; and the salty, deep yellow butter). We went to New England when I was eight (fried Ipswich clams, lobster rolls, drawn butter, creamy clam chowder, and golden Indian pudding).

But as the years went on, travel increasingly meant time that my dad was away for two or sometimes three weeks at a time. Understandably, my mother was lonely and upset during his absences. Though I rarely let on, I was sympathetic to her. We were fond of playing competitive games of Scrabble, and we sat down together each and every weeknight at five-thirty to watch Walter Cronkite deliver the *CBS Evening News*. Like her, I was absorbed by the day's events, reading the conservative *Globe-Democrat* every morning and the liberal *St. Louis Post-Dispatch* every afternoon. Vietnam, the antiwar movement, civil rights, Lyndon Johnson's beleaguered presidency, the return of Richard Nixon, and of course the St. Louis Cardinals then dominated the news. The two of us were on the same page politically, and those moments were a sanctuary in our relationship. But in those days I reflexively defended my dad for anything and everything, and as my parents' relationship grew more and more strained, so too did mine with my mom. I found myself, painfully, in the middle of our family's growing rift. But as the middle child, torn in every possible direction, I was developing useful skills for shuttle diplomacy, negotiating, and contending with adversity. These skills would later serve me well in business and in life.

Partly because of my physical development, and partly because of my insatiable hunger for new foods (and the comfort I got from eating them), I put on some weight at about age twelve. I remember my mother taking me to Famous-Barr to shop for clothes in what used to be called the "husky" department. Increasingly, she expressed concern over how much I was eating. But being asked to watch what I ate felt like a punishment and only impelled me to eat more. Back then, people dieted primarily by counting calories, and so Grandpa Irving gave me a book listing the caloric value of practically every food on earth. He offered to pay me $1 for every pound I lost and challenged me to keep a chart with a running total of all calories I'd consumed each day. My mom began to serve my sandwiches open-faced, on super-thin slices of Pepperidge Farm white bread.

But on Sunday mornings, my brother Tom (often my partner in culinary crime), and I would wake up at six o'clock and very quietly tiptoe to the refrigerator in search of leftovers. We'd make melted American cheese sandwiches in the broiler (frying them would have produced a buttery aroma strong enough to awaken everybody). Or, without breaking the seal on the butcher paper, I'd deftly open a new package of Usinger's Milwaukee braunschweiger, a staple in our home; snag a slice; and then carefully reassemble the package. We were never apprehended by my otherwise omniscient mother.

Despite the tension surrounding the topic of food during my early teens, no one eventually took more pleasure in the success of my restaurants than my mother—except, perhaps Irving, who had initially advised me to stay out of such a "rotten business" but later expressed enormous pride in the restaurants until the day he died, at age ninety-four, in 2004. Ironically, by making me keenly aware of what I ought to eat and not eat, the two of them were unwittingly reinforcing my love and passion for food: the taste of it and what it meant to me both as nourishment and as a symbol of love.

When I attended Camp Nebagamon in northern Wisconsin, where I spent six magical summers, I learned to cook over an open fire. It was an exceptional all-boys camp that my father, uncles, and cousins from both sides of the family had attended. Camp Nebagamon reinforced the same ethical and moral codes I learned at home. The Sunday night campfire, known as the council fire, was a weekly ritual in which campers were encouraged to present skits that focused on ethics. These skits taught me to make a spiritual connection to nature and the environment.

Friday night was cookout night, and we learned to chop our own logs; forage for kindling wood; prep our ingredients; and grill, smoke, and roast meats in a Dutch oven or in handmade foil pockets buried under the coals. We learned how to bake cakes in an aluminum "reflector oven" that was set up adjacent to the pit, and designed to reflect the heat of the open fire down onto the cake pans.

Each cabin elected a representative to vie for supremacy in the camp's annual Chef's Cap competition, Nebagamon's top culinary honor. I was chosen to be my cabin's representative when I was twelve, and I did everything but take reservations: I painted a sign, dug the pit, raked the surrounding area, and designed the campsite to look as neat and welcoming as an outdoor restaurant. I prepared, cooked, and served an entire three-course meal. When it was over, I was judged not just for the food, but by how well I cleaned the pans and plates, put out the fire, refilled the pit, and—most important—by whether I would be able to "leave the campsite neater than I had found it." (That concept remains, for me, one of the most significant measures of success in business, and in life.) For the competition, all the camper chefs were given identical bags filled with ingredients: four potatoes, a whole chicken, four lemons, a stick of butter, two ribs of celery, two carrots, one tomato, a box of cake mix, and some salt and pepper.

We cooked all day, and I wanted to win badly. I made a juicy lemon chicken and potatoes cooked under the coals in a Dutch oven, served with a well-seasoned tomato salad and a vanilla layer cake baked over the open fire; and I won. Actually, I tied for first place. My chicken was by far the best-looking and best-tasting. (The truth should now be told—I'd rubbed the bird with a tablespoon of lemon-pepper seasoning, surreptitiously supplied to me by one of the camp nurses I had befriended at the infirmary, called the Waldorf-Castoria.) But I was docked several points because at the last minute one of my two cakes slid off its shelf in the reflector oven and fell into the fire. I managed to save the cake, but I was unable to brush off all the ashes before applying the frosting. Still, each bite provided an interesting texture and smoky flavor!

As a young teenager back home in St. Louis, I cooked for friends. I would take something as simple as a hot dog or a knockwurst and slice it down the middle, stuffing it with cheese and wrapping it with a slice of bacon before grilling it in the barbecue pit. I created my own signature barbecue sauce by mixing Open Pit with ketchup, crushed garlic, Worcestershire sauce, brown sugar, a dash of cayenne, and loads of cracked black pepper. I learned to make pizza from scratch. I was proud of my recipe for tacos. My friends enjoyed what they ate when they came to our house (except for my mother's broiled chicken livers), and most of them seemed to get a kick out of the fact that each visit would be spent playing basketball, football, hockey, or Ping-Pong—and then cooking.

During my adolescence, food continued to figure prominently

in my social life. In the tenth grade I took cooking lessons in home economics, and as one of only two guys in the class I furthered more than just my culinary interests. That year I had transferred from the all-boys St. Louis Country Day School, where I had been a top student, to its coed archrival, John Burroughs School. Burroughs was an excellent and highly demanding independent school—presenting me for the first time with female distractions in the classrooms and hallways. My academic performance dipped dramatically. I was now fifteen years old, and what mattered to me most were girls; pickup games of street hockey; football on the lawn; tennis; and going to bed with my transistor radio tuned to KMOX and glued to my ear, as Jack Buck called that night's St. Louis Cardinals game or Dan Kelly announced for the St. Louis Blues. Yet a constant theme in my life was always food: Imo's pizza, Ted Drewes frozen custard, and Steak 'n' Shake. Steak 'n' Shake seemed to be where my friends and I all ended up every weekend night, throwing back shoestring fries, steak burgers with cheese, and shakes. Were those necessarily the best hamburgers to be found anywhere? It didn't matter, because the nights at Steak 'n' Shake with curbside service in our own cars were the best hamburger experiences I had ever known. (Decades later, my memories of Ted Drewes and Steak 'n' Shake inspired me to create Shake Shack in New York's Madison Square Park.)

For more upscale fare, I took dates to Giovanni's, in the Italian neighborhood known as "the Hill." The toasted ravioli, cavatelli, and veal saltimbocca were always delicious, but the food was almost secondary: the owner, Giovanni Gabriele, made me feel like a young VIP in front of my dates, and the clincher was that I had check-signing privileges because my dad, a regular, loved the place and had his own house account there. Occasionally I'd accompany him to Giovanni's. He'd always order a bottle of Gattinara, Nozzole Chianti Classico, or Corvo; and though I was underage, I always managed to get a lesson in red wine, which of course required that I consume at least half a glass when the waiter wasn't looking. My father would take care of the rest of the bottle. It was wonderful being with him in a place where his self-esteem was so high, and where he was treated like the king he wanted to be.

Now, many years later I know that I maintained an almost unnatural loyalty to my father long after it was healthy to do so, sometimes against my own best interests. One way I managed to keep him propped up on his pedestal as his businesses and marriage failed was not to beat him at anything. We would play card games like casino or cribbage, and he would almost invariably beat me. There were years when I was good enough at tennis to play varsity singles, but still I would not allow myself to beat him. Whatever the transaction, the deck of the subconscious was stacked against me: I would choke and he would win.

AS MY SENIOR YEAR AT John Burroughs School began, my underachieving high school performance culminated in my applying to only three colleges. On the day acceptance letters were received, I was in for a crushing disappointment: Princeton and Brown had both rejected me, and I had done no better than earn a spot on the waiting list at Trinity College in Hartford, Connecticut. Irving called with an offer to get me into University of Chicago, where he was an active donor. I didn't want to do that and in fact couldn't even contemplate it; my father would have viewed my going to Chicago as a defection to the other team. Furthermore, I didn't want to start life on my own at the beck and call of my powerful grandfather.

I knew what I had to do: I got down on my knees and wrote a pleading, heartfelt letter to Trinity. My effort paid off and I was accepted. This spared me the disaster of being accepted nowhere. But the message was clear: the slumbering athletic, competitive spirit within me finally needed to wake up and come out of hibernation. Once I graduated from John Burroughs in 1976 and left home, it did.

I got nearly straight A's during my first term at Trinity. I felt an intense need to prove to Trinity, and to myself, that it had been mistaken not to accept me outright. I was motivated both by personal pride and by anger. I remember on many occasions taking inspiration from my childhood baseball hero Bob Gibson on the mound for the Cardinals, brushing back a player who'd hit a home run in his previous at-bat. To this day, my surest form of motivation comes from someone telling me I'm not measuring up.

Following my sophomore year I went to Rome to work as a host at Caesar Associates and a guide for my father's interline tours. (All three Meyer siblings got to take this job upon reaching age twenty: my sister Nancy, having already been a foreign exchange student in Denmark, chose to work in Copenhagen; and my brother Tom, having been an exchange student as a teenager in France, went to Paris.) Our three packages in Italy varied, including visits to Naples, Sorrento, Capri, and Pompeii, and an intensive tour of Rome. Our premier trip was the "Gran Giro d'Italia," a comprehensive bus tour to Assisi, Florence, and Venice, and then back to Rome.

To me this was hospitality boot camp, a rigorous but excellent training for satisfying the emotional needs of my dad's customers, who would typically arrive jet-lagged and crabby. After meeting them at the airport following their overnight flight to Rome, we'd board a tour bus, and I'd get on the microphone to describe the trip ahead. Next it was on to the hotel, where I'd help them all check in and settle into their rooms for a nap. Then after a few hours, I'd gather the woozy bunch together for an afternoon welcome meeting over Asti Spumante and rum cake. My first priority was to identify the crankiest clients and win them over. Having discovered a number of mom-and-pop Roman trattorias on my own (my favorite was La Taverna da Giovanni, where I spent even my days off happily feasting on *spaghetti alla carbonara* and roast pig), I could tell my travelers that I knew of an amazing family-run place that very few tourists ever found. They loved that. I improvised on my dad's official itineraries when I could, and steered the travelers to lunch or dinner at one of these authentic restaurants. Not only would I get to eat for free, but the owners would typically pay me a commission (*una mancia*) of 1,000 lire for every guest I delivered. A thousand lire bought me a cappuccino, a brioche, and a *sugo d'albicocca* (apricot nectar) for breakfast at my favorite coffee bar. I loved earning tips, and this was an easy and enjoyable way to earn extra cash, not just from the trattoria owners but also from my grateful tourists, who rewarded me handsomely for making their visit special, and for just being nice.

My father, thanks to a specious deal he had struck with Lineas Aereas de Nicaragua (LANICA) making him a "consultant" for the airline (at a fee of $1 a year), now qualified himself for those incredible interliner airfares. And as a child of a consultant for LANICA, I also qualified to fly to Europe for just $44 dollars round-trip until I was twenty-one; throughout my college years I could not afford *not* to fly Pan Am to Italy for any long weekend. I would just call my dad, and he'd handwrite a $44 ticket and mail it to me. I learned Italian by taking classes at school and from traveling in Italy. I fell madly in love with Rome, Florence, and Venice.

During my sophomore year at Trinity College, in 1977, my parents at last separated. Another painful issue was that by this time, my dad was increasingly expressing himself loudly in public settings, driving somewhat recklessly, and drinking more than he could handle. He continued to make foolish choices in his business life. We were drifting apart. As my family divided, I increasingly comforted myself with food.

By the second semester of my junior year I was headed back to Rome. This time it was to spend four months at Trinity's campus there, ostensibly to study international politics, the Italian language, and art history. But my real interests were, first, being far away from home; and second, as I would soon learn, eating. I memorized every Roman entry in the red Michelin Guide to Italy (even though most of Michelin's selections were fancier than the kind of trattorias I preferred). I was living in a small room in a convent that Trinity rented for its American students on the Aventine Hill. I slept under a glow-in-the-dark crucifix (I reckoned I was the first Jew from St. Louis to have done so), and it was a special day when the new pope, John Paul II, chose our convent as a place to come and bless. (I'll never forget getting knocked off a chair by the stiff arm of a papal security guard as I stood above the crowd and snapped photos of my classmates being blessed by the pope. Evidently one does not stand on chairs during a papal blessing!)

I went out for dinner almost every night, wandering every obscure *via*, alone or with friends, reviewing the menu boxes outside every trattoria. I was always searching for the one unique thing at any restaurant. While I was living in and later returning often to Rome (thanks to my IATA card), I was intrigued to discover that every trattoria had basically the same menu. Each had *spaghetti alla carbonara*, its *bucatini all'amatriciana*, its *melanzane alla parmigiana*, and its *coda alla vaccinara*. I could see that trattorias in Rome distinguished themselves by nuances: how each chef cooked a classic dish. Furthermore, the trattorias possessed a subtle quality that was every bit as important as the food: a genuinely welcoming spirit that led to the formation of a community of regulars.

It's hard not to fall in love with a society that is confident about and content with its traditions, so that it doesn't need to eat a different kind of food every day at lunch and every evening at dinner. I came to love the ritual of dining each evening at the same time with the same people and eating the same foods. This runs counter to the compulsion in our culture to continually change channels. When it came time for me to open my own restaurant for New Yorkers, there was no question in my mind that I would embrace all I had learned in Italy and that the Roman trattoria would be my richest inspiration.

But I wasn't there yet. After graduating from Trinity in 1980, I moved to Chicago, where, after a brief stint at the public station, WTTW-TV, in pursuit of a possible career in journalism, I became the $214-a-week Cook County field coordinator for John Anderson's presidential campaign. Anderson, the nominee of the Independent Party, was running against Jimmy Carter and Ronald Reagan. It was a brutally intense experience that fired up my passion for politics and also taught me a thing or two about management—even though my candidate was on the wrong end of a landslide.

Learning to manage volunteers—to whom, absent a paycheck, ideas and ideals were the only currency—taught me to view all employees essentially as volunteers. Today, even with compensation as a motivator, I know that anyone who works for my company *chooses* to do so because of what we stand for. I believe that anyone who is qualified for a job in our company is also qualified for many other jobs at the same pay scale. It's up to us to provide solid reasons for our employees to want to work for us, over and beyond their compensation.

I decided that my next stop had to be New York, a city I had always loved to visit for stimulating weekends while I was at Trinity. I'd drive down for a day of museumgoing or horse racing, and an evening of restaurants, Broadway theater, or jazz. I loved the pulse of New York and decided to try living there for a year or so. This time I didn't object to Grandpa Irving's help, and he lined up a job with Checkpoint Systems, a small but growing company that manufactured and sold electronic tags and pressure-sensitive labels to stop shoplifters. (My grandfather had been an early principal investor.)

I was hired as a special projects manager at a salary of $16,500 in January 1981; and I spent most of my time assisting the sales force. By the end of my first year, another position opened up and I was offered a sales job in charge of the entire New York territory. I soon became Checkpoint's top salesman, covering the New York metropolitan area and earning nearly $100,000 in commissions. I quickly got to know every branch of every family tree of every New York retailing family that owned drugstores, clothing stores, grocery stores, coat stores, and shoe stores. I was making cold calls, meeting people, and getting to know every obscure corner of New York. As I had learned during Anderson's campaign, I was reaching out and building a constituency.

This was another indispensable lesson that would serve me well as a restaurateur.

I also became Checkpoint's expert on training grocery store chains in the ways and means of preventing loss. Thereafter, I was sent out to travel and train around the United States. Naturally, I spent every free moment checking out local restaurants, and I made some important gastronomic discoveries. In Detroit, I visited the Golden Mushroom and the London Chop House. In California, I tasted food cooked by the chefs Wolfgang Puck, Alice Waters, Mark Miller, and Jeremiah Tower, who were at the forefront of the "new American cuisine." At Spago, I tried Puck's new wave pizza with duck sausage and shiitake mushrooms. This was no fancy restaurant, but it was fun—an exciting place to experience an emerging unfussy American cuisine based on the simple, fresh Italian and French cooking that I had grown up loving, combined with seasonal local California produce. A lot was happening out west, while New York was still primarily rooted in old-school French and Italian cooking.

Still, I preferred New York to any other place. I was Checkpoint's top salesman for three years running and was consistently motivated by the competitive urge to lead the pack. Earning top commissions was the icing on the cake; and with no one to support but myself, I was putting money in the bank. I loved art and went to the Museum of Modern Art as often as possible taking advantage of my grandfather's annual gift to me of a membership there. By attending opening parties at the museum, I also learned that New York's social life consisted of more than Upper East Side bars. The joy I was experiencing each day by setting my own personal and professional agenda made it increasingly clear to me that I would never go to work for someone else. Even at Checkpoint, where I officially reported to sales directors, I worked for myself out of my own walk-up apartment on the East Side. I had built my own little business within a business, creating my own schedule, plotting my own tactics, and exceeding whatever goals were set for me. My dad and both of my grandfathers had worked for themselves, and they were all presidents of their companies. My mother had owned her own art gallery. I had an uncontainable drive to win that was now in high gear. What I loved most about Checkpoint was that my hard work and independence provided financial rewards and opportunities for seeking my own pleasure. I was devouring New York. I could take myself on little adventures all over town, and I loved being able to eat out and learn. I'd map out an entire day of sales calls, basing my schedule on where to eat in whatever borough I had to visit that day. It could be a Greek diner in Astoria, a Jewish deli, or Popeye's Fried Chicken in Brooklyn, or even an Olive Garden in Peekskill (that was the best restaurant in Peekskill at the time). By night I'd dine, following the advice of the *New York Times*'s restaurant critic Mimi Sheraton, or, better still, making a sport of discovering new places on my own. I was still taking opportunities to travel to Europe (now flying for $149 each way on People Express) so that I could explore food. I took one seventeen-day road trip with two close friends—Connor Seabrook and Zander Grant—driving from Paris to Rome and back. The itinerary had to do exclusively with finding great places to eat. This gastronomic adventure had been largely designed for us by my father, and it felt good to reconnect over something he was so good at. The dollar was very strong, enabling three ravenous young men to eat abundantly and well for modest prices. I loved finding good value in places off the beaten path; in fact, I was uninterested in dining at the most expensive places. I always drank Saint Veran instead of Pouilly-Fuissé, pinot bianco instead of pinot grigio, and Saint Aubin instead of Puligny-Montrachet.

Back in New York I was cooking like crazy out of cookbooks and *Gourmet*. I lived in Yorkville, a neighborhood famous for its German butchers and Hungarian spice stores. I took cooking classes from an exceptional cook, a dynamic woman named Andrée Abramoff. She was an Egyptian-born Jew who had split her childhood between France and Egypt; and her restaurant, Andrée's Mediterranean Cuisine, was one of my favorites. She taught cooking out of her townhouse on East Seventy-fourth Street, which also housed Andrée's. There, I learned to make spanakopita, bouillabaisse, and rack of lamb. I enrolled in a restaurant management class at the New York Restaurant School with Connor, who was in U.S. Trust's bank training program. We discussed opening a restaurant together; he'd be the money guy and I'd be the food and wine guy. That plan fell apart when Connor dropped out of the class after just two sessions. He thought better of going into the restaurant business and decided to get an MBA instead. Sad for me; wise for him.

In late 1983, Checkpoint asked me to lead the launch of an office in London. I was at a crossroads. Working abroad was a tempting opportunity, but my dream as I was growing up had never been to catch shoplifters, on any continent. My years at Checkpoint had been a period of great personal growth. I had learned that it was important to me and hugely enjoyable to compete in the business arena. I had learned how good it felt to earn, have, and spend my own money and not have to ask or feel obligated to anybody else for it. I had gained a world of independence and a new self-confidence. I was in my early twenties, making $125,000 a year, with no obligations except to myself. Each year, I invested a good chunk of the commissions I had earned in Checkpoint's publicly traded stock, which during my tenure there soared from around $2 to nearly $12 dollars per share. I was earning money for and from the company, and that had felt great. But it was time to move on to something different. It was time to grow up and pursue my life's career. I enrolled in a Stanley Kaplan prep course for the law boards. My new plan was to practice law as prelude to a career in politics or public service. That was my fantasy. In reality, I was lost. The night before taking the LSAT, I had dinner at Elio's on Second Avenue with my aunt and uncle, Virginia and Richard Polsky; and my grandmother Rosetta Harris. I chose not to drink wine because the test was being given early in the morning. I told my uncle, "I can't believe I'm doing this LSAT thing tomorrow. I don't even want to be a lawyer."

"So why are you?" Richard Polsky asked in an exasperated tone. "You know you don't want to be a lawyer. Why don't you just do what you've been thinking about doing your whole life?"

"What's that?" I asked him.

"What do you mean, 'What's that'? Since you were a child, all you've ever talked or thought about is food and restaurants. Why don't you just open a restaurant?"

The idea felt, at the same time, both foreign and like an absolute bull's-eye. The next morning, completely relaxed, I took the LSAT, and then I never bothered to apply to a single law school. From that moment on, I was off to the races.

IT WOULD BE NEARLY two years before I would have a location, a name, or a menu for my restaurant, but instinctively I knew how I would run the business. It would reflect the confluence of interests, passion, pleasure, and family dynamics that had shaped my life.

I would enter the restaurant business with a potent combination of my father's entrepreneurial spirit and my grandfathers' legacies of strong business leadership, social responsibility, and philanthropic activism. And I would have a chance to give others two things I craved: good food and warm hospitality. I had begun to understand that business and life have a lot in common with a hug. The best way to get a good one was first to give one.

I would also have the good fortune of entering the restaurant industry during its fertile period of revolutionary change. Only in the past two decades has being a restaurateur become viewed as a valid entrepreneurial pursuit and also a career that fascinates people. Not only are chefs and restaurateurs celebrated; restaurants themselves have become celebrities in their communities. That transformation has given me a chance to pursue and accomplish some truly exciting things.

CHAPTER 2

In Business

My FIRST JOB IN the restaurant business began in the bitterly cold, snowy January of 1984, as daytime assistant manager at Pesca, a San Francisco–inspired–Italian seafood restaurant on East Twenty-second Street. Among my tasks were taking reservations, typing out the daily specials, running to the copy store to get them Xeroxed, and stuffing them in Lucite holders to be presented at each table. I would check in waiters, host lunch by greeting and seating mostly regular guests, and—when I was really lucky—get to sit in on menu-planning meetings or wine tastings in the kitchen.

The busy restaurant—which had a successful eight-year run—was good, and ahead of its time. It offered fresh, imaginative "Cal-Ital" seafood dishes; had a breezy style; and was in an emerging trendy neighborhood. I adored meeting many fascinating people from the worlds of advertising, publishing, and photography—the new denizens of a neighborhood that had just been named the "Flatiron district" by *New York* magazine. My paycheck—$250 a week, down a bit from the $125,000 a year I'd earned as a commissioned salesman—did take some adjusting to and getting used to. But I had to pinch myself: at last I was in the restaurant business, and I was jazzed.

I was at Pesca for just eight months, but in that short time I worked alongside some extraordinary people who would change my life. On my very first day on the job I literally ran into the woman who would become my wife, four years later, and then the remarkable mother of our four children. I was pounding down the narrow staircase to the basement office to pick up Pesca's ringing reservation line when I encountered a beautiful, perky waitress named Audrey Heffernan making her way up. For three seconds we looked intently into each other's eyes, and then we moved along. Suddenly I felt very optimistic about my new vocation. I couldn't wait for day two on the job.

The next day, however, she was gone. A regional theater and commercial actress who had performed leading roles in *Babes in Toyland, Fiddler on the Roof,* and *Oklahoma!,* Audrey was on the road, this time to play Sarah Brown in a production of *Guys and Dolls* in Indianapolis. She had been at Pesca for two years and was so beloved by the owner, Eugene Fracchia—who called her "Saint Audrey"—that there was always a place for her when she came back to New York. I happened to be manning the reservation lines one day when she called Eugene to tell him she'd soon be home and wondered when she could get back on the waiters' schedule. I wasted no time delivering the message to the general manager, Douglas Scarborough, who found a way to put Audrey back on the schedule almost immediately. She and I flirted for months without acknowledging our feelings or making any kind of move. In late April, as a ruse to get Audrey to see my apartment, I sent out invitations to a dozen members of Pesca's wait staff for my annual "Meyer at the Wire" Kentucky Derby party. I was utterly dismayed to learn that her brother was getting married on that very day. I would have to wait a little longer to see her outside the restaurant.

Another person whom I met at Pesca and who had an enormous influence on me was the restaurant's bar manager, Gordon Dudash. He possessed a soul of pure hospitality that was exquisite and innate;

behind his elegant good looks and warm smile was a welcoming aura you could sense half a block away. When I opened Union Square Cafe, he was the man I hired to be my bar manager, and eventually he became our general manager. I was devastated when, in 1989, Gordon died of complications from AIDS. (AIDS eventually claimed the lives of several of my former colleagues at Pesca, including the restaurant's owner, chef, general manager, and bar manager, and at least one of the waiters.) Gordon made a profound impact on my appreciation of the importance and power of genuine hospitality, and I have always been grateful that he lived just long enough to see Union Square Cafe earn its first three-star review in 1989.

I also met a young chef named Michael Romano. Michael had just returned from a six-year culinary stint in France and Switzerland and was learning Pesca's system as co-chef because Eugene wanted him to become the chef at Lola, a new restaurant he soon would be opening a couple of blocks west on Twenty-second Street. Sensing a rare talent and knowing that Michael and I would not be together at Pesca very much longer, I vowed to learn every possible thing I could from him. His deft chef's skills were apparent. I had never seen anyone handle a knife the way Michael did; every dish he cooked just seemed to look and taste better than anything else I had previously seen at Pesca.

I was determined to get into the kitchen. Though the managers weren't ready to let me give up my lunch shift at the front door, I finally persuaded them to let me put on kitchen whites and cook during the dinner shift. The cooks welcomed me with bemusement, and it was trial by unsavory work: I was responsible for such tasks as "cleaning" boxes upon boxes of live soft-shell crabs, a euphemism for snipping off their faces and removing their guts, during Pesca's hugely popular annual soft-shell crab festival. I worked my way up to a more permanent position on the line, stirring seafood risotto and tossing seafood pastas. After just a few weeks my suggestions for daily specials were welcomed—even by the very serious Michael Romano—and

I was at last allowed to cook the staff's meal. One night a week I was taking a course at L'Académie du Vin, taught by Melissa and Patrick Serré and housed in the basement of Lavin's restaurant, one of the early New York restaurants to feature a deep selection of California wines. Each week our curriculum focused on wines from a different part of the world. I couldn't take in the information quickly enough, and I'd eagerly share my enthusiasm with colleagues at Pesca whenever I could get anyone to listen.

Soon I had demonstrated enough palate proficiency and taste memory that I was at last trusted to weigh in on the restaurant's wine selections. As much as I wanted to talk to Michael about my love for food, he wanted to talk with me about wine. Michael told me he had accepted the interim position at Pesca with mixed feelings: what he really dreamed of was to parlay his years of training into becoming the executive chef at a classic French restaurant in midtown. We formed a friendship based on food, wine, and mutual respect.

While attending L'Académie du Vin I had become friendly with a lanky young journalist named Bryan Miller, who'd recently left his job at the *Hartford Courant* to write about food for the *New York Times*. Soon he was assigned to launch a new Friday column called "Diner's Journal." His job was to uncover new restaurants, and he called on me frequently, both as a source for ideas and as a dining companion. (In those days before the Internet, it was part of a newspaper's mission to be the very first to let the public in on new places. Today, we need only go to any one of several restaurant blogs to get even more up-to-the-minute information.)

Bryan once invited me to share a table at the opulent Russian Tea Room with the venerable food writers Craig Claiborne and Pierre Franey. Among such icons, I alternated between being attentively humble and showing off. I have no idea if they thought I was interesting company or just a tagalong sycophant. But I was getting a priceless education by dining out with and hearing the thoughts of some of America's most knowledgeable culinary giants. With Bryan I went to places as diverse as the intimate, chef-driven La Tulipe, the patron-driven *ristorante* Primavera, and the Chinese-style Pig Heaven. One night, following a horrible meal at a now defunct restaurant notable for its disastrous service, we saved the evening by going to Le Cirque with Pierre Franey, just for dessert. Sirio Maccioni, the legendary restaurateur (and a front-of-the-house master), showered us with ten desserts and glasses of his favorite Sicilian dessert wine, Malvasia delle Lipari. I'm certain that I was all but invisible to Sirio, who was peerless at coddling his rich and powerful regulars. But I was *there*.

Despite the success of the Maccionis of the world, in 1984 embarking on a career as a restaurateur was still frowned upon, at least by families like mine. This was considered blue-collar work not befitting a liberal arts background. In those early days of "new American" cuisine, the one legitimate path to owning a restaurant was through the kitchen door, as a number of bold young chefs were already demonstrating. Whenever I mentioned to people that I might become a restaurateur, they nodded politely and then winked, smiled, or gestured under the table. The common perception was that restaurants were a shady, cash-driven racket where money was always being passed illicitly and everybody kept two sets of books. This was not the career for which suburban parents sent their kids to college. (They were more than happy to dine at the establishment of a great chef. But allowing their own children to pursue such a career was another story.)

Yet during the early 1980s many American culinary stars were being recognized and celebrated. I began to follow the careers of Wolfgang Puck, Alice Waters, Paul Prudhomme, Jeremiah Tower, Joyce Goldstein, Mark Miller, Bradley Ogden, Michael McCarty, Larry Forgione, Jonathan Waxman, Anne Rosenzweig, and Barry Wine. These people were generating change and excitement, and they often had impressive university degrees. Tower founded Stars in San Francisco after earning a degree in architecture from Harvard and working at Chez Panisse. Mark Miller had studied anthropology and Chinese art at the University of California–Berkeley. Joyce Goldstein had graduated magna cum laude from Smith College and had earned an MFA from Yale. The new celebrity status of chefs, enhanced by their appearances on morning television shows that had features on cooking, was turning a few talented, charismatic chefs into household names, long before the advent of the Food Network.

So after eight months of building my own constituency of lunch regulars at Pesca in the new Flatiron district, I decided it was time to walk through the kitchen door and see where it might lead me. I made arrangements through a variety of resources, including my Roman family at La Taverna da Giovanni; my cooking teacher in New York, Andrée Abramoff; and my father, to study cooking in Italy and France for the next three and half months.

These plans at last nudged Audrey and me into action. When she heard I was leaving Pesca, she blurted, "What?" Though we hadn't had even one date at this point, we had been involved in a quiet but determined courting dance. We were the only people to whom we had not acknowledged our mutual attraction. "I think we need to go out to dinner before I leave," I said. On the eve of my last day at Pesca, we went out, putting together a jam-packed all-night date that was a harbinger of our eventual style as a married couple—never enough hours for all we want to accomplish. We started with drinks at the Algonquin Hotel, barely made the curtain for *Noises Off* at the Brooks Atkinson Theatre on Broadway, took a cab down to Tribeca for dinner at the Odeon (then perhaps the liveliest and most delicious late-night dining spot south of Canal Street), sauntered over to Le Zinc for after-dinner drinks, and walked all the way up to the West Village for more drinks and conversation at another late, favorite restaurant, Texarkana. We meandered up to Audrey's apartment on Twenty-second Street, which was across the street from Pesca, where we listened to tapes of her singing Broadway tunes and talked until four in the morning. At that point I took a cab uptown to my own place; I was due at work at the restaurant in just a few hours. I got just enough exuberant sleep to have the wherewithal to write a thank-you card (my mother's lessons were at last paying useful life dividends), which Audrey found slipped under her door when she woke up later that morning.

Pesca had been an invaluable experience both for the things it taught me to do and for the things it taught me *not* to do. Ownership and top management were highly secretive about the restaurant's finances. We had no idea what a budget was, much less how to compute a food, beverage, or labor cost. We could only assume, rightly or wrongly, that the restaurant was profitable. Also, the owners ran the restaurant more emotionally than professionally, with their prevailing mood being the primary cues for our performance that we were given on any given day. The owners dined and entertained frequently in their own restaurant; and for those meals no money was exchanged, no records were kept, and no tips were offered to the employees. Some servers were favorites of the management; others were not. Job interviews often began with an up-and-down physical assessment before any dialogue took place. In fact, that's how my own job interview had begun. I'm amazed that I got the job, when I consider my preference for wearing Wallabees and corduroys. I was a sponge with eager eyes, and I noticed everything. It was now time to leave, and to gain other perspectives on how to run a restaurant.

I SPENT THE LAST 100 days of 1984 soaking up culinary life in Italy and France, much of the time as a *stagiaire*, or chef's apprentice. That's a romantic way of saying I did those kitchen tasks no one else wanted to do, and in which there was no fear that my rudimentary kitchen skills might lead to disaster. In Rome, I worked with and learned cherished recipes from the wonderful family at La Taverna da Giovanni. I was twenty-six years old, and I seized every free moment to eat my way through the Eternal City, as well as Florence, Bologna, Genoa, Piedmont, and Sardinia. It was heaven. My two bibles were Victor Hazan's groundbreaking book *Italian Wine* and the blue pocket-size *American Express Guide to the Restaurants of Italy*.

I spent mornings wandering through food markets such as Florence's overflowing *mercato centrale* or Bologna's supernal kitchen specialist Tamburini, feeling vegetables, smelling fruits, eyeing the oils and vinegars, ogling strange creatures from the sea, marveling at unusual cuts of meat and hung game, sniffing wild mushrooms, and savoring salami, cured meat, and cheese. My brother Tom joined me for two of those weeks as Scrabble partner, comrade, and, as important, extra mouth and stomach. We stayed in cheap *pensioni*, as I had vowed to spend my limited budget not on my pillow but only on my belly. Everywhere, I scrutinized menus and analyzed restaurant design. I scribbled in my journal, chronicling and decoding every component that defined the distinctive allure of a trattoria or ristorante.

Beyond describing dishes I had loved, the journal entries included notes and sketches for lighting fixtures, menus, architecture, flooring, and seating plans, and—tellingly—notes about how I felt treated wherever I slept or dined. I was developing my vision of my future restaurant by getting to know myself. Never before had I been alone for so long, and the experience was forcing and allowing me to think about and feel what truly mattered to *me*.

The next chapter of my training began inauspiciously in Milan, where I spent three of the longest weeks of my life apprenticing with a cooking teacher named Savina Roggero. Andrée Abramoff had put me in touch with Savina, whom she described as the "Julia Child of Italy." After about two minutes with Savina, I had my doubts about the analogy. Savina was overweight, perspiring, disheveled, and exactly two hours late for our first meeting, owing to a car accident she had been involved in that day. She asked me to forgive her and assured me that tomorrow would be another day. But the next morning brought more of the same: I showed up at the appointed hour, but there was no Savina. Even though she was charging me what seemed like a huge sum of money for the privilege of learning from her— $500 per week—she was only rarely present in the kitchen to instruct me. I did most of my cooking with her willing, wide-eyed assistant,

Pina, who fortunately was a gifted cook and a patient teacher. I did end up with a handful of very good recipes. Still, although Savina had indeed published nearly thirty cookbooks, she was no Julia Child. Perhaps I caught her at the wrong end of her career, but in any case *la signora* Savina was not delivering the goods for which I had journeyed to Milan. To make matters worse, I was renting a tiny room in a depressing, industrial neighborhood; and autumn in Milan was wet, cold, and gray. At night, I could pick up a crackly, faraway radio station that broadcast the presidential debates between Walter Mondale and Ronald Reagan, and then Geraldine Ferraro and George Bush. And I missed Audrey, to whom I was writing regularly. I longed for the rendezvous we were planning in November, though I didn't quite believe it would ever occur. I couldn't wait to leave Milan.

I was relieved to finally board an overnight train for Bordeaux. My experience had done nothing to dampen my deep affection for Italy, but to this day I have little interest in visiting Milan.

In planning this culinary adventure, my father had insisted vehemently that I commit at least as much time to France as to Italy. Before leaving, I hadn't been sure if he was trying to quell my burgeoning passion for Italy or if, perhaps, his incantations about France were on the mark. In the end, I had decided to trust him and assume that he both wanted and knew what was best for me. He had allowed that Italian cooking was brilliant in its simplicity—combining just a few extraordinary ingredients—but he was orthodox in his insistence that I go to France if I truly wanted to learn technique. He called on a number of his friends from Relais et Châteaux and eventually connected me with an acquaintance who owned La Réserve, a hotel and restaurant in the town of Pessac; and the restaurant Dubern in the center of Bordeaux. Luckily, it was the autumn harvest, the most compelling season to be there; and I could soon see that my father's advice was sage: I was in for a powerful and unforgettable education. Both of the restaurants were closed on Sundays, so on that day I would drive to selected châteaux with La Réserve's maître d'hotel to get a lesson on the great vineyards of Bordeaux. We began at a little-known château in Saint-Émilion, moving on to bigger players like Château Lascombes in Margaux and Château Léoville-Barton in Saint-Julien. My most memorable Sunday excursion was one we took to Château Mouton-Rothschild, where we "robbed" and tasted the first growth from barrels, and where I first learned of a new collaboration being formed with Robert Mondavi, to be called Opus One. We traveled west to the coastal village of Arcachon, where I learned to slurp down briny blue-fleshed oysters along with dried sausage, brown bread, and butter. Each morning at dawn, I accompanied La Réserve's short, bespectacled head chef, Pierrot, to Bordeaux's food market to learn how he selected all the products for his larder. I visited Château Guiraud in Sauternes and went hunting for *palombes* (wild pigeon) and foraging for girolles (chanterelles) and cèpes (porcini). Building on my experience at Pesca gutting soft-shell crabs, I advanced to tasks like opening oysters, carving lemons, chopping shallots, and plucking feathers from dead birds. Occasionally I was invited to cook meals for the staff. Ironically, the young French cooks loved my recipes from Savina Roggero. But their favorite dish of mine was *côtes de porc*—also known as my grandmother's version of St. Louis spareribs.

One day, La Réserve collaborated with Château Calon-Ségur to cater a grand luncheon in a beautiful palace in Bordeaux. I was bursting with pride to be part of the kitchen brigade when we received applause at the end of the meal. And for the first time, I felt accepted by the *équipe* when I was allowed to join the cooks in drinking every remaining drop of the 1979 Calon-Ségur that had been left in the bottles.

After my *stage* ended in November, I took the train up to Paris for the week I had so eagerly anticipated: Audrey was flying to Paris for an eight-day rendezvous with me. As usual, I had turned to my father for his advice on both my culinary and my romantic itinerary.

The night before Audrey arrived, anxious, I had eaten myself silly dining solo on a massive copper pot of cassoulet at Lamazère. I remember sleeping for all of three hours that night, both because I was stimulated with excitement and because of the three portions of cassoulet I had consumed. (Every time the incredulous waiter had offered more, I'd smile and say, "*Oui, merci.*") The cassoulet was expanding in my stomach as I rolled around perspiring in my lumpy bed. Audrey and I continued the Parisian eating affair. We began with foie gras and Sauternes in our shabby hotel room; and we dined at the two-star Chez Michel, the one-star Pile ou Face, the brasseries Vaudeville and Au Pied du Cochon, and the bistros Allard and Benoît. From Paris, we took the overnight Orient Express to Venice, where we feasted on razor clams and *seppie* at Corte Sconta, and risotto with tiny clams at Osteria da Fiore. Then it was on to refined tasting menus at La Frasca in Castrocaro Terme, not far from Bologna; and at Enotecca Pinchiori in Florence. There were also more rustic dinners of *finocchiona* (fennel-flecked salami), *coniglio arrosto* (rabbit), *bistecca alla fiorentina*, and endless portions of *fagioli* drowned in deep green olive oil and black pepper in the trattorias Acqua al Due, Del Fagioli, and Anita. From there, we motored down to Torgiano in Umbria, and then on to Rome, so that I could introduce and show off Audrey, my *ragazza*, to my Italian family at La Taverna da Giovanni. Of course, they approved, and began whispering to me that she should soon become my *fidanzata*, or fiancée.

Audrey flew back to New York, and exhausted, I dragged myself by train back up to Florence for the much anticipated family celebration of my mother's fiftieth birthday. My advice on where to shop, eat, and sightsee was in great demand, and it was then that I realized just how much I had learned over the past several months. My time in Italy and France had provided a crucial introduction to the real work of restaurants, and nothing I had seen or learned had dissuaded me from continuing to follow my passion. I liked the kind of people I kept meeting in the business, felt blessed being around so much good food and wine, and was intoxicated with the idea of taking an unexpected career path. In my many solitary moments during those 100 days, I'd had ample opportunity to contemplate, feel, and envision the kind of restaurant I now knew I had to open.

One role I decided not to play myself was chef. Though I had fantasized early on about leading the kitchen (and in fact had seen being a chef as my only legitimate avenue into the business), it increasingly dawned on me that as much as I loved to cook, I was much more suited to becoming a restaurant generalist. My culinary education in Europe had provided the necessary foundation with which to communicate clearly about food with chefs in their own language. Firing myself as chef (or at least abandoning the notion that I might one day become a chef) turned out to be one of the smartest business decisions I have ever made. My flight home from Rome was a scribble-fest. There were barely enough minutes within the eight-and-a-half hours for all the notes I was making on my time in Europe, and my plans for New York.

BACK IN THE CITY, I was a twenty-seven-year-old guy from St. Louis who'd worked in the restaurant business for a mere eight months. I knew just a few people in the industry, and very few people beyond the walls of Pesca knew of me. What I did have was an intense desire, a burning sense of urgency, and—having sold my Checkpoint stock—enough cash to get things going. According to my calculations, I'd need somewhere between $500,000 and $1 million to open the kind of restaurant I had been dreaming of. The good news financially was that I was thinking of something rustic, not refined, in an off-Broadway rather than a Hollywood style. I knew I would need to raise some additional money in order to open, but I wouldn't know how much, or from whom, until I first found the ideal restaurant space.

I scoured the city, sometimes with brokers, but more often just hunting on my own for unlisted places—seeking the right place in the right location. I had two nonnegotiable needs: I wanted to open in an emerging neighborhood; and I wanted to have the right to assign my lease to someone else if my restaurant should go out of business. Having experienced my father's bankruptcies, and knowing something about how many new restaurants went belly-up, I was soberly aware that failure was a real possibility.

With regard to the first point, I wanted to be in an area that could provide a strong lunch business. (I had learned from Pesca that a vibrant lunch service could help a restaurant to meet fixed costs, and furthermore that the kind of business clientele attracted by lunch could give the place an added identity.) I also wanted a neighborhood where a modest rent would allow me to offer excellent value to our guests. Part of the adventure of dining out, for many people, is venturing to new surroundings. A dynamic neighborhood would bestow a freshness that could rub off on the restaurant. As for the lease, my dad, now a restaurateur himself—he had opened a French bistro, Chez Louis, in St. Louis—had consistently pointed out that if my restaurant were to fail, the lease itself would be my only tangible asset. (To this day, getting an assignable lease is the first piece of advice I give any new restaurateur.)

In my search for the ideal spot I had visited more than 100 prospective restaurant sites in at least ten distinct downtown neighborhoods. One place that captivated me was just off Union Square, an old, stale-smelling vegetarian restaurant on East Sixteenth Street called Brownies. I had been to Union Square just once or twice since I began living in New York, so I was only vaguely aware of its greenmarket—then a small twice-a-week outdoor gathering of cash-crop farmers and a specialist in heirloom apples. This was the closest thing in New York to the markets I had fallen in love with in Italy and France. Though only six blocks from Pesca, Union Square felt half a city away. At night, I knew Union Square as the stomping ground of Andy Warhol, Max's Kansas City, and The Underground nightclub. By day, the neighborhood was home to the men's garment industry, and the side streets off Fifth Avenue were clogged with rolling racks of slacks and coats. There was a seedy-by-day, dangerous-by-night feel to the area. Where Zeckendorf Towers now stand there was a faltering S. Klein department store. An equally outdated landmark was May's department store on Fourteenth Street; a few doors to the east, Luchow's restaurant was in the twilight of its life. I still wasn't sure the neighborhood's future was promising, but the deteriorating conditions made me believe that it would at least offer an opportunity for an excellent lease. The farmers' market was intriguing, and according to Ellen Giddins, the real estate executive who first urged me to follow my instinct on Union Square, this was precisely where the advertising and publishing industries would soon be relocating to escape the escalating rents in midtown.

I had never even heard of Brownies, and no brokers had ever listed it. In the front window was a middle-aged Hasidic Jew sitting in a creaky swivel chair at the cash register, ringing up the bills after people had eaten at the very long lunch counter or in the restaurant's dark, low-ceilinged dining room in the back. Just to the west of Brownies was a vitamin store of the same name. Drawing on my salesman's skill at cold-calling, I approached the cashier and asked if the owner was there. He peered suspiciously at me and said, "No, the owner's not here, why you ask?" I explained that I was looking for a restaurant space. I gave the cashier one of my old Checkpoint business cards with the phone number of my home office. "If the owner should ever be interested in selling, I might be an interested buyer," I said. There was no doubt in my mind that the word *chutzpah* had crossed his mind.

The penetrating cold during that winter of 1985 was relentless. Primarily on foot, I scoured Tribeca, the area around Lafayette Street (I liked the idea of being near the Public Theater there), and even considered Little Italy, the West Village, and the meatpacking district, which was then very rough. Disillusioned with what I was and wasn't seeing in New York, I even contemplated going home to the Midwest. I checked out Chicago's River North neighborhood—it was being gentrified—and briefly imagined what opening there would feel like. Audrey reluctantly agreed to visit it with me, but the Chicago winter—six degrees Fahrenheit, with a wind-chill factor that made the temperature feel like minus twenty-five degress—made New York seem warm by comparison. Also, Audrey's family lived on the East Coast. Both factors put the kibosh on any fantasies I had about returning to Chicago.

Despite all the uninspiring spaces I was seeing, I continued to reject the prevailing maxim: "Location, location, location." This is the idea that you somehow need an upscale address to be considered a great restaurant. But to afford an acceptably swank location, restaurants had to pass on their huge overhead to the guests, charging way too much money for lunch and dinner. Back then, an excellent restaurant was too often confused with an expensive restaurant.

I was determined to go against the grain. I was no expert in New York real estate, but I understood on a gut level that if I handicapped the location correctly, and could successfully play a role in transforming the neighborhood, my restaurant, with its long-term lease locked in at a low rent, could offer excellence *and* value. This combination would attract smart, adventurous, loyal customers, in turn giving other restaurants and businesses the confidence to move into the neighborhood until a critical mass had been reached and the neighborhood itself changed for the better. Moreover, were I to go belly-up after a few years in such a neighborhood, I was confident that I could find someone else who would be eager to pay my below-market rent on the remaining years of my lease. I sensed a lot of upside and felt protected against the downside.

One bone-chilling Saturday night in February—still without a site—I decided to bundle up and trek from Union Square all the way downtown. Maybe I'd get lucky and fall in love with a location that gave hints of being available. If you weren't busy on a Saturday night, I reasoned, you were for sale. I began on West Fourteenth Street and downed a kir at the bar of Quatorze (packed) before crossing the street for a Dos Equis at a Mexican joint (full enough). I wandered through the meatpacking district along the cobblestones of Gansevoort Street. I thought it resembled a hauntingly beautiful stage set, and I remember thinking that it had the potential one day to be a great restaurant neighborhood, but not just yet.

Using the illuminated towers of the World Trade Center as my compass, I continued on foot all the way down to Chambers Street, stopping at a few places along the way, hoping to gather some intelligence as to their desirability and availability. Soon I was in Tribeca, where I tossed back my fourth or fifth drink of the night at El Internaçional (which years later became El Teddy's). I sat at the lively tapas bar and took in the layout: the long bar, a square dining room toward the back, and another rectangular dining room through a doorway off to the side of the bar. The place felt like one big party, with all kinds of more intimate episodes unfolding within. Then it hit me: El Internaçional's layout was a virtual mirror image of Brownies, if only the wall between the vegetarian joint and its next-door vitamin shop could be torn down and the spaces combined. Until that moment, I had actually put Brownies out of my mind. But suddenly I began feverishly scribbling and sketching on the tiny, translucent paper napkins provided for tapas.

First thing Monday, I called Eugene Fracchia at Pesca; he had a penetrating eye for design, and I asked him to visit Brownies with me. We tried to be inconspicuous as we walked in. Eugene took one look and gave the space a thumbs-up: "Why is it that you'd wait? Of course you can tear the wall down!"

When I came back later by myself, the cashier remembered me. "The owner's here," he said. "He'd be happy to see you now."

Minutes later out came Sam Brown, a short, balding man who looked to be in his seventies, wearing brown sandals with socks. In a soft voice he told me he had opened Brownies, the first vegetarian restaurant in the United States, in 1936. Back then Union Square was the locus of frequent workers' protests, and vegetarianism was considered a left-wing political movement. A kind man suffering from what sounded like an asthmatic cough, Mr. Brown was planning to retire and told me he was open to discussing a deal.

We hit it off and agreed after only our second meeting that I would purchase the last fourteen years of Brownies' twenty-year lease. Two meetings later we consummated a deal. To celebrate, Sam, now the former owner of America's oldest vegetarian restaurant, took me to Sparks Steak House on East Forty-sixth Street. He was a neighbor and friend of Pat Cetta, who, with his brother Mike, had founded Sparks in 1966 on East Eighteenth Street. For a decade, I learned, Sam had been sneaking out of his own vegetarian restaurant to splurge on sirloin steak at Sparks.

That night at Sparks, Pat Cetta sat down with Sam and me for three scintillating hours of steak, storytelling, red wine, and repartee. Somehow, Pat also decided to adopt me as a mentee. He regaled us with stories about getting screwed by restaurant critics (and how he'd screwed them back) and stories about his favorite restaurateur, Barry Wine of the Quilted Giraffe; and he swore he would never use any ice cream other than Bassett's from Philadelphia. He took pride in the coarse, dust-free black pepper he served, in the magical way his waiters changed their tablecloths between the entree and dessert, and in how unbelievably much money he was making selling steak.

When I think back on it now, and when I consider all the things that can and do go wrong when you're starting a restaurant, it's amazing how many things just fell into place in the process of launching Union Square Cafe. One day, early in the spring of 1985, trying to learn more about the neighborhood in which I would open my new restaurant, I made a cold call on a construction space I'd passed on Fifth Avenue at Thirteenth Street to learn if a restaurant was being built there. I wanted to know if I'd have more competition. After the workers told me it was to be a clothing store, I introduced myself to the construction manager, Tom Hanratty, who was both genial and helpful. He said his crew was actually looking for its next project. I called him a few days later, followed up on a couple of references, met his boss, and then hired them to build my restaurant. I now know how critically important it is to be careful in the selection of a construction crew; but at the time, I just wanted to get started, and fortunately my naïveté went unpunished.

I also had no clue how to find a good architect on my own. As I was discussing the situation with my grandfather and his second wife, Joan Harris, she mentioned that she knew the Kander family from her hometown, Kansas City. (John Kander and Fred Ebb wrote such Broadway classics as *Cabaret* and *Chicago*.) Joan mentioned that she had heard that Warren Ashworth (husband of Susan Kander), was a terrific architect whom I should meet. Susan's brother, John, had taught me tennis at Camp Nebagamon. That was that: I felt comfortable enough, after just one interview, to hire Warren and his boss Larry Bogdanow to design Union Square Cafe. Larry was earthy, cerebral, and intense. Warren was dry, irreverent, and sharp. Each was brimming with imagination and enthusiasm for the project. The two had little experience with restaurants (they spoke of only two very small projects to date), and they reacted politely when I told them I wanted to design a restaurant that looked as if no architect had ever been there.

I suppose I could have picked my favorite trattoria in Rome and instructed Warren and Larry to go there and simply reproduce it in New York. Other restaurateurs have done that brilliantly. (Years later, Balthazar, in Manhattan's SoHo district, became such a perfect reproduction of a brasserie that I would almost rather go there than to half a dozen authentic brasseries I know of in Paris.) That is an awesome accomplishment, but replicating something already in existence isn't where my own business or design sense has ever guided me.

Instead, I had asked my architects to create a restaurant that would be easy, comfortable, and timeless—that would look as if it had been there forever. (On the occasion of Union Square Cafe's twentieth anniversary in 2005, Larry wryly observed, "Now it *has* been there forever.")

Given what I presented them to work with, my instructions may have been easier than I knew; there was only so much an architect on a modest budget could do with this awkward three-level space. The kitchen is cramped, and if you're a waiter you literally can't make coffee or cut bread without being bumped into by somebody carrying food out of it. The coatroom is claustrophobic and the bathrooms are minuscule. The dining rooms are low-ceilinged. The wooden staircase to the balcony is narrow and steep—and half of the meals eaten at Union Square Cafe require someone to carry plates up the stairs. To the dozens of couples who have gotten engaged at our "most romantic table," it may come as a surprise to know that their cherished table 61 on the balcony sits on the former site of Sam Brown's lavatory. The balcony itself was for nearly half a century his office.

Union Square Cafe is the least sexy and most ergonomically clumsy restaurant space that I own. But Warren and Larry came to understand that I wanted a look that would endure, rather than something frozen in the prevailing design trends of 1985. The restaurant remains today an odd amalgam of their aesthetic sense combined with notes I scribbled in journals in Italy and France and on tapas napkins at El Internaçional. I believe it became a wonderful restaurant *because* of its imperfections, which helped build the kind of team character necessary to overcome adversity. One of the core business lessons I have taken from the continued success of Union Square Cafe is that willingness to overcome difficult circumstances is a crucial character trait in my employees, partners, and restaurants.

The combined cost of paying for the assigned lease, the design, and the construction of this 5,000 square foot restaurant in 1985 was just a little over $700,000—an absurdly gentle figure by today's standards. With my $350,000 of cashed-in Checkpoint stock, I still needed to raise an equal additional amount. Even though my family (except, of course, for my uncle, Richard Polsky) continued to think I was crazy to be getting into the restaurant business, there was evidently enough loving confidence in me that I managed to raise almost all the additional backing from the family, much of it in the form of loans, allowing me to retain most of the equity. A couple of associates of my grandfather Irving Harris helped me to figure out how to put the deal together, and also how to explain the investment to various members of my family. I decided not to invite my grandfather to be a financial participant, despite his offer to help. That was, in a sense, one final protective measure to avoid my father's resentment. And even though my father seemed to be back in the black, I chose not to ask him to invest either.

I did, however, take my dad's advice on a name for the restaurant. During my months in Europe I had passed a lot of idle time sitting in piazzas or on trains, dreaming up prospective (and remarkably forgettable) restaurant names, like Bimi (my grandmother's nickname), Blue Plate Cafe, Gorgonzola, and—once I had the location—Piazza del Unione. Wincing at these ideas, my father had a straightforward suggestion for me: "Why don't you just call it what it is? It's Union Square Cafe. In San Francisco Union Square is *the* premier address."

"In San Francisco, yes, it is," I said. "But in New York, Union Square is not an especially prized location." I described what I knew of the fringe neighborhood with some unsavory details.

"You can help make this square a premier address in New York," he persisted. "Name the restaurant Union Square Cafe!"

Construction began on Memorial Day and was completed in less than five months. The experience was a cliff-hanger. We had settled on October 21, 1985, as our opening date, but with one week to go, we were still finishing the cherrywood floors and applying wainscoting to the walls. It was impossible to lead any kind of meetings or training sessions amid the noise, smells, and chaos. I conducted all staff interviews on the sidewalk while sitting on a sawhorse next to a Dumpster. Intuitively, I was searching for employees with the kind of personal style I'd find compatible with my own. My brain was look-

ing for people with restaurant skills, but my heart was beseeching me
to cultivate a restaurant family.

The job application form I wrote was idiosyncratic. I typed questions like, "How has your sense of humor been useful to you in your
service career?" "What was so wrong about your last job?" "Do you
prefer Hellmann's or Miracle Whip?" If you're trying to provide engaging hospitality and outstanding technical service, there must also
be a certain amount of fun involved, and those bizarre questions gave
me an idea of whether or not applicants had a sense of humor. They
needed one, too, as our training sessions necessarily took place in the
middle of Union Square Park. I'd buy a bushel of Jonagold apples
and we would sit on the grass, munch on apples, and play-act service
scenarios.

One day in the park, I looked over my shoulder to see Bryan
Miller and Pierre Franey taking notes on what we were doing. While
I was cooking in France, Bryan had written to tell me that he had
been named Mimi Sheraton's replacement as chief restaurant critic
at the *New York Times*. I wrote back, congratulating him and telling
him of my concrete plans to open a restaurant in New York. Upon
my return in January 1985, we dined out together just once, but the
dinner proved uncomfortable for each of us. The restaurant that Bryan
had picked to review that night was La Caravelle, whose new chef
was my former colleague at Pesca, Michael Romano. I felt uneasy to
be surreptitiously complicit in the judgment of my friend's cooking,
and I felt unscrupulous to be a future restaurateur dining with the
current restaurant critic of the *New York Times*. Though Bryan and I
had become good friends, we agreed that night not to speak for a
long while, and to cease dining out altogether. I was beginning to
feel the heat.

I didn't hire the opening chef for Union Square Cafe until well
after I had signed the deal for Brownies. (Though I had already decided against it, on some level I was still flirting with the fantasy of
being my own chef.) Months before, Bryan had introduced me to

a robust Frenchman named Marc Sarrazin, the top meat purveyor to French restaurants in New York, who also served as an unofficial headhunter for restaurants and adviser to the city's top culinary talent. Marc knew all the chefs, especially in the French houses; he visited them in their kitchens and knew which talented young cooks were interested in making a move. Marc also knew where the job openings were. He was a rainmaker, and so I asked him to help find me a chef. Within days, he introduced me to a young, baby-faced fish cook named Ali Barker. Ali had been the saucier and *chef poissonnier* at La Côte Basque, which at the time was a great training ground for a number of promising young chefs including Todd English and Charlie Palmer. I was also interested in two sous-chefs: Scott Campbell, a young cook recommended by a culinary teacher named Peter Kump (whom I had also met through Bryan); and Marcie Smith, a cook at Barry and Susan Wine's four-star Quilted Giraffe.

I arranged tasting auditions in the kitchen of my apartment on East Eighty-fourth Street. Taking a page from the outdoor cooking contest I had competed in at camp as a twelve-year-old, I gave each cook a chicken breast, some butter, an onion, garlic, fresh herbs, and a tomato to see what he or she would do with them. Ali's chicken was juicy and seasoned just properly; impressively, he subsequently used the chicken bones and onion to make a delicious stock. When I hired him as executive chef, we agreed that he would give the job two years—which was acceptable to me since it was about as far into the future as I could see.

Staffing was a study in the blind leading the blind. I hired a chef who had never been a chef or sous-chef—and who was even younger than I was. Naively, I made myself the opening general manager, responsible for things I knew little or nothing about, like setting the staff's schedule, overseeing repairs and maintenance, and conducting performance reviews. I'd lured Gordon Dudash from Pesca to be my second in command as manager, but he'd managed only an inanimate bar before, never a live staff. Our bookkeeper was an incredibly nice man with no previous bookkeeping experience, and one of our waiters surprised me during our two days of training by insisting on opening a bottle of champagne with a corkscrew.

One day, a week or two before we opened and while the restaurant was still under construction, Uncle Richard brought by an acquaintance to offer me some advice. This white-haired culinary lion—who was in charge of the food and beverage program at New York's Harvard Club—looked down his aquiline nose at me and asked, "Just what kind of restaurant is it that you are planning to open?" He cleared his throat.

"I'm not really sure what you would call it," I said.

"I see. Well, then, what kind of food will you be serving at your restaurant?"

"We're going to offer some pastas in small appetizer portions. I've got this idea for filet mignon of tuna marinated with soy, ginger, and lemon. We'll also have a couple of French things like confit of duck with garlic potatoes. And—"

"It'll never fly," he said with conviction.

I paused for a moment before continuing: "We'll be serving my grandmother's mashed turnips with fried shallots as a side dish and black bean soup with a shot of Australian sherry."

"Stop! It won't work," he sputtered. "When people go out to eat, they say, 'Let's go out for French, or Italian.' Or maybe even Chinese. But no one says 'Let's go out for eclectic.' You'd really better rethink your concept."

This expert had scared the shit out of me. With days to go before opening, I couldn't tinker with my menu even if I wanted to. The fact was that I didn't know what kind of restaurant this was going to be. What I did know was that I was champing at the bit to share my enthusiasm for the foods and recipes that I loved—and to treat people the way I wanted to be treated. Wasn't that enough?

On the evening of October 20, 1985, we served our opening-night party. It was a numbing, surreal moment, and an emotionally loaded night for me. I broke into tears as soon as the doors flew open, realizing that this moment marked the culmination of a lot of professional research as well as a lifetime of personal development. Seventy-five people showed up, all of them friends or family members. There was something bittersweet in the air as well. My dad was not present. He apparently had gone on a business trip. Were my tears in part about his not being there? Or were they because I now knew that I didn't need him to be there? In any case, this was my moment to achieve something on my own. I had spent nearly two years doing my best work ever as a student, and now it was up to me to show what I had learned and what I was capable of doing on my own two feet. However the restaurant might ultimately fare, this opening night was a breakthrough, in my career and in my life. These were tears of intense joy and sadness, relief and release.

CHAPTER 3

The Restaurant Takes Root

IN THOSE FIRST WEEKS and months it didn't take me long to learn
that very little makes guests madder than having to wait for their
reserved table or their food. That was happening a lot, because the
phone was ringing with increasing frequency and I was saying yes to
almost every request for a reservation.

Though the restaurateur in me was obsessed with hospitality, the
entrepreneur in me was becoming addicted to volume. I was always
trying to see how many covers—customers, in restaurant parlance—
we could serve on a given day. This was also important, since a higher
volume meant more tips for the servers. I could not afford to lose the
few good servers we had, but I would lose them if they weren't able
to make a living wage. The restaurant had 135 seats, and each night my
goal was to set a new "personal best" for covers. We were consistently
hovering around the one-turn mark—seating each table just once per
night—and we had plateaued at around 140 for several weeks. Then, I
almost brought the kitchen and restaurant down one night when we
shattered our record and served 171 guests. Each high-water mark led

to another. I charted out a manual reservation system, assigning two hours for each deuce, an additional thirty minutes for each four-top, and three hours for a party of five or more. This was clearly maximizing covers, but I did not yet understand the art of pacing tables. The problem was that with a kitchen as undersized as ours, seating more than twenty or so guests every fifteen minutes would invariably clog it up; it was like shoving too much mass down the tube part of a funnel, stopping the flow of food altogether.

On the first night that we served actual paying guests, two parties left because their food never arrived. In the weeks going forward, excruciating waits and walkouts were the norm more than the exception. We realized that the broad number of items on the menu was far too ambitious for our small kitchen and our inexperienced cooks. I hated having to edit dishes I loved from the menu, even if only temporarily—but I did remove them. On most nights, there would come a point when I would leave the dining room and stand sweating in the kitchen, because I couldn't face the fuming guests anymore. Watching Ali try to expedite his way out of a wall of "dupes"—each one representing a table of hungry guests—was safer than subjecting myself to the slings and arrows in the dining room.

In my obsession for big numbers, I'd created hideous logjams. But it was oddly exciting to manufacture challenges and then surmount them. (In fact, that was and continues to be a pattern in the way I work.) I drew up new reservation sheets, adjusted the seating chart, reassigned waiters' "stations," and sharpened my calculations of the turn time for each table—all with the goal of maximizing volume without compromising our ability to deliver excellence. As a puzzle, this was both an art and a science, and each dinner service brought new opportunities to make adjustments in pace, flow, and progress.

I was developing what I would call an "athletic" approach to hospitality, sometimes playing offense, sometimes playing defense, but always wanting to find a way to win. On offense, we'd figure out creative ways to enhance an already good experience (extra desserts with inscriptions written in chocolate for birthdays; dessert wine for regulars). Playing defense, we got better and better at overcoming our frequent mistakes or at defusing whatever situations the guests might be angry about. Increasingly, their anger was over not getting a reservation at a specific time. I was good at dealing with that, guided by my instinct to let the callers know I was on their side. "I'd love to put your name at the top of our wait list for eight o'clock," I would say. Or, "There are literally no tables at eight. Is there any way I could do this for you at eight-forty-five?"—which I knew sounded a little earlier than "quarter of nine." Or, "Can you give me a range that would work for you, so that I can *root* for a cancellation?" The point was to keep the dialogue open while sending the message: I am your agent, not the gatekeeper!

For those who had to wait too long, there was often a reward—a generous supply of dessert wines on the house. We had resuscitated an old refrigerator from Brownies in the back bar that we named the "Medicine Cabinet," the medicine being our ample collection of dessert wines, which we dispensed liberally by the glass as an apology to guests. Except for the most hostile, the medicine generally worked. Back in 1985 one rarely saw dessert wines by the glass on a menu in New York—this was still much more of a European custom—but I began offering an extensive list of dessert wines by the glass. It was an important early lesson in applying defensive hospitality when things don't go according to plan.

While we weren't giving away Château d'Yquem, we did offer an assortment of world-class sweet wines like Château Raymond-Lafon, Château Guiraud, Moscato d'Asti, Malvasia delle Lipari, and Verduzzo di Cialla. Our most popular dessert wine was from Tuscany Vin Santo—an amber-colored Madeira-like wine into which we'd encourage guests to dunk almond biscotti. The Italian tradition of *biscotto bagno* ("biscuit bath") was new to most of our guests in 1985, but it was an after-dinner delight I had enjoyed learning about while working as a tour guide in Rome back in 1978.

Though it was nearly impossible for me to concede, some parties were beyond winning over. I distinctly remember one table that wouldn't abandon its anger, despite five attempts at trying to overcome our mistakes. "I really want you to know how important it is to me that we earn back your trust," I pleaded. "I know we made you wait too long for your food. Your time is valuable and I feel horrible. Is there anything I can do to earn back your patronage?"

"There's nothing you can do," one of the men at the table said. "We're never coming back." I still remember the lump in my throat. "OK, but when you go," I said, making one last attempt, "just know that I would have done anything to earn back your faith in us."

That outcome, happily, was rare. Instead, guests began coming back and asking for dessert wine. And they paid for it. Those early days were filled with unexpected lessons in management. One day, soon after opening, I went to the kitchen in search of chef Ali. Unable to find him there, I descended our narrow stairway to the basement prep area. No Ali. I resorted to the last option and opened the door to the walk-in refrigerator. There was Ali—with his sous-chef, Marcie Smith, locked in an embrace next to the oyster bushel shelf. None of us said a word as I backed out of the walk-in. Up until that moment, I'd had no idea that Ali and Marcie were romantically involved, and it was a delicate situation I knew I'd have to handle quite carefully. I called my father for advice (this being a safe topic). He said, "Whenever you get attractive people together in the intense environment of a restaurant, they're either going to fight or fall in love. This is probably the better option." I still didn't know what to do.

One evening, some weeks after we opened, I was proudly showing off Union Square Cafe to Tom Carouso, a good friend from Trinity College who had just returned to New York after living in Africa, who couldn't believe I had actually followed through on my dream of opening a restaurant. The two of us were surveying the restaurant from the balcony overlooking the back dining room with its twenty-five-foot ceiling and its huge mural along the back wall. As I began to describe how the artist Judy Rifka had painted it, I suddenly heard a piercing crack, and a boom, as one end of a thirty-foot track lighting rod ripped out of the ceiling and swung down like a pendulum. The heavy steel rod and its fixtures smashed into the wall with a grotesque thud, gouging a three-inch gash in the plaster wall, perilously close to the head of a woman who was dining. If it had been two inches to the right it could well have killed her, and would surely have put me out of business for good.

The woman was in shock. My heart skipped several beats. I ran downstairs and offered to move her into the other dining room and to buy her dinner. We were both shaking. She was far too upset to stay, and as soon as she could catch her breath, she and her date went home. I don't think I even had the presence of mind to ask for her name, address, or phone numbers so that I could follow up. Our contractor had some very serious explaining to do.

I also recall the Friday after Thanksgiving, just five weeks after opening. Business had been decent, but we hadn't yet been reviewed, and I had anticipated a slow holiday weekend. I gave both chef Ali and his sous-chef and girlfriend, Marcie, the weekend off so that they could go to Pepper Pike, Ohio, where Ali would be presented to Marcie's parents—his future in-laws. (My inexperienced way of dealing with their relationship was not to deal with it at all but just to pray for the best.)

My prediction of a slow weekend was absolutely wrong, and on Friday night, overcome with a slew of last-minute reservations, we were so busy that I needed to throw on kitchen whites, over my suit and tie, and cook. The kitchen was swamped, and guests were waiting thirty minutes for their appetizers and at least that long for their main courses. I was overheated and perspiring and my red Brooks Brothers tie began bleeding all over my wrinkled white button-down shirt. I became lightheaded, not having bothered to eat all day. At one point I walked out of the kitchen into the dining room and saw a drunken patron stumbling around loudly ranting about not being able to order a baked potato at this "crappy restaurant."

My judgment was cloudy from fatigue and hunger, and I chose to confront the man on his own terms. When I told him we wouldn't serve him another drop of anything, he blurted, "You can't cut me off."

"Yes, I can," I replied. "Your check is on the way."

"You can't make me pay my check," he countered.

"Maybe not," I said, "but I *can* tell you to leave my restaurant."

We continued our conversation—"'Fraid not," "'Fraid so"—while dancing chest to chest through the dining room and then up the stairs toward the bar. As we neared the front door, he threw a nasty punch that hit me squarely in the jaw. I punched him back as hard as I could. I then managed to push him toward the door and out into the vestibule. But from there he was able to grab the door handle and next my head, which he slammed between the door and the doorjamb. That was painful—and when he began to come at me again, I instinctively wound up and kicked him as hard as I possibly could in the nuts.

He managed to crouch his way outside to the sidewalk on East Sixteenth Street, where his two dining companions, who had been lurking around uselessly during the altercation, finally picked him up off the sidewalk and stuffed him into a taxi.

The next week I opened the *Daily News* and learned for the first time that its restaurant critic, Arthur Schwartz, had been in the restaurant that raucous evening and had witnessed the entire fracas. (Remarkably, he omitted any mention of the fisticuffs in his review, but he later told me he had seen the whole thing. He hoped I was feeling better.)

Schwartz became the first critic in New York to suggest that Union Square Cafe had tremendous promise and that we were doing something groundbreaking and fresh. His review was the first to put us on the map. Meanwhile, I was looking over my shoulder for Bryan Miller. Bryan was now the most powerful restaurant critic in America; and since we had a tacit agreement not to be in contact, I had no idea when, or even if, he'd ever show up in our dining room.

IT WAS CRUCIAL FOR me that Union Square Cafe express a sense of boldness and innovation. I wanted to blend the best of European fine dining with the ease and comfort of American style. I imagined Union Square Cafe as a combination of three very different kinds of restaurants one encountered in the late 1970s: first, the earthy, seasonal, local, food-loving places in Berkeley and San Francisco; second, the refined gastronomic temples of Paris; and third, the mama-and-papa trattorias of Rome. In California, there were passionate men and women working together; sometimes living together; breaking rules, boundaries, and traditions; and loving it. In Paris refined excellence was the only relevant criterion and everyone knew exactly what was expected of him or her—accountability to precision, and to hospitality. In Rome, one family ran the restaurant for the pleasure of its extended family of regulars. I was determined to find a way to "emulsify" those three ingredients to create an ambience of relaxed excellence. I was convinced that I could blend the best of California, Paris, and Rome and have it all ways: refined technical service paired with caring, gracious hospitality, and soulful seasonal cooking.

Going against the grain of the high-flying 1980s, we always looked for low-key, straightforward ways to celebrate with the guests in our dining room. One easy way to set ourselves apart in that era, when lofty menu tabs convolutedly conferred superior status, was to offer exceptional value. I was willing to accept legitimate criticism for any aspect of the restaurant, but if anyone ever accused us of overcharging for our product, I was mortified. My views on this had been shaped by my own early experiences at restaurants with my family, when I had been urged to read the menu "from right to left"—that is, prices first. My dining forays in Italy and France in my early twenties had also shaped my ideas. The dollar had been very strong then, and I was used to downing appetizer bowls of the world's best pasta for, say, $3 or $4. I was appalled that in America some restaurants charged $18 for entree

portions of only passable pasta. And I saw offering value as a great opportunity to distinguish us from the rest of the pack. But it was in the
late 1980s, several years after Union Square Cafe had opened, that I
had my epiphany as a restaurateur. Audrey and I were in Paris, making
our first visit to the three-star Taillevent. The seamless service and exquisite hospitality were superior to anything I had ever experienced,
and the polished staff members also possessed a confident sense of
humor about themselves while providing pleasure for the guest. This
was the first time I had ever dined at a Michelin three-star restaurant
that, in addition to serving ethereally good food, was actually fun!

It is no coincidence that Taillevent has maintained its three-star
rating for more than three decades. If there's a better restaurateur in the
world than Taillevent's Jean-Claude Vrinat (whose father created the restaurant), I have yet to meet him or her. Self-deprecating to a fault, Monsieur Vrinat brushed off my gratitude for an evening of perfect service.
"We have fun taking service seriously," he said. "And as for perfection,
we just hide our mistakes better than anyone else!" That was a refreshing
insight for me as I continued to hone my own version of hospitality.

After leaving Checkpoint in 1983, I had treated myself to a memorable fortnight in London. I used the Gault Millau Guide to ex-
haustively research the local restaurant scene (which was still sleepy
at that point, but fascinated me nonetheless), and dined out alone
every night. The trip added a new wrinkle to my understanding of
hospitality. Half the restaurants I selected simply refused to accept
my reservation once they learned I was a party of "just one." After
a series of rejections, I decided I was no longer going to take no for
an answer. I would call back the same restaurant and simply make a
reservation for two. Then I'd arrive, be seated, and after a while look
disbelievingly at my watch and say, "It seems my guest isn't showing
up." This approach worked at a series of highly rated restaurants, all of
which had initially refused to take "just me." These experiences led
to a determination that in my restaurant solo diners would be treated
with extra courtesy and respect.

Although at some places the maître d' and servers looked down their noses at me, other waitstaffs served me warmly. I was viewed either as an economic nuisance, occupying a table that could otherwise have generated more revenue, or as someone paying the restaurant a compliment by choosing to eat there. On one occasion I was treated so dismissively—ignored for at least twenty minutes after receiving my menu and wine list—that I decided to try an experiment. I summoned the haughty sommelier and proceeded to order a very expensive bottle of wine, bringing my tab to far more than what a typical deuce would have spent. Not surprisingly, I was soon deemed worthy of his attention. He may not have learned a lesson, but I had. I swore always to treat the guest who orders Soave exactly as I would the one who orders Chassagne-Montrachet.

That trip sensitized me to the idea that solo diners could be an important part of our business and should be welcomed accordingly. When I thought about how much time and care I put into choosing where to take myself to dinner, and how often I recommended those places that treated me well (and conversely, how strongly I warned everyone off the inhospitable ones), I knew that treating solo diners as royalty was both the right thing to do and smart business. Union Square Cafe began serving the full menu at the bar, mostly to single diners and couples, long before others in the city did this. I have always felt that solo guests pay us the ultimate compliment by joining us for a meal. Their visit has no ulterior motive (it involves no business, romance, or socializing). These guests simply want to do something nice for themselves, *chez nous*. Why wouldn't we reward that?

But the most significant and lasting way for us to set ourselves apart was the way we defined and delivered hospitality. Union Square Cafe opened in 1985 during the first blast of the "masters of the universe" culture. There was a combination of abundant money floating around and a lingering effect of the velvet rope at Studio 54: the more expensive or exclusive something was, the more coveted it became.

I don't remember ever having particularly enjoyed a place just because I'd been afraid that it wouldn't have me, so I was appalled to think that by charging people too much money and putting up barriers to entry, some restaurants had actually created an inflated demand to be part of their scene. However, these candles had short wicks. The discos of the 1970s had given way to the coked-up nightclubs of the early 1980s, which in turn gave way to stadium-size restaurants where the food was really nothing more than a prop in an ersatz nightclub scene. This was happening a lot, particularly as people started to gravitate downtown and take over lofty warehouse-like spaces. At the other extreme of the dining culture were celebratory, serious French restaurants such as La Grenouille, Le Cirque, La Côte Basque, and Lutèce. What you didn't see much of was excellent dining in a setting of down-to-earth comfort. I sensed that there was in New York a community of food lovers who would be happy to be welcomed warmly and charged fair prices. In fact, conceiving Union Square Cafe as an excellent version of a neighborhood restaurant was, in retrospect, not very challenging. It turned out that there was a tremendous gap in the dining culture that allowed us to open in a comparatively uncrowded field. We were doing something new and unexpected, and it was attracting an intelligent, self-confident clientele.

The 1980s were also the decade of the "service economy." Virtually all of corporate America was being challenged to respond to a cry for more service—from rental car companies to banks to the U.S. Postal Service. That trend appeared in our industry as well—sometimes, paradoxically, at the expense of hospitality. In the prevailing view of service, guests were to be treated to more coddling, more choices—and more interruptions. Did restaurants really need to offer a choice of four breads, two butters, and any number of special knives at dinner? Did the one-bite premeal morsel known as the *amuse-bouche*, or in some restaurants the *amuse* (a gift from the chef) really require a one-minute description of every ingredient and cooking method? Every choice meant another needless intrusion by the waitstaff on guests' time and attention. What mattered most to me was trying to provide maximum value in exchange not just for the guests' money but also for their time. Anything that unnecessarily disrupts a guest's time with his or her companions or disrupts the enjoyment of the meal undermines hospitality.

The beautiful choreography of service is, at its best, an art form, a ballet. I appreciate the grace with which a table can be properly cleared. I admire the elegance with which a bottle of wine can be appropriately opened, decanted, and poured. There's aesthetic value in doing things the right way. But I respond best when the person doing those things realizes that the purpose of all this beauty at the table is to create pleasure for me. To go through the motions in a perfunctory or self-absorbed manner, no matter how expertly rendered, diminishes the beauty. It's about soul—and service without soul, no matter how elegant, is quickly forgotten by the guest.

Understanding the distinction between service and hospitality has been at the foundation of our success. Service is the technical delivery of a product. Hospitality is how the delivery of that product makes its recipient *feel*. Service is a *monologue*—we decide how we want to do things and set our own standards for service. Hospitality, on the other hand, is a *dialogue*. To be on a guest's side requires listening to that person with every sense, and following up with a thoughtful, gracious, appropriate response. It takes both great service and great hospitality to rise to the top.

When you are seated at the precise time of your reservation at the exact table and with the waiter you requested, that is a reflection of good service. When the right food is delivered to the right person at the right table at the right temperature at the right time—that's service. When you see a member of the waitstaff decanting a bottle of wine with care and grace, that's service. When your empty plate is cleared from the table in a graceful manner, that too is service. When, in answer to your question, the waiter can explain the nuances of the wines on our list, that's service. But hospitality, which most distinguishes our restaurants—and ultimately any business—is the sum of all the thoughtful, caring, gracious things our staff does to make you feel we are *on your side* when you are dining with us.

Our restaurants are not selective in doling out hospitality—we strive to treat first-time visitors as well as many restaurants treat their regulars, and we do not give priority treatment exclusively to the privileged. This fact has been often cited to me as criticism. But far from being a problem, our democratic approach to how we treat guests has become a core value of our business philosophy. I still remember a review in a column called "The Restaurant Rotator" that appeared in a hip weekly of the mid-1980s called 7 *Days*, about two years after we opened. The writer, who called herself The Rotator, compared her dining experience at Union Square Cafe to being served by the Stepford wives. I had to look up the reference; at the time, I didn't know what she meant.

She apparently found it objectionable and disingenuous that we were hiring naturally friendly people and allowing their personalities to shine through in the dining room. This cynical review stung me, but it didn't hurt the restaurant or in any way change the way I chose to do business. If a guest refused to sit at a particular table, I'd say, "Sure. Which table would you prefer?" Many didn't know how to respond to this, because they'd been conditioned to expect, "Sorry. That's the only table we have available."

I had already learned that the trick to delivering superior hospitality was to hire geniune, happy, optimistic people. The Ritz-Carlton hotels are deservedly famous for their focus on service; they don't call it hospitality. But as a guest there, I have occasionally sensed a rote quality in the process, when every employee responds with exactly the same phrase, "My pleasure," to anything guests ask or say. Hearing "My pleasure" over and over again can get rather creepy after a while. It's like hearing a flight attendant chirp "Bye now!" and "Bye-bye!" 200 times as passengers disembark from an airplane. Hospitality cannot flow from a monologue. I instruct my staff members to figure out whatever it takes to make the guests feel and understand that we are in their corner. I don't tell the staff precisely what to do or say in every scenario, though I do have some pet peeves that I don't ever want to hear in our dining rooms. I cringe when a waiter asks, "How is everything?" That's an empty question that will get an empty response. Also, I can't stand the use of *we* to mean *you*, as in, "How are we doing so far?" I abhor the question, "Are you still working on the lamb?" If the guest has been *working on* the lamb, it probably wasn't very tender or very good in the first place. And if a guest says "Thank you" for something, the waiter should *not* answer, "No problem." Since when is it necessary to deny that delivering excellent service is a "problem"? A genuine "You're welcome" is always the appropriate response.

IN THE FIRST THREE months we were open, I left Union Square Cafe just one night—to celebrate Audrey's birthday with a dinner uptown at the four-star Lutèce. It was our first grown-up restaurant date in months. As I watched Lutèce's peerless chef André Soltner make his rounds welcoming guests in the dining room, I was hoping wistfully that he would greet us the way he did his best regulars. He didn't know me, but our mutual friend Marc Sarrazin had arranged for our reservation—which otherwise would have been impossible to get—and had told chef Soltner that I was a budding downtown restaurateur. Table by table, Soltner said hello to every one of his guests. And then he arrived at our side. Turning to Audrey with a broad smile, he said, "Happy birthday to you." To me, with a mock stern look, and in a pronounced Alsatian accent, he said, "What the hell are you doing in my restaurant tonight when you should be working in your restaurant?" Sheepishly, I smiled, looking down at my bowl of *écrevisses* in tomato cream. It was clear that I had a very long way to go.

I didn't go out for a long time after that. I was fairly certain that Bryan Miller was going to come in to review us one night, and I absolutely wanted to be there when that happened. We were beginning to build a nice business, already serving more guests than I had ever imagined, learning to do it a little better every day. But I was so stressed over the impending review by the *New York Times* that I developed a case of Bell's palsy. I was just two months into the restaurant business, and the left half of my face had become paralyzed and the left half of my tongue had lost its ability to taste. I couldn't flare my left nostril or close my left eyelid. The best I could muster was a half smile. And even that was only half sincere: Bell's palsy is scary, and it hurts. My doctor told me that 80 percent of all cases go away within two weeks, but 20 percent don't. So for half a month I had no idea in which group I'd end up. That made me really worry, and worrying added more stress and made everything worse. During the first New Year's eve at Union Square Cafe, in 1985, I could barely smile when the noisemakers rang out and confetti whirled at midnight. I couldn't even manage to cry. When my face began to regain its full movement after the first two weeks of 1986 I did cry, with relief.

Over the next month, Bryan, at last, came in five times (for two lunches and three dinners). I was there every time. One night I knew I should expect him because although he had made the reservation under a new alias, he had used the same callback number as on a previous visit. I remembered from the wine class we took together that he hated overchilled white wines. I tried to guess what he'd select in advance, because our bar refrigerator was malfunctioning, nearly freezing the bottles of wine. Knowing his tastes, I predicted that he'd choose to begin with an Italian white. I even remembered which Italian white wines were his favorites.

Five minutes before Bryan's expected arrival, I pulled five bottles from the refrigerator so that they would be less cold by the time he ordered. He did come, and just as I'd expected, he turned to the section of Italian whites on the wine list. But when the waiter sent in his order I was terrified to see that Bryan hadn't picked any one of the five wines I had preselected. He had ordered one that was still in the freezing refrigerator, a Tocai Friulano from Ronco del Gnemiz, and the bottle was frosty.

Cursing under my breath, I went over to the bar, well out of sight of his table, and stuck the icy bottle of Tocai between my thighs to warm it up. Five minutes later Bryan's waiter approached me nervously. "Where's the Tocai? He's asking where it is!"

Feeling the bottle, I said, "I think it's ready right now," and handed it over. My pants were wet and very cold. A minute later the waiter returned to the bar with a defeated look, grasping the bottle: "Mr. Miller wants another bottle of Tocai. This one is too warm."

FOR BRYAN'S FIFTH AND final visit, he and his wife, Anne, brought as their co-tasters the actress Mariel Hemingway and her new husband, Steven Crisman, a restaurateur. They had just opened a hopping spot called Sam's Café. This was after her appearance as the buxom centerfold in *Star* 80, and it was impossible for me not to notice that she had had her breasts augmented. Bryan was going all-out and began his meal by ordering oysters and champagne. After I poured Mariel a glass of Billecart-Salmon, I slowly slid the glass closer to where it should be—while irresistably gazing down at her cleavage. Had I not been ogling her, I might have noticed that the tablecloth was poorly pressed and was stiffly creased where it had been folded. As I slid the glass, the foot of the top-heavy champagne flute caught on the crease and tipped over, pouring cold champagne all over Mariel's dress and lap. I now had two strikes, both involving wine.

On the night of January 23, 1986, Ali Barker and I camped out at the *New York Times* building on West Forty-third Street. At precisely

11:04, stacks of the next day's early edition papers were tossed from a truck and then unbundled in the lobby. We noticed a few other people waiting for the paper—some who wanted the first crack at the classified want ads, and others whose plays were being reviewed. Plunking down 35 cents, we tore through the paper to the back of the Friday weekend section to find the review of Union Square Cafe. Bryan had given us two stars: "very good." We were beyond ecstatic. Two stars really did mean "very good" in those days, and it read like a money review. He praised the food and the décor, calling them "genuine and eclectic"; and he said that the seafood risotto was "rousing," the spaghetti alla puttanesca "generous" and "boldly seasoned," and so on.

Two of Bryan's observations really hit home. The first was that we were "fast becoming a lunch haunt for the downtown publishing crowd." To this day, I always want any new restaurant I open to become a "lunch haunt" for some core group of loyal customers. To the degree that a restaurant can serve as an unofficial club for any constituency, it takes on an additional mystique that leads to more and more business. Second, Bryan wrote that the sensitive design made Union Square Cafe feel like "part of the neighborhood, not something imposed on it." Reading his words helped me understand that what I was doing intuitively was actually working. I have made that an intentional strategy for every single restaurant I've opened since.

That first review in the *New York Times* had more revenue impact on Union Square Cafe than any subsequent review has ever had on any of our restaurants. Business spiked 60 percent overnight. In later years Bryan confided that because of our friendship, he had actually been tougher on us than he might otherwise have been, to avoid any appearance of a conflict of interest. He had also had conversations with his boss at the *New York Times* about how to proceed with the review. He could avoid reviewing us altogether, but that wouldn't be fair to his readers or to the restaurant. In the end, he and his boss agreed that if he hated the restaurant he'd probably omit the review.

If he liked it, he'd err on the side of understating his enthusiasm. He wanted to give the restaurant a chance to exceed expectations. That was a gift.

IN THOSE EARLY DAYS, I benefited hugely from an unexpected mentor who helped me clarify and execute my vision. The larger-than-life co-owner of Sparks Steakhouse, Pat Cetta (the same man who helped celebrate my deal with Sam Brown), would often simply appear at the doorstep of Union Square Cafe, out of the blue. He never showed up at a convenient time, but, strangely, it was always the right time. I was struggling with my inexperience as a boss and a manager, and with learning how to operate a busy restaurant. Pat had a sixth sense for knowing precisely when I needed to be dressed down, or to be helped. He was equal parts genius and ruffian; charming and vulgar; teddy bear huggable and frighteningly cantankerous. I don't think I ever saw Pat without a red wine stain on his tie or a button missing from his shirt. His unusually wide-set eyes had permanent crow's-feet, the kind that come from a combination of loving and laughing at life while chewing people out at the same time.

One day Pat arrived for one of his impromptu visits, and I promptly showed off a new dish I thought was a clever idea: fried oyster Caesar salad. We sat down together at table 61, and I confidently had the kitchen send one out to sample. No one else was serving fried oyster Caesar salad, and this was long before every casual restaurant in America started offering even chicken Caesar salad.

"This dish," Pat said, scowling, "is nothing more than mental masturbation. You're clearly doing it just to get noticed by Florence Fabricant"—in the *New York Times*. "And the bad news," he went on, "is that *she* won't even like it. I guarantee you that shit is coming off your menu within two months—and if I were you, I'd take it off in two minutes. You know better than that bullshit, luvah!" He was right and I quickly retired the dish.

Though we were cut from completely different cloth, Pat's vision of hospitality, service, and excellence was quite similar to mine. It was amazing to watch him work his own dining room, which was always full. He did this (and is probably still doing it, wherever he went after he died) every weekday night. Pat wanted people to have a great time in his restaurant, and he focused all his energy and passion on making certain that his staff missed no detail. We did differ profoundly, though, in our philosophies on honoring dinner reservations. To Pat, a reservation merely meant, *We are expecting you.* But when you were seated was quite another matter. Guests at Sparks might typically wait anywhere between fifteen and ninety minutes for their reserved table. If Union Square Cafe is as much as thirty minutes late on a reservation, people are ready to write me a letter of complaint and send a copy to every restaurant critic in town. But Pat, who died in 2000, always got away with it because people loved eating at Sparks and because he somehow made the wait part of the expected experience. (In later years, that gave me the confidence not to fret too much over the long lines at Shake Shack. They're part of the experience.)

Another priceless mentor I gained in those early days is the brilliant wine importer Robert Chadderdon. Bob was among the extraordinary people I first met while I worked at Pesca in 1984. Even then, he already had a nearly mythic reputation for being difficult and iconoclastic, because he was supposedly selective about which wholesalers, restaurants, and wine stores he would and would not choose to do business with. In his clients, he required a high standard of excellence and integrity along with humility and faith in him—criteria that ruled out all but a very few. Beyond the fact that he had worked for the legendary Frank Schoonmaker, I didn't know much about him before we met. But I had always loved (and had never been let down by) any bottle of wine bearing his label: Robert Chadderdon Selections. Before I knew much about wine, I looked for his label at wine stores and at the few restaurants that displayed their bottles; it was a virtual guarantee of quality. One day when general manager

Douglas Scarborough announced Robert's arrival at Pesca, it was as
if visiting royalty had stopped in for lunch. Douglas would not allow
me to taste Robert's wines with them, but I did get to look Robert
in the eye for a brief moment at the bar. (Douglas did save me a taste
of some of the wines, and I'll never forget my first sips of Mercu-
rey Blanc and St. Joseph Blanc, two obscure, high-value, delicious
wines.) This first encounter with Robert Chadderdon impressed me
so much that a year later, when I was putting together the opening
wine list for Union Square Cafe, I gathered the courage to pick up
the phone and call him. After giving me the third degree over the
phone, to determine if I seemed worthy of selling his wines ("You're
opening what? Where? Who's the chef? What's your background?"),
he agreed to meet me for dinner. We met in Greenwich Village at the
bistro La Gauloise on Sixth Avenue. As he looked me squarely in the
eye, his opening question was, "How old are you anyway?"

"Twenty-seven," I said, taken aback. "Why? How old are you?"

"Thirty-seven," he replied, without missing a beat, "and I've forgotten more about wine—and life—in the last ten years than you
may learn in the next twenty." Then and there, I decided that this
was a man from whom I could learn, from whom I wanted to learn,
and with whom I could enjoy the learning process. He immediately became an important adviser and ally, something between a
father and a brother; and we eventually worked closely together, even
making several trips to France and Italy, where I was privileged to get
intensive training and an advanced degree in wine and food. Robert
is now twenty years wiser, and he hasn't stopped teaching, pushing,
and loving me since that first night.

Robert Chadderdon is, to be sure, a man who steadfastly walks
down one path in life: his own. He's not interested in submitting his
wines to be reviewed, even by publications as influential as the *Wine
Spectator* or Robert Parker's *Wine Advocate*, because he doesn't need or
want publicity. He has an extraordinary stable of winemakers and vineyards and has developed lifelong relationships with leading producers,

who have been growing their grapes in prized vineyards for generations. He gets into their blood, taking an interest in their families and their lives. He advises them on every step as they make their wines. Nothing is more important to him than quality, integrity, and trust. A Robert Chadderdon wine is not a commodity one sees listed at discount in a newspaper advertisement. Each bottle is a living extension of a living human relationship. Thanks in part to Bob, I first discovered the pleasures of some of the world's most phenomenal wines—Château Rayas, Vouvray's Domaine Huet, Burgundy's Marc Colin and Robert Arnoux, Château Simone in Provence, Tuscany's Querciabella and Grattamacco, Piedmont's Bricco Manzoni, and the Veneto's incomparable Giuseppe Quintarelli. And then there are Billecart-Salmon in Champagne, Château Clos Floridene in Graves, and Sancerre from George Roblin and Roger Neveu. Those wines and many others have helped our restaurants earn high praise for their wine lists.

But to view Robert Chadderdon as just an expert on wines would be missing the real story. The man is indeed blessed with a pitch-perfect palate, an uncanny taste memory, and an exquisite sense of inherent quality; but he also possesses a rich store of life knowledge, wisdom, and judgment to draw from. There is no one in all these years from whom I have learned more about excellence, food, wine, or life than Robert Chadderdon.

OUR THIRD FULL YEAR, 1988, brought important transitions. For the first time, we broke into the *Zagat Survey*'s list of New York's top-forty favorite restaurants—we were number twenty-one—and Union Square Cafe was described as a "triumph of imaginative American cookery." In August 1988, after having been together for four years, Audrey and I got married. And by early fall, I made a long-considered change in the kitchen.

Ali Barker, having promised me two years at his first job as chef, had now given me three. He had achieved everything he could for himself (including finding a wonderful woman to be his wife) and had contributed every ounce of raw culinary ability and effort he could muster, despite having no previous experience as a chef. We had an honest and open conversation about the future. I told him, "You have too much potential not to go and learn some more. And Union Square Cafe has too much potential not to benefit from having an even more experienced leader in the kitchen." I urged him to spend some time cooking in France. The discussion was painful and tearful for both of us. We had become good friends and together had injected heart and soul into the place. Though Ali understood exactly what I was saying, it wasn't easy for him to welcome my conclusion. But I knew this was the right decision; today, many years later, we remain friendly, and he has built a successful restaurant career and meaningful life with his family in the town of St. Joseph, Michigan, on the eastern shore of Lake Michigan.

In early October, I hired my old colleague Michael Romano, who had been turning heads at La Caravelle with his solid yet light approach to the French classics. It had taken me a long time to persuade Michael that he should consider making a move downtown, and even longer to get him to say yes. Ultimately, what sold him was the allure of cooking in a restaurant that would let him return to his Italian roots, even if it meant moving away from the refinement he had so diligently achieved as he built his career. During his first month at the restaurant, I prohibited Michael from changing our menu. "Get to know the staff, the guests, the facility, and the restaurant's rhythms. Work on making our existing menu items look better than ever. Use the daily specials as an opportunity to try out new dishes. We'll know which ones work, and we can add them one by one to the menu later on."

And that's precisely what we did. In May 1989, Bryan Miller returned to review the restaurant once again, this time awarding it three stars and calling Union Square Cafe "a paragon of a new breed of restaurants that might be called international bistros." Mentioning

Michael's passion for northern Italian cooking, Bryan described our menu as "the best roster of dishes I've encountered here," and "reasonably priced" as well. Our wine list, he wrote, was one of the city's best ("many uncommon treasures"); our tables were "spaced well to allow easy conversation"; and the dining room, down a few steps off the bar area felt "inviting and countrified." In October, Zagat promoted us from number twenty-one to number thirteen on the list of New York's favorite restaurants. Crushingly, 1989 was also the year that our beloved general manager, Gordon Dudash, succumbed to complications from AIDS. He had hung on long enough to see the fruits of his labor: a restaurant that was increasingly adored as much for its welcome as for its cooking.

I was just four years into the restaurant business, and the fire inside me was only beginning to burn. My vision for Union Square Cafe was being realized, from its cozy décor and ambience to the outstanding value we offered. To this day, Union Square Cafe remains the purest expression of me and most clearly represents the mission of all my restaurants: to express excellence in the most inclusive, accessible, genuine, and hospitable way possible.

CHAPTER 4

Turning Over the Rocks

I HAVE BEEN FLY-FISHING ONLY once in my life. It was in Woody Creek, Colorado, outside Aspen, and I went with a young guide who had come highly recommended by the original chef at Eleven Madison Park, Kerry Heffernan (no relation to my wife, Audrey), an expert fly-fisherman. My guide, displaying wisdom that belied his age, called me over as he waded into a clear, rushing stream, and picked up a small rock. He turned it over and smiled. From a distance, I noticed nothing unusual on its slick underside. I had no idea what he was looking for, or at.

"Here, come look," he said. He pointed out dozens of tiny aquatic insects hatching on the rock. This told him precisely which fly to tie because, as he explained, the trout would only bite on an artificial fly that resembled what was actually hatching. The guide then put the stone back exactly where he had found it. I was intrigued. There was a world of information under that rock, if only one knew or cared enough to look for it.

I took a valuable business lesson back home to New York. There's always a story behind a story if you look for it; and you can augment your success at "hooking" customers by taking the care, time, and interest to look. On my rounds in our dining rooms, I'm constantly turning over rocks, hunting for those details—a guest's impatient look or a glance at a watch, an untouched dish, a curious gaze at our artwork. These details could indicate that someone is bored, impatient, in need of affection, puzzled, interested, or just daydreaming. But each gesture is a potential opportunity for me to visit the table and provide some hospitality.

It's human nature for people to take precisely as much interest in you as they believe you're taking in them. There is no stronger way to build relationships than taking a genuine interest in other human beings and allowing them to share their stories. When we take an active interest in the guests at our restaurants, we create a sense of community and a feeling of "shared ownership."

Shared ownership develops when guests talk about a restaurant as if it's *theirs*. They can't wait to share it with friends, and what they're really sharing, beyond the culinary experience, is the experience of feeling important and loved. That sense of affiliation builds trust and a sense of being accepted and appreciated, invariably leading to repeat business, a necessity for any company's long-term survival.

And it all starts by turning over the rocks.

I'm constantly reminding our staff members to initiate a relationship with our guests whenever it's appropriate. For example, it's amazing how powerful it can be simply to ask guests where they are from. Often, that leads to making a connection because we know someone in common, or we've enjoyed the same restaurant, or we can share a sports story. The old game of "Do you know So-and-so?" is a classic example of turning over rocks to further human connection. And it works. When you are considering several restaurants for dinner, other things being equal, you'll choose the one whose maître d' went to the same school as you, or roots for your sports team, or has the same birthday as you, or knows your second cousin. You'll also tend to choose a restaurant whose chef came out to greet you on your last visit, or who saved you the last soft-shell crab special, knowing it was a favorite of yours. The information is always there if it matters enough to look for it.

Making my rounds in the dining rooms involves, more than anything else, my ability to see, hear, and sense what's going on so that I can connect intelligently with our staff and guests and make things happen. I don't have a standard approach for every table, but I often start with a gut sense that a patron is ready for a visit. That's what springs me into action. I might just walk over to a table and say, "Thanks for being here." That puts the ball in the other court. The encounter either does or doesn't advance from there. But once the rock is turned over and a dialogue begins, I start to learn something, and I always act on what I learn. (And sometimes I learn that the person just wants to be left alone to eat dinner.)

One night in April 2002, soon after opening our barbecue restaurant Blue Smoke, I noticed a couple in the back room gazing out at the trees in the courtyard. I could sense that they were debating whether they liked their ribs, so I went over to greet them. "Where are you from?" I asked.

"We're from Kansas City," the man said.

"We're going to have a tough time living up to the barbecue standards of your hometown," I replied.

As we chatted, I also learned that they had recently moved to New York and that they were very happy to have discovered a real pit barbecue place in their neighborhood. "I only wish we didn't have to make reservations for barbecue four weeks in advance," the man said. I told him that we had just decided to leave half the tables open for walk-ins as a way of encouraging spontaneous visits to the restaurant. That news pleased them. Then the man added, "You know, in Kansas City they give you more than one kind of sauce. Would you ever consider serving a sweeter and spicier sauce than this?"

My hunch was right: something had been on their minds. Now I knew what it was, and also how to make a connection. "It's interesting to hear you say that, because we're actually working on a Kansas City–style sauce right now in the kitchen. Would you like to be the first guests to try it?"

I went to the kitchen for a pitcher of that sauce and brought it back out to the table. The man poured some on his brisket (something a Texan would *never* do). "This," he said beaming, "takes me home!" I asked for his business card, and later wrote him a note when Blue Smoke began offering Kansas City–style barbecue sauce.

I'm certain that this couple felt a sense of ownership in the restaurant after our encounter. As far as they were concerned, they were in part responsible for our putting the new sauce on the table. That's the kind of dialogue we want to have. Hospitality can exist only when there is human dialogue. This particular dialogue provided great customer feedback and helped us forge a bond with two customers—not a bad investment of six minutes of my time!

I try to be in the restaurants as often as possible. For nearly twenty years, until the opening of The Modern on West Fifty-third Street, all my restaurants were within a ten-minute walk of one another and my apartment—and I made it my business to visit every one of them during lunch. I'm not there just to greet and shake hands. I'm building daily communities within the restaurant's larger community.

The best way to do this is to first gather as much information as I can about our guests. I call this collecting dots. In fact, I urge our managers to *ABCD—always be collecting dots.*

Dots are information. The more information you collect, the more frequently you can make meaningful connections that can make other people feel good and give you an edge in business. Using whatever information I've collected to gather guests together in a spirit of shared experience is what I call connecting the dots. If I don't turn over the rocks, I won't see the dots. If I don't collect the dots, I can't connect the dots. If I don't know that someone works, say, for a magazine whose managing editor I happen to know, I've lost a chance to make a meaningful connection that could enhance our relationship with the guest and the guest's relationship with us. The information is there. You just have to choose to look.

I always try to sense opportunities to glean information, and it's not limited to information about our guests. I will often just stand on the periphery of the dining room and watch. I gauge the temperature of the room, the smell, and the noise. Most important, I watch my staff members. Are they enjoying one another's company? And are they focused on their work? If the answer to both questions is yes, I feel confident that we're at the top of our game.

Think about every time you've walked into a restaurant or an office, or even looked into the dugout at a baseball game. When the team is having fun *and* is focused, the chances are very good that the team will win.

I study the faces of our guests. If I see that the direction of their eyes intersects at the center of the table, I know that they are actively engaged with one another and I'm confident that everything is fine. This is an inopportune time to visit. Guests dine out primarily to be with one another, and their eyes tell me they are doing precisely what they came to do.

Whenever I see that the direction of someone's eyes is not bisecting the center of the table, then a visit may be warranted. I am not certain that something is wrong, but I am certain that there is an opportunity to make a connection without feeling like an intruder. It could be that a guest has been waiting too long for his or her food and is looking for a waiter. It could be that someone is simply curious about the architecture, a work of art on the wall, or, for that matter, an attractive guest across the dining room. Or a guest could be momentarily bored, or just taking a pause, or having a fight with a companion.

I also look for solo diners. From my own experiences dining alone, I know that solo diners have a straightforward agenda: to treat themselves to a gift of quality, contemplative time, and to do so at our restaurant. I consider that the ultimate compliment, and I'm also hoping that today's solo diner will host tomorrow's party of four.

A little perception goes a long way. Hospitality can, in the right instance, involve little more than standing nearby and allowing my body language to smile at the guests. If I catch, say, a woman's eye, she may beckon me to the table and let me know that she needs water, a waiter, or the check. If I thank her for coming to the restaurant, she might say, "You're very welcome. This place is so much better than your other restaurants!" Or, "We were wondering when you opened this restaurant." Or, "It's nice to be back. It's gotten much better. Last time, the service was so slow." Or, "We hadn't been back since you opened. It was so loud then! How did you fix that?"

In these exchanges I'm collecting information not just about who our guests are, but about how they feel about our product. One advantage a restaurant has over many other businesses is that we can get instant feedback while our consumers are consuming our product. People have an emotional attachment to food and to their money, and they come to our restaurants with high expectations. To the degree that they believe we are on their side, we usually don't have to work very hard to get candid reactions.

If our customers love what they've ordered, I can tell by looking at their faces (and their plates). If they aren't happy, they're going to let me or my staff know—as long as we've built the right relationship with them. One night in Blue Smoke, I noticed that some diners had finished eating but had left most of their onion rings untouched on the plate. They could simply have been full, but I went over to say hi and to have a closer look. Sure, enough, the rings didn't look crispy. "You didn't love them," I said, gesturing to the rings.

"You know, you're right," the man answered. "They were the only thing I thought could have been better. I wish they'd been crispier and spicier."

"Well, then," I said, "you're not paying for them." A moment later, as they got up to leave, the man handed me a $100 bill. "This is for the waiter," he said. Good as this waiter was, I knew that the generous gratuity was in part a reflection of the fact that the guests appreciated our taking a special interest in them and caring for them. In the end, we decided to take the onion rings off the menu, because we couldn't get them consistently right without incurring a very high labor cost to produce them. That, of course, led to a spate of new complaints: "Bring back the onion rings!"

IT HAD OCCURRED TO me in Woody Creek that until my fishing guide turned over that rock, I'd have been content to stand at the edge of the running stream enjoying the dreamy valley and mountains. But in business, turning over the rocks and reading the water, as a fly-fisherman might do, gives you crucial information so that you can take an even deeper interest in your customers, and encourages them to do the same with you.

Since I opened Union Square Cafe in 1985, guests who have dined with us there and in our other restaurants are presented with both a check and a comment card, an idea I had first seen while I was at Pesca. (There, guests were asked for their name and address, but feedback and comments were not solicited.) If guests write their name and address on the front of the card, we place them on the mailing list for our newsletter. That way, as promised on the comment card, we can "keep them informed of upcoming events," such as our "morning market meetings," "wine and food dinners," and cooking classes. On the back of the card there's room for guests to share their opinions about the food, wine, ambience, service, and anything else on their minds—an ideal opportunity for us to collect dots. Early on, I responded personally to every comment card, but today that is the job of our chefs and managers, who read up to 100 cards a week. It's an excellent way to build trust, encourage and enrich dialogue, and give our guests the confidence that, at our restaurants, their suggestions are taken seriously.

It may seem obvious now, but in the 1980s using a comment card to compile a mailing list for a fine restaurant's newsletter was an innovation of sorts. You would rarely if ever see comment cards distributed in fine restaurants—that was more the domain of places like Denny's. But within two or three years I began to notice that the wording I chose for our first comment card—"We want you to return to Union Square Cafe and eagerly seek your comments or suggestions"—was being adopted almost word for word in all kinds of restaurants. Today, we have collected well over 150,000 names on our mailing lists. The lists have proved to be an extremely effective way to build a community and stay connected with our guests and friends all over the country—and even worldwide. Today, of course, the entire marketing profession is out to collect e-mail addresses to stay in touch with existing and prospective customers. We do that too, but in my judgment nothing can or will replace the meaningful contact that happens with a personal note or newsletter sent the old-fashioned way.

One of the oldest sayings in business is "The customer is always right." I think that's become a bit outdated. I want to go on the offensive to create opportunities for our customers to feel that they are being heard even when they're *not* right. To do so, I always actively encourage them—when I'm on my rounds, in our comment cards, and in letters or e-mail to us—to let us know if they feel something's not right. When they do, I thank them.

I HAVE ALWAYS VIEWED excellence as a journey rather than a destination. Taking that journey demands a form of athleticism. It is the athlete's nature to call on all resources to compete and win. I believe it's possible to apply to business the same athletic skills I would apply on a tennis court or a baseball diamond. I see this as a combination of innate ability, focused training, and a persistent zeal to win.

A friend once told me a story about an athletic display by Governor Jeb Bush of Florida. My friend, who is a very successful businessman—and, I should note, a Democrat—opened an office in Florida with about forty employees. On the day the company was incorporated, out of the blue, he received a personal phone call from Governor Bush (whom he had never met) thanking him for doing business in Florida. "Here's a special number," the governor said, "that I want you to use if you ever need any roads moved or bridges built for your company." My friend remains a Democrat, but he left that transaction very impressed with Governor Bush.

Whatever your politics, that's an inspirational business story. It's the kind of unexpected gesture that sends a clear message to the governor's constituents: *I'm not taking one vote for granted.* In my business, which is so dependent on repeat customers, I never take a vote for granted either. I'm campaigning for a core constituency of regulars. I don't know too many businesses that can survive without one.

If I see a new area code or zip code on our reservations list, or if I notice that some guests come from as far away as, for instance, St. Paul, Minnesota; Highland Park, Illinois; or Cambridge, Massachusetts, I will make sure that these guests get special attention. We might ask them how they heard about us. We might ask them if they are in town on business or a vacation. We will ask where else they'll be dining while they are in New York. That opens a dialogue with them, as well as an opportunity to send them to one of our other restaurants—where they can expect to get another special welcome. The hope is that when they return home, they'll spread the word about each of our restaurants.

How do you get customers to come back for more? That's the question facing every business owner, whether the business is a bowling alley, pharmacy, computer company, or tattoo parlor. There are two processes at work—*trial* and *repeat*. And it's critically important to prevail in each of them. If you own a restaurant and you're fortunate enough to persuade someone to give it an initial try (no small feat), you'd better make a great impression and win the first round. I think that most businesses are better at coddling regulars than they are at focusing on first-timers. But both are crucial to any business; although it's obviously important to keep your steady clientele happy, life depends on auspicious beginnings! In tennis, you can't possibly win a tournament without first having won each of the earlier rounds. If we can get to the third round with a guest, we've got a good shot at moving him or her into the important group of patrons who become cherished regulars.

It's always fascinating to see which people choose to become regulars at any one of our restaurants. We don't necessarily have the same core of habitués at each place. In fact, only a very few patrons love everything we do with equal enthusiasm. More typically, we've found that a dyed-in-the-wool regular at one of our restaurants loves one or two of the others, and that's it. This is usually a matter of chemistry, and of preferences in food and design.

Even so, our batting average is pretty good. I'd guess we succeed at earning repeat business over 70 percent of the time. It's significant that the older our businesses become, the more popular they become—and not just according to the *Zagat Survey*. With few exceptions, our restaurants have also enjoyed increased revenues each successive year they've been open. I know that popularity is not in and of itself a measure of excellence but it is one reliable measure of how many people you're pleasing, and how well you're pleasing them.

If an avid restaurant-goer in New York dines out three times a week, that's twelve times a month. People love discovering new experiences when they dine out, so I assume that about eight of those times they'll decide to try a place where they've never been, whether it's an establishment that has just opened or one that has been around for years.

That still leaves four meals per month to return to old favorites. I don't expect anyone to eat at any of our restaurants every day or even every week (though we are remarkably fortunate to feed and serve a substantial number of seriously devoted, loyal creatures of habit). I'm deeply grateful when regulars who dine with us three or four times a week think of our restaurant not just as another destination but also as their club—or better still, as an extension of their family and home.

My goal is to earn regular, repeat patronage from a large number of people—40 percent of our lunch business and 25 percent of our dinner business—who will dine at our restaurants six to twelve times a year. Unlike a Broadway show, which most people will see just once no matter how much they've enjoyed it, a solid restaurant experience should make you want to return for more. There are always more dishes to sample, more waiters by whom to be served, and more tables from which to view the ever-changing scene. At its best, a restaurant should not let guests leave without feeling as though they've been satisfyingly hugged.

If you can do that, regardless of what product you are offering, you've built a solid foundation for your business. Those satisfied customers become not just your regulars but also your apostles. They'll proceed to sell your product for you by telling the world how much they like it. Automobile companies and watchmakers have long understood that people buy their products not just because of how the product itself performs, but to tell a story about themselves. Almost any watch tells time; every car can get you from point A to point B; and every restaurant can feed you. Just as my choice of a watch to wear and a car to drive (and be seen driving) says something about me, so too does my choice of where I dine frequently. We want as many of our guests as possible to be proud to identify themselves with our restaurants. Our job is to give people a story worth telling.

For us, building a community of regulars has become more efficient, with computers and online reservations, than it was in our early days, when we maintained a standard paper-and-pencil reservation book. I receive computer-generated copies of the detailed reservation sheets from each of our restaurants first thing every day. My assistant also reviews the sheets in the morning, looking for tidbits of information that can help us offer our guests more hospitality. Knowing who is dining where—and when—helps me determine how to plan and plot out my day. It also gives me the opportunity to get involved with seating and greeting plans. We look for opportunities to create chance encounters by strategically seating people with similar business interests near one another. We also try to create privacy for those who want it. I happen to love maps. I view our reservationists as cartographers, the reservation sheets as a map, and the dining experience as a brief vacation for our guests. As with any trip, there are lots of routes one can take; and it's our job to draw a map with the greatest possible detail. The more specific information we can gather ahead of someone's dining experience, the greater the chance that we can create a "rave" experience. Is it a special occasion? A first visit? Does this guest prefer a quiet table? Was there any problem the last time this guest visited? Does any guest have an allergy? This guest loves red wine! That guest is a columnist for *Newsweek*. Another is going to a Knicks game. And so on.

Our telephone reservationists, who are our first line of offense in delivering hospitality, listen carefully and then input whatever data they receive from a caller into our Open Table reservation and "guest notes" database. (In the old days, we'd also gather information, but it was simply written in pencil on the reservation sheet for the day. That system made it unlikely that we'd ever be able to retrieve the information again.) This information tells our hosts, maître d', managers, and servers a lot about a guest's needs, and helps us to customize our service and hospitality.

We also make sure to enter into "customer notes" any previous mistakes we made ("overcooked salmon on 7/16, spilled wine on purse 5/12"). We also indicate all "special requests" ("likes table 42; bring hot sauce with food; loves corner table; ice on side always with cocktails; allergic to shellfish; serve coffee *after* dessert"), which then show up on our computer reservation screen. As long as we make it clear that we're interested in knowing through active listening, most people are delighted to tell us exactly what they want or need.

When a reservation indicates that a guest is dining at one of our restaurants for the first time, we'll make sure the host knows. If we are to stand any chance of creating a new regular, it starts here. We'll need to win that trial round!

It's even possible to use the reservations sheets to begin the hospitality experience before anyone sets foot in the restaurant. One day I noticed on a reservation sheet that a couple would be coming in that evening to Gramercy Tavern to celebrate their twentieth anniversary—a big-deal night, for sure. That morning I picked up the phone to call them and thanked them for sharing the special occasion with us. "Bring a good appetite," I said, "and enjoy your anniversary." The woman on the other end of the line was happily surprised to hear from me, and said she was just about to confirm her reservation. "No need to call," I said. "It's taken care of."

After we hung up, I confirmed the reservation at Gramercy Tavern and instructed the restaurant to send a complimentary midcourse to the couple that evening. Knowing it would be something delicious delivered by a wonderful waiter, I was confident we would create an evening worth talking about.

That is being proactive about offering hospitality, and it's what our managers do when they're performing at their best. Many businesses depend on word of mouth. People talk about where and how they celebrate anniversaries, birthdays, and holidays ("What did you do for your birthday? Where did he take you for Valentine's Day?") and so those special occasions are especially rich opportunities to build word-of-mouth business.

Reviewing the reservation sheets that same morning, I learned that a regular guest was coming for dinner at Tabla, having visited three of our other restaurants over the previous two days. These included Jazz Standard, our music club downstairs from Blue Smoke, where this guest had enjoyed hearing the wonderful pianist Bill Charlap. It is absolutely critical to know such details. I called Tracy Wilson, our general manager at Tabla, and urged her to acknowledge how much we appreciated his loyalty.

Then I saw on another reservation sheet that a couple I knew who were coming in for dinner that night at Blue Smoke had indicated that they wanted to give their best regards to me. Why wait? I promptly picked up the telephone, called them, and left a message on their answering machine: "Hey, Helen and Paul, this is Danny Meyer. I noticed that you're coming to Blue Smoke tonight, and I just want to let you know how much your loyalty means. I won't be able to be at the restaurant to greet you personally, but I hope you're both well and that you'll enjoy Blue Smoke tonight."

I realize that I don't have to do this kind of thing, but there is simply no point for me—or anyone on my staff—to work hard every day for the purpose of offering guests an average experience. I want to hear: "We love your restaurant, we adore the food, but your people are what we treasure most about being here." That's the reaction that makes me most proud and tells me we're succeeding on all levels. I encourage each manager to take ten minutes a day to make three gestures that exceed expectations and take a special interest in our guests. That translates into 1,000 such gestures every year, multiplied by over 100 outstanding managers throughout our restaurants. For any business owner, that can add up to a lot of repeat business.

In the late 1990s, when I first started hearing about Web-based electronic reservations books, I was very resistant to the whole notion. I thought that by taking online reservations, we would be losing the advantage we had always had with our warm, human telephone staff. We would be like every other restaurant.

Then I changed my view, for one reason: to close that window of access to people who preferred making their reservations online would be poor hospitality. It may be more convenient for them to reserve at eleven-thirty at night when they're sitting at their computers than during our regular business hours. It would let them check out the availability of a table without making a single call, without the frustration of a busy signal, without being put on hold—and without eventually being told that there's nothing available.

Once I finally accepted the inevitability of online reservations, I fell in love with the process and its benefits. Every time somebody makes a reservation on the Internet, that's one less telephone call for our reservationist to handle. As a result, the reservationist can more often avoid making the annoying request, "May I put you on hold while I take another call?"

The information we receive—whether a booking was made by telephone or on the Internet—is instantly added to the file of guests' preferences that we once recorded manually on reservation sheets or occasionally on file cards.

Now, thanks to the vast record-keeping capacity of the computer, I can measure the degree to which guests are regulars. I can know what their favorite table is, or if they have a favorite (or least favorite) server. I can know when a guest's birthday or anniversary is. I can know if guests are regulars at our other restaurants—in which case I'm even more pleased to see them coming in to try another one of our restaurants for the first time. All this adds up to a gold mine of information, which allows us to connect all sorts of dots.

Online reservations also allow guests to make their own comments. One guest, describing himself as a "super-Eleven Madison Park regular" and wine enthusiast, was making, by his own count, his 149th visit. If we see that guests qualify for VIP status for Open Table, meaning that they've made a huge number of online reservations at all sorts of other restaurants, we know that we're welcoming people who frequently dine out at other fine restaurants. That's a valuable opportunity to turn proven restaurant aficionados into our own regulars.

Occasionally, there are angry, demanding, or even abusive callers who do test our reservationists' patience. We have designed a short-hand system to give us a heads-up about a potentially difficult situation. It's another way we take a proactive, athletic approach to hospitality. If a reservationist has had to work especially hard to calm down or ac-commodate an irate caller, we may use the notation WFM ("welcome from manager"), which means that the guest may need some extra attention from a manager. When people let us know that they don't wish to be interrupted unnecessarily, the notation is "do not disturb" or "drop and go"—that is, deliver the food and leave them alone. This note is passed on to the host and waitstaff. Our job is not to impose our own needs on our guests: it's to be aware of their needs and to deliver the goods accordingly. In hospitality, one size fits one!

When I spent my summer as a tour guide working for my dad in Italy, I reported to his manager in Rome, Giorgio Smaldone, a proud, chain-smoking native of Salerno who taught me a lot about the essence of hospitality. Giorgio's favorite expression about how to treat tour group members, delivered in his special form of English, was: *"There is to make them feel important. Always start with the one who most need feel important!"* Many years later, a wonderful server who had been at Union Square Cafe for more than a decade told me that when she had previously worked for Mary Kay Cosmetics, Mary Kay would teach the salespeople that everyone goes through life with an invisible sign hanging around his or her neck reading, "make me feel important." Giorgio and Mary Kay had it right. The most successful people in any business that depends on human relationships are the ones who know about that invisible sign and have the vision to see how brightly it is flashing. And the true champions know best how to embrace the human being wearing the sign.

DESPITE HIGH-TECH ENHANCEMENTS, RESTAURANTS will always remain a hands-on, high-touch, people-oriented business. Nothing will ever replace shaking people's hands, smiling, and looking them in the eye as a genuine means of welcoming them. And that is why hospitality—unlike widgets—is not something you can stamp out on an assembly line. But its powerful impact can be taught, and teaching it with hundreds of colleagues is the best way I've found to extend my reach.

One reality of our business growth is that I cannot be everywhere at all times. I compensate for the fact that there's only one of me by studying the maps and responding. I'll often run into somebody on the street and be able to say, "I understand you were at Tabla last night. How was your dinner?" People immediately feel good and are surprised that I would know this. But why wouldn't I? If I want our guests to take an interest in us, I'd better take an equal interest in them.

I also use this information to bring together people from similar professions, or to connect people who I know share some common ground—whether it's from the art world, financial services, politics, the culinary business, book publishing, journalism, advertising, or design. I call this *planting like seeds in like gardens* in order to extend our community. I'll purposely make certain that these people are seated near, but not next to, one another. Or I may simply introduce them, hoping that something positive, beyond a good meal, may come out of the "chance encounter." A publisher who sees another publisher dining at Union Square Cafe will logically assume: "This is where publishers come for lunch." A food journalist who sees a well-known chef dining two tables away may conclude: "This place must be good if *he* eats here." I call this form of dot-connecting "benevolent manipulation." Everyone wins, including us.

Through the years I've had plenty of help from our loyal friends in building communities. Roger W. Straus Jr.—the brilliant book publisher and world-class bon vivant who cofounded Farrar, Straus and Giroux and led that company for nearly six decades until his death at age eighty-seven in May 2004—became one of our best and most devoted patrons soon after Union Square Cafe opened. By our estimate, Roger ate some 3,000 lunches there—his favorite dishes were oysters on the half shell, black bean soup, smoked steak sandwich, and vitello tonnato—and almost all of those lunches took place at table 38, where he held court an average of three days a week for nearly two decades.

Roger was proud of the people with whom he dined—erudite editors, Nobel Prize winners, best-selling authors—and it was always important to him to introduce them to his other friends. Sometimes we'd be chatting at his table and he'd lean forward to ask me if I knew "who the son of a bitch was over there" at table 30 or table 36. When I'd say no, he was always kind enough to introduce me. Seeing Roger lunching at table 38 made any other author, editor, agent, or publisher aware that Union Square Cafe was *the* downtown haunt for the literary trade. It also didn't hurt that across the room sat another legend in the book world: Paul Gottlieb of Harry Abrams, a leading publisher of art books and other literary works. Through the years, many other tables in that dining room began to be filled by other publishers, many of whom are important fixtures at the restaurant.

Sometimes I'll see a name and remember that it's a guest who once held a book party at Gramercy Tavern or Eleven Madison Park. I can then remind the maître d' to welcome him or her back. One day I'll see that novelist Richard North Patterson, a longtime friend of our restaurants who dines with us whenever he's in town from San Francisco, is coming in. I recall that handgun control is the subject of his latest novel, and when I notice that Donna Dees-Thomases, a founder of the Million Mom March, is eating in the restaurant as well, it's natural that I'm going to seat them near each other, setting up a chance for a beneficial outcome.

Google (or any online search engine, for that matter) is one of the best dot-collecting tools ever invented. I might see a name on the reservation list I think I recognize. I can then check Google to find out who the person is. It's a remarkable tool for hospitality and for drawing even more detailed maps. Google proved to be amazingly useful during the Republican National Convention of 2004. We served a late-night dinner party at Eleven Madison Park for about a dozen media people who included NBC's Tom Brokaw, the *New York Times*'s R.W. (Johnny) Apple, Maureen Dowd, Todd Purdum, plus Purdum's wife, Dee Dee Myers, Bill Clinton's former press secretary. Following a marathon evening at the convention, they all finally sat down to a five-course dinner at eleven-forty-five. Before I left at one o'clock in the morning, I said, "If you folks stay long enough, we'll have to serve you scrambled eggs for dessert." And Johnny Apple, who's from Akron, Ohio, said, "I can tell you're a Midwest boy, probably attended a bunch of coming-out parties." I smiled. "In fact," I said, "it was by going to debutante parties as a nineteen-year-old in St. Louis that I first learned about eating scrambled eggs at two in the morning."

"But I bet you've never had 'eggs daffodil,'" he said. "That's the real thing." He had me there.

As I was leaving for the night, I said to my team, "You guys need to go online and figure out what 'eggs daffodil' are, and I want you to make sure to put a bowl of them on the table by two o'clock in the morning." After all, if you believe that word of mouth makes the world go around, here were eleven people who had fairly big, powerful mouths.

Googling "eggs daffodil" revealed just a vague description, but it was enough to inspire Eleven Madison Park's chef, Kerry Heffernan, who improvised what he imagined eggs daffodil to be, creating an inspired recipe that included zucchini blossoms and cheese. They were brought out at two o'clock and served in a copper pot to Johnny Apple, right around dessert time, as the journalists were making some toasts. (Brokaw and Apple would soon be retiring and were each covering their last political convention.)

The next day Kerry told me the eggs daffodil "blew them away." Kerry loved the recipe—he had cooked the eggs and cream slowly, put them in a blender with some *beurre fondue,* and then gently heated them up again, stirring in some zucchini blossoms—and said he had decided to put it on our brunch menu. The *ABCD* strategy—*always be collecting dots*—had once again strengthened a sense of community and had challenged our staff to express more caring and creativity than our guests could have expected. It also provided an opportunity to add more value by listening, using our imagination, and executing.

We had served a wonderful dinner as it was. But when Johnny Apple made that remark about "eggs daffodil," it was as if he had presented us with a rock with all kinds of life growing underneath it, and we were then able to tie the right fly to catch the fish. Two years later, I saw Tom Brokaw at a dinner party, and he told twelve other people the story of eggs daffodil. Ask Johnny Apple or the others what they remember most about that evening's menu. I guarantee it's the eggs daffodil.

CHAPTER 5

Who Ever Wrote the Rule. . . ?

IT'S BEEN ONE OF my life's greatest pleasures to conceive and launch a new business venture. It's exhilarating to dream, to plumb the depths of my own experiences and piece together things that excite me to create something that never existed before. But I will throw myself into a new venture only when certain criteria are met:

- I am passionate about the subject matter (i.e., early American folk antiques, modern art, jazz, barbecue).

- I know I will derive some combination of challenge, satisfaction, and pleasure from the venture.

- It presents meaningful opportunities for professional growth for my colleagues and me.

- The new business will add something to the dialogue in a specific context, such as luxury dining (Gramercy Tavern), museum dining (The Modern, Cafe 2, and Terrace 5 at the Museum of Modern Art), Indian dining (Tabla), barbecue (Blue Smoke), or burgers and frozen custard (Shake Shack).

- Financial projections indicate the possibility of sufficient profit and returns on our investment to warrant the risk we're undertaking.

My wife, Audrey, an experienced mother of four children, has remarked that watching me in the process of creating a new restaurant reminds her of what she goes through becoming and being a mom. Like restaurants, kids are a lot of fun to conceive and significantly less fun to gestate over the next nine months. You don't get much sleep for the first six months after they arrive, and you feel as if you're never going to get your nose above water. Then, if you're really lucky, after about a year they start to pay lifelong dividends. And we are willing to do it all over again only because we have built-in memory erasers that allow us to forget how painful the whole process was.

My ultimate mission for any new restaurant is always to begin with a subject I love, zero in on what I enjoy most about it, and then envision a new context for it. I take something that is already accessible (such as frozen custard) and try to make it better; or I take what's excellent (a selection of artisanal cheeses or a wine list) and try to present it in a more user-friendly context. I'm never out to invent a new cuisine. Instead, I'm interested in creating a fresh "hybrid" dining experience; and then, like a museum curator, I strive to put a complementary frame around it, find the right wall to hang it on, and aim just the proper lighting on it. The care with which we design our restaurants and the thoughtful way our chefs create the food on our menus are two elements that add significantly to the artistry and the handcrafted feel of a new restaurant.

I feel the entrepreneurial spark when some instinct tells me that a certain dining "context" doesn't currently exist but *should* exist. I then ask myself a series of questions that force me to examine and challenge the status quo—and then change it. Each question begins with these five words: "Who ever wrote the rule . . . ?" Who ever wrote the rule, for example, that you shouldn't be able to enjoy a refined dining experience, with the finest ingredients, served on Limoges china, in a rustic tavern? Or that you can't serve slow-smoked pulled pork with a glass of champagne or Chianti Classico, just off Park Avenue? Or that you can't create a classic burger-and-shakes drive-in in New York City, where no one drives? Or that live jazz sounds good only in a late-night club and only if everyone around you is smoking?

Each venture has taken shape differently. It could be that I know of a chef I really want to work with and now must search for an idea and a location (Gramercy Tavern); or I could have what I think is a compelling idea and then look for a location and a chef (Union Square Cafe); or I could be in love with a specific location and need to find the chef and the idea (The Modern).

Context is everything. What has guided me most as an entrepreneur is the confluence of passion and opportunity (and sometimes serendipity) that leads to the right context for the right idea at the right time in the right place and for the right value. I have never relied on or been interested in market analysis to create a new business model. I am my own test market. I am far more intuitive than analytical. If I sense an opportunity to reframe something I'm passionately interested in, I give it my absolute best shot.

The commitment to add something fresh to an existing dialogue informs every decision my colleagues and I make, from the locations we select to our staff uniforms to virtually every dish we serve. Whether the topic is poached striped bass, tuna tartare, a BLT, or a cup of hot chocolate, I challenge my chefs to tell me exactly what they're planning to do differently from or better than the next guy.

Years ago, for instance, we knew that we needed to offer steak on the menu at Union Square Cafe—in a city that already claims some of the world's greatest steak houses. I also knew there was no way we could outdo Sparks, The Palm, Peter Luger, Smith and Wollensky, or any of the other temples of beef. So we came up with the idea of our smoked steak—a great piece of meat, cold-smoked, grilled, and then served with world-class mashed potatoes and topped with fried leeks. Sirloin steak could have been a kind of "every restaurant needs a steak" throwaway on our menu. Instead, our smoked steak became a reason people return over and over again to Union Square Cafe. Still, in reframing something that people are familiar with, the outcome must be excellent and must never seem contrived.

I always ask our chefs to explain why they think this or that presentation is just right for *their* restaurant. When I asked Tabla's chef, Floyd Cardoz, to explain why heirloom tomatoes belonged on his Indian-inspired menu, he replied, "That's easy. I'm using them in a salad with fresh grated ginger, lots of black Tellicherry pepper, and balsamic vinegar." No one could call Floyd's heirloom tomato salad derivative, and it belonged at Tabla. He continually seeks sensible ways to innovate, in the Indian idiom, demonstrating that you can experiment while remaining grounded in solid traditions, seasonal ingredients, and traditional cooking methods. He's done the same with guacamole, infusing the avocado salad with toasted Indian spices and substituting crispy lotus root chips for tortilla chips.

I do not want to see a dish like tuna tartare (which became ubiquitous in New York during the 1990s) on any of our menus unless our chefs are doing something singularly excellent with it. That challenge led us to come up with an impressive signature dish for Eleven Madison Park: tuna tartare seared on one side. Served with sliced avocado and a radish salad, it looks and tastes different from any other version I've had in town, and—most important—it's addictively delicious. "What makes ours different and special?" is the question we ask and try to answer every day, and not just with food. It adds interest to your work, and it can give people a reason to do business with you, no matter what business you're in. Otherwise, who really needs your product, and what value are you really adding or selling?

One reason Union Square Cafe became so eclectic was that for nearly a decade it was the sole outlet for all my culinary ideas—ideas that I hoped would enrich our guests' experiences. Whenever I traveled I tasted all kinds of food, and Union Square Cafe was the only place where I could try out my new discoveries.

The restaurant was my laboratory, and I pounced on every possible opportunity to experiment with something new. For example:

- We built up an extensive international wine list (when others were focused on wines from just one or two countries), pioneered a new way of organizing that list (by flavor profile rather than appellation), and presented guests with seasonal wine-and-food dinners.

- I wrote a biannual newsletter that became a conversation with our guests and helped to ensure continued patronage.

- By the late 1980s, we were open for Sunday dinner. At the time, that was unusual among fine restaurants.

- In late 1990, I decided to eliminate smoking in our dining room. For years I had permitted smoking in various parts of the restaurant. But smoke drifts, and I couldn't stand mediating arguments night after night between the smokers and nonsmokers. The airlines had a similar problem—there was always one nonsmoking row just ahead of the last smoking row. In 1991, I eliminated smoking from Union Square Cafe altogether, four years before New York City passed a partial ban on smoking in restaurants (the Smoke-Free Act of 1995) and a decade before the more stringent version of 2002.

My voluntary ban on smoking at the restaurant was controversial, though for me it wasn't a matter of telling anyone else what to do. It's my opinion that you can do anything you want in your own place of business. I didn't need a law. Rather, I was sensitive about this issue because Audrey's mother had died of lung cancer at age sixty-one, and then my father had died of it at age fifty-nine. My grandmother, Louise Meyer, had been a lifelong smoker, so although my dad had quit smoking himself when he was in his twenties, he had grown up breathing secondhand smoke. Another motivation for me was concern for my health and that of our employees. And above all, my instinct told me to get out ahead of the pack and take a strong, activist stand in something that affected human health. Some people thought I was crazy, but for me, hospitality must be enlightened: we must care for our own staff first. Interestingly, after our self-imposed ban on cigarettes, business improved, and the restaurant grew more popular than ever.

DESPITE THE CONTINUED SUCCESS of Union Square Cafe, for almost nine years I was firmly against opening a second restaurant. Owing, in large part, to my experience of my father's tumultuous career and his two bankruptcies, I always thought of expansion as dancing on the edge of failure. It wasn't until after my father died that I began to give myself the freedom to expand my business. It was almost as if my fear of repeating his defeats was softened by the fact that he wouldn't be around to see the outcome. Another factor was that for years I had protected myself from the perils of growth by establishing three prerequisites that I knew would be almost impossible to meet. First, any new restaurant would have to be as excellent within its niche as Union Square Cafe. (In my mind, the success of Union Square Cafe had been a fluke, and I was fairly certain I'd never have a hit like that again.) Second, the opening of the new restaurant could in no way compromise or diminish the excellence of Union Square

Cafe. (Restaurant sequels can diminish the original, perhaps because the management's focus and capacity may be spread too thin.) Third, I would open another restaurant only when I was sure that I would also achieve more time for myself and Audrey. (That seemed unlikely, as I was already working up to fourteen hours a day.)

At this point in our lives, Audrey and I were married but still without kids. Audrey had successfully transitioned from a career as a stage actress to become a leading member of the publishing and sales team at *Gourmet* magazine. Since we had met in the restaurant business, neither of us had to adjust our expectations about what demands my career would place on us as a couple. But with each year of Union Square Cafe's progress as a prominent restaurant, I found myself working harder and longer to exceed increasingly ratcheted expectations—the public's and my own. We were intent on having kids, all the more so because each of us had lost a parent. I did a lot of soul-searching, asking myself whether taking on more business and more stress would be wise for me or my marriage, or even for my business. To her credit, Audrey left the decision to me.

In the early 1990s, I was doing a lot of thinking about how much I enjoyed luxury dining. I was inspired by Michelin-starred restaurants in France and Italy, especially the two-star restaurants, which seemed able to combine refinement with genuine warmth. I was also increasingly impressed by the improved quality of cooking here in the United States. I loved the food and wine served at these great restaurants, but I was less moved by their customary pomp and circumstance.

So I was presented with a dilemma in 1992 when the restaurant Mondrian closed. Mondrian had received a three-star rating from the *New York Times*, and I knew and greatly admired its chef, Tom Colicchio. Now Tom asked me if I would be interested in starting a new restaurant with him. I was not thinking about opening a new restaurant—but how could I say no to a collaboration with such a gifted, passionate chef? I knew he was the right choice; and with Audrey's encouragement, I began to plan a new restaurant with him.

We agreed that we wanted to combine the elements of luxury dining that we most loved, but to present them within a new framework. I had in mind the lovely restaurants I had enjoyed in the French and Italian countryside, as well as the taverns that Audrey and I had frequented in and around Bucks County, Pennsylvania (Audrey grew up there), and in New England. She and I had become addicted to the hunt for early American antiques. While we were childless, our routine on many weekends was to travel in search of shops and auctions in Maine, Vermont, Connecticut, and Pennsylvania; find a historic tavern for dinner in the evening; and stay overnight at a bed-and-breakfast. Though the food in the old taverns rarely rose above, say, mixed salad with raspberry vinaigrette, duck with cherry sauce, and chocolate mousse, I always found the folk-style atmosphere appealing. Exploring the idea of the "tavern" and imagining how to apply it in a fresh way was becoming a fixation.

So Tom and I began by asking, "Who ever wrote the rule that the only way to enjoy luxurious fine dining is in the environment of a stuffy restaurant with tuxedo-clad waiters and a stiff, hushed atmosphere?" And, "Who ever wrote the rule that a rustic tavern couldn't be a setting for truly outstanding modern food?"

Union Square Cafe had become known as an excellent version of a neighborhood restaurant, so it occurred to me that Gramercy Tavern might succeed as a neighborhood version of an elegant restaurant. In one case the goal was to take some element of dining that was already accessible and make it better; in the other, it was to take an element of excellent dining that was rarefied and make it more accessible. Some people expect a stuffy ambience at Gramercy Tavern, but when they walk in they find an animated community hall—with excellent food and drink. This setting immediately puts guests at ease and makes it somewhat easier for the restaurant to exceed expectations.

We worked with Peter Bentel and his remarkably talented and focused family of architects (whom I had met serendipitously through the contractor who completed Audrey's and my apartment). The Bentels were famous for designing churches and libraries, but this would be their very first restaurant. We began with a fantasy that what we were designing had always been the tavern for the Gramercy Park community, and that we had continued to update it over the past century. Now, as Gramercy Tavern, it would continue to play its earlier role as the community's best place to meet, eat, and drink. As we pounded the pavement looking for a site, my one requirement was to be as close as possible to Union Square Cafe and the greenmarket.

One day Tom Colicchio urged me to come to see a place he had seen through a Runyonesque real estate broker named Augie Hasho. It was on East Twentieth Street and had been a warehouse for military uniforms. The company that owned the building (coincidentally called "N.S. Meyer") also manufactured and sold military medals. The huge storefront space—6,000 square feet—housed a giant version of the type of conveyor hanger system typically used by dry cleaners. The site was a short four-block walk from Union Square Cafe and just three blocks from the greenmarket, which by now included more farmers than before and was open four days a week. And the Gramercy Park–Flatiron district seemed ready for this kind of restaurant. For some reason it had lagged behind nearby developments; it had just a few decent eateries. The contiguous Union Square neighborhood was just starting to emerge as a restaurant row. The time was right to move. The location was perfect. And the price was right: we negotiated an incredibly favorable rent, just $20 per square foot.

With that vast open space we could start from scratch. I hoped that by working with the architects Bentel and Bentel, we could create a restaurant design that would compensate for all the physical shortcomings of Union Square Cafe. If we succeeded, the coatroom would actually have adequate space for a night's worth of coats, the kitchen would have enough space to cook for large numbers of guests, and there would be a private dining room. The restrooms would be commodious and lovely. The offices would be generously sized and would enable the managers to work efficiently. The chilled wine cellar would have a capacity of 7,500 bottles. In the dining rooms there would be no bad tables. And bartenders would actually have enough area to work together behind the bar without bumping into each other every time they mixed a drink.

In our earliest conversations with Bentel and Bentel, we decided to use authentic antiques—and no reproductions. Where we did not use antiques, we would hire craftspeople to create their own artistic interpretations of, say, original tavern sconces and chandeliers. "Inject your own personality," I told these artisans. "But keep it real." In this way we stayed true to our vision and avoided the forced, artificially thematic "ye olde tavern" that we might otherwise have ended up with.

With help from friends and experts in antiques like Peter Ermacora, Evan Hughes, and Dorothy and Leo Rabkin, the treasure hunt yielded some gorgeous early American finds—mirrors, portraits, tavern signs, Amish quilts. We discovered hand-cut bricks from an eighteenth-century foundry in the Carolinas. We found a pie chest from North Carolina; a counter from a general store in Connecticut that we placed between the kitchen and the dining room; a schoolteacher's desk from Massachusetts (which became our maître d's stand); a primitive cabinet we'd use for storing linens; and a nineteenth-century granary wheel to hang in our private dining room. Those items were hard to find and expensive to buy; in fact, the cost to design, build, and outfit Gramercy Tavern was over $3 million— more than four times what it had cost to open Union Square Cafe. But each dollar spent contributed to the aura of authenticity and enhanced the meaning and value of the word "tavern."

The name Gramercy Tavern was first suggested to me by the writer and television producer Peter Kaminsky, a longtime bar lunch regular at Union Square Cafe, who was writing an article for the *New Yorker* about the process of opening our restaurant. (At the last moment and after months of work, his story was canned by Tina

Brown, who was then the magazine's editor. But two weeks before our opening, Peter sold the story to *New York* magazine. Its editor, Kurt Andersen, made Gramercy Tavern his cover story on our opening day. This story had a powerful effect on us, both positive and negative, but I'll talk about that later.)

Tom and I each had something to prove at Gramercy Tavern. Tom's cooking at Mondrian had received wide acclaim—including the three stars from the *New York Times*—and he was determined to show the world that Mondrian's failure to survive was caused by the bad economy of the early 1990s, rather than by a flawed menu or mismanagement. And I needed desperately to prove to myself that Union Square Cafe had not been a "one-hit" fluke.

There had been many changes in New York in the nine years since I'd opened Union Square Cafe. President Clinton's "new economy" had taken off, crime rates were beginning to recede, and the category of "casual-excellent" restaurants like Union Square Cafe was becoming saturated.

Business at Gramercy Tavern was intense from the start. In fact, there was a lively media buzz about the restaurant, and we couldn't come close to meeting the demand for reservations. Nor were we coming close to meeting the expectations our guests brought with them—especially after the cover story in *New York* magazine, which pondered whether Gramercy Tavern might be "the next great restaurant." Everyone, it seemed, wanted to judge for himself or herself the answer to the cover. The good news was that we were booked every single night. The painful news is that we were far from being a great restaurant, and plenty of people told us as much.

Actually, I felt like a miserable failure in 1994–1995. Union Square Cafe appeared to be getting worse (it dropped from number two to number three on Zagat's list of most popular restaurants). Gramercy Tavern seemed less excellent and less safe than Union Square Cafe, and I was beset with complaint letters and irate phone calls from disappointed guests—many of whom identified themselves as regulars at Union Square Cafe. And I was running around like one of the Three Stooges with less, not more, time for myself and my family, which by now included a one-year-old daughter, Hallie. Audrey, who loved Gramercy Tavern almost from the outset, couldn't fully understand why I was pulling my hair out. Of course, she had begun to reprioritize her own talents now that she was a mom, and our beautiful new daughter was far more important than my bellyaching about either the new or the old restaurant.

I knew that Audrey was right, yet I still had the sense of being close to a dangerous outcome. Was I now treading down the same path my father had taken—expansion to bankruptcy? Had I blown it?

I began to look all around me for ways to regain direction and control of both restaurants. In 1995, after intense internal debate, I went through an unpleasant professional divorce from a managing partner. Talented as he was, we had entirely different styles, and different approaches to running the business. I felt constrained by his emphasis on making profitability the top priority. I realized, too, that my own hands-on managerial style was not particularly effective in operating two restaurants at the same time under pressure. I managed by example, and I had yet to learn how critically important it is to lead by teaching, setting priorities, and holding people accountable. I was beginning to feel defeated. Gramercy Tavern was not performing like a champion, and I was becoming painfully aware that my own leadership was to blame. And then personal disaster struck. One Saturday night in the summer of 1995, Audrey suddenly went into premature labor with twenty-two-week-old twins. We grabbed two-year-old Hallie from her crib; rushed uptown to Lenox Hill Hospital; and after the taxi driver urged us to "have a nice day," we tore up to the maternity ward where, despite heroic efforts to halt the labor, Audrey gave birth to two tiny babies—a boy and a girl—each weighing no more than a pound. Within eight hours, both had died.

It was a crushing blow that challenged our marriage and our lives; and if we had not resolved to use every form of therapy available—

and in my case additional intense work with a men's group—the loss almost certainly would have brought us down individually and together. Facing up to the real meanings of life, death, perseverance, survival, and love gave me and Audrey an enhanced sense of urgency and a new perspective on how we spent our time.

At this point, I was in a fighting mood, and the object of my focus was Gramercy Tavern. It was time to win, at any cost. It was time for me to become even more precise in describing what kind of managers we'd hire, and even more articulate in communicating what was expected of them. At this moment, "enlightened hospitality" was born. In a meeting of the entire staff of Gramercy Tavern, and with full agreement and support from Tom, I began to outline what I considered nonnegotiable about how we did business. Nothing would ever matter more to me than how we expressed hospitality to *one another*. (Who ever wrote the rule that the customer is always first?) And then, in descending order, our next core values would be to extend gracious hospitality to our *guests*, our *community*, our *suppliers*, and finally our *investors*. I called that set of priorities enlightened hospitality. Every decision we made from that day forward would be evaluated according to enlightened hospitality. We would define our successes as well as our failures in terms of the degree to which we had championed, first, one another and then our guests, community, suppliers, and investors.

One by one, the staff lined up behind us (those for whom this way of doing business held no interest left for other restaurants) and grew more confident. We were profitable, and at last we were getting good reviews. Ruth Reichl, now restaurant critic for the *New York Times*, promoted us to a rating of "excellent"—three stars. "It takes a while for a restaurant to hit its stride," she wrote, "there is no timetable for this; each proceeds at its own pace. It can take a year or two or more before everything comes together in one smooth motion. But when it finally happens, everyone knows it: one step through the door and you can feel the energy running through the room."

I conducted the same meeting next at Union Square Cafe, and my first restaurant almost immediately regained its upward course. The staff members rallied to something they could believe in, follow, and support. Perhaps most important, I had learned to trust my own instincts, and to make them explicit for others. What had once been intuition—ripples I'd leave in my wake—could now be transformed into intentional waves. I'd written a new set of rules for my business, and I was at last ready to read them aloud.

CHAPTER 6

No Turning Back

Now I wanted to turn my attention to Michael Romano. Michael had been somewhat dejected when I corrected all of Union Square Cafe's design flaws by building a new facility at Gramercy Tavern. Though he had invested his own money in Gramercy Tavern, he was envious when he saw that the new restaurant's shining kitchen had everything his didn't have. Even though neither of us was really sure that Michael actually wanted to play a role in launching another restaurant, it was important at least to explore the option. For my part, my own growth as a leader had allowed me to strengthen the foundations of both Union Square Cafe and Gramercy Tavern. It had also helped me become more confident as I contemplated further expansion. I was ready to go for it. By 1995, there were no great or affordable spaces left along Union Square Park, and so I decided to take a look around Madison Square Park—a run-down plot of splotchy green which was a stone's throw from Union Square and Gramercy Tavern, and which had all the potential upside in the world.

I thought we might be able to contribute something new to the traditional bistro or brasserie, so I asked Michael to accompany me on a research trip to Paris, seeking new ideas and inspiration for creating a French version of Union Square Cafe. (Union Square Cafe itself being an Italian version of Union Square Cafe). This research proved to be a punishing form of pleasure. On day one, we dined at two different Michelin three-star restaurants (lunch at Robuchon, followed by dinner at Lucas Carton), and over the next forty-eight hours we ate at six other classic bistros and as many brasseries. Was there anything fresh to express in this niche?

The space I had my eye on in New York was at the base of the gorgeous old Gift Building at 225 Fifth Avenue on the northwest corner of Madison Square Park. Since it was a fairly small storefront, the only realistic plan for adequate seating at 225 Fifth was to extend the ground floor outward by building an enclosed sidewalk annex or cafe overlooking Madison Square Park and the Flatiron Building. I knew that the park had been center stage for New York's social elite at the turn of the nineteenth century, and it was still one of Manhattan's most significant confluences—Fifth and Madison avenues, Broadway, and Twenty-third Street. I met with three officials of New York City to seek approval for the sidewalk annex, assuring each one that if we could make a restaurant work there, it would let us lead an effort to revitalize the downtrodden park outside our front door.

The park itself was poorly landscaped, dirty, and unsafe—not unlike Union Square Park circa 1985, but without even a spark of retail activity on its perimeter. Twenty-third Street had a hodgepodge of fast-food places, shoeshine shops, and delis; and the three-block stretch of Madison Avenue, as well as Twenty-sixth Street and Fifth Avenue, was practically barren. As I became more enthusiastic about the idea of opening a third restaurant, the possibility of playing a role in reviving Madison Square Park made it even more compelling. This would be a chance to make a bet on an emerging neighborhood while the rents were still affordable—about 50 percent lower at that time than for comparable spaces around Union Square or in the Flatiron district. Why wouldn't we want to create a wonderful restaurant overlooking what could once again become a majestic park? I was indeed motivated to open a French-style restaurant with Michael, and a voice within me urged me to be a pioneer in another new community.

In 1995 we began negotiating a lease with the Japanese owner of 225 Fifth Avenue, but we made just a little headway on an agreement over the next several months. Meanwhile, a real estate consultant contacted us to say that she had been hired to find a nationally known restaurateur for the ground-floor space at 11 Madison Avenue, the MetLife Building. MetLife was upgrading this historic art deco building into "class A" office space and had already signed leases with such high-end tenants as Credit Suisse First Boston (CSFB) and some major advertising agencies. When my assistant told me that she had informed the developer that we were already looking elsewhere, my first reaction was "That's a mistake!" It was important to take a look at 11 Madison. Even if we were to close a deal and one day open a restaurant at 225 Fifth, a competitor would eventually take the space at 11 Madison, and I felt we should at least learn what kind of deal that potential competitor would get. (*ABCD!*) Meeting with the developer not only would gain us information about a prospective rival but also would be a hedge against losing the deal at 225 Fifth.

My hunch soon proved prescient, when we got some deal-breaking news: there was an enormous Consolidated Edison transformer directly beneath the sidewalk at 225 Fifth that would make the construction of an enclosed outdoor café impossible. The huge grates over the transformer were plainly visible; but in my inexperience and ignorance, I had never noticed them or thought to ask about them. Instead, I had wasted six months of our time telling the city officials how much a new restaurant there would add to the neighborhood.

Still, the time had not been spent entirely in vain; on the contrary, whatever time and effort had been used examining Madison Square Park and selling ourselves on its future had been very well spent. I had become consumed with the neighborhood and had gotten to know and become known by leading public officials in the process. I was more determined than ever to open a restaurant directly across from the park, and to invest in its future.

We immediately started talking seriously with the agent for the project at 11 Madison. The primary notion of restoring the park was to bring beauty and life to the neighborhood and provide the community with a reason to use the park. That idea reflects one of my core business philosophies: *invest in your community, and the rising tide will lift all boats.*

I invest in your community. A business that understands how powerful it is to create wealth for the community stands a much higher chance of creating wealth for its own investors. I have yet to see a house lose any of its value when a garden is planted in its front yard. And each time one householder plants a garden, chances are the neighbors will follow suit.

In mid-1996, I attended my first meeting with executives at MetLife to negotiate a lease. There were all kinds of financial and real estate terms to discuss, but first I made my own agenda—the big picture— clear to our prospective landlord. "Before we discuss any details of a lease," I said at this meeting, "it's important for me to know that you will first commit to partnering with me in rebuilding and restoring Madison Square Park—to where it was in its heyday." He may not have fully realized what he was getting his company into, but the MetLife executive, Dom Prezzano, replied, "I don't think you have any idea how many people have tried to do this and for how long; but if you have the energy to lead, we'll lend our financial support."

The city's social elite and a concentration of capital had long ago converged on the park to bring it early iconic skyscrapers like Madison Square Garden (1890), the Flatiron Building (1903), and the MetLife clock tower (1906). But ever since the Great Depression of the 1930s, Madison Square Park had been in decline. After months of being urged by Audrey to read Caleb Carr's best-selling historic mystery *The Alienist,* I finally did so and became fascinated by his description of what the area around Madison Square Park had been like in its days of glory. I was also captivated by what Carr wrote about New York's prominent turn-of-the century restaurateur, Charlie Delmonico, who had always opened the next Delmonico's restaurant in whatever neighborhood he believed was going to become New York's most prominent. In 1876, he had opened a Delmonico's on the corner of Fifth Avenue and Twenty-sixth Street. That inspired me—a little over a century later—to try my hand at doing the same.

Since the 1970s, it seemed, local business leaders had been disappointed by broken promises from New York City to rebuild the park. Good intentions, it seemed, had always been followed by downturns in the city budget. By the time I started asking questions about reviving the park, most people I spoke to in business or government expressed doubts at best, and cynicism at worst.

I knew that 11 Madison could be majestic, but it came with significant financial and architectural obstacles, and the talks with MetLife went on for nearly a year as we ironed out these issues. Because the building was a designated landmark, we would need to satisfy the requirements of the National Register of Historic Places, to preserve and restore existing elements of its historic design—an enormous and costly undertaking. We would need to restore ceiling moldings that were chipped or missing, and repair and restore a thirty-five-foot-long art deco fluorescent light fixture even though we'd never use it. We even had to design lighting fixtures that would surround but not replace the space's original hanging fixtures and sconces, to meet historic preservation requirements. All this work would add at least 30 percent to the normal costs of building a restaurant, and this extra cost would delay any possible return on investment for our shareholders, of whom there would need to be a lot more than the usual few if we were to pull this off. And there was an even more difficult challenge: a massive wall bisected the first floor of the MetLife Building. Since the historic requirements of the building prohibited us from taking it down, we'd have to create *two* different restaurants, one on either side of the dividing wall.

People began telling me that it would be insane to create, design, staff, and open two restaurants simultaneously in the same space. It was becoming abundantly clear to me that I would need to take on more investors and more managing partners, and I did. I did not have the personal funds to build two large restaurants in the space; nor did I have the gumption to go it alone without partners at my side. I began to think intently about where I'd seek financial assistance. I recruited two new colleagues to become my managing partners—David Swinghamer, from Chicago's Lettuce Entertain You Enterprises; and Richard Coraine, from San Francisco, who had worked for years with Wolfgang Puck at Postrio, and had then opened his own restaurant, Hawthorne Lane.

BRASSERIE

When I looked at the two adjoining spaces, it struck me that the larger rectangular room—which had thirty-foot-high windows on the park—offered the perfect volume for the heady bustle of a brasserie. This would be the result of all those conversations with Michael Romano in Paris. There's nothing particularly refined about brasserie standards—oysters, escargots, pigs' feet, soupe à l'oignon, and steak frites—or about the breezy brasserie style of service; it's just meant to be fun. But then I asked myself: "Who ever wrote the rule that just because you're having all that fun, you can't simultaneously have exquisite food and an extensive list of fine French wines?" That was

followed by the question: "Who ever wrote the rule that just because it's a brasserie you have to serve soupe à l'oignon and steak au
poivre?" How could we combine a brasserie's winsome atmosphere
and French culinary accent with an urbane New York point of view
to create something unexpected? I wasn't entirely sure of the answer;
but whatever it was, that would be restaurant number one.

Now, however, nearly a year after our trip to France, Michael said
that he did not want to open another restaurant—his true joy was
to focus entirely on Union Square Cafe. So together we hired a chef
for our forthcoming restaurant, Brian Goode, who had previously
been a talented sous-chef for Michael at Union Square Cafe, and
had recently opened as the executive chef at Firebird, a new Russian
restaurant in the theater district. We sent Brian to France for a month,
with a long list of all kinds of restaurants we wanted him to visit and
an ample sack of Francs for meals and lodging.

I described the new restaurant to my friend Robert Chadderdon.
Although he himself is a Francophile, he told me: "Don't use French
in the name. Americans are tiring of French restaurants. Call it something in English."

"How about Madison Square Cafe?" I said, recalling a conversation I'd had with my father more than a decade earlier.

"You can do better and be more original," Robert countered.

"Madison Park Cafe?" I asked.

"No. Call it Eleven Madison Park. That's what it is."

Not long after Brian returned from France, and while he was
working intently on the kitchen plans and the construction of the
restaurant, it occurred to him that this place was becoming very costly.
He was concerned about whether it could be a safe financial bet for
his own future. He didn't see how the restaurant would ever be able
to pay off its debt or its investors, and that made him nervous. When
construction delays arose, he grew increasingly impatient and ill at
ease. With just six weeks to go before opening Eleven Madison Park,
we parted ways. I immediately consulted with my business partners,

and Tom Colicchio pointed me toward Kerry Heffernan. Kerry had been Tom's sous-chef years earlier at Mondrian, and had built a solid resumé as an executive chef since then. Tom told me that Kerry was the best cook he had worked with, and I also knew that the two were fly-fishing buddies. Kerry had just moved to Tavern on the Green from the Westbury Hotel when its restaurant, The Polo, had closed. I liked what I knew of Kerry, and he was ready to join our team. I hired him after just two interviews, and without even asking him to prepare a tasting.

INDIAN

That left restaurant number two. I still needed to come up with an idea for the smaller space on the other side of the historic wall. One day I was hanging out in Michael's office, and I asked him what he thought we should do there. He shrugged, rubbed his left sideburn, and returned to the cookbook he was intently perusing. "Whatever it is," I said, "I want it to be a leader within its niche." I began flipping through the *Zagat Survey* for 1997, looking in the section on categories. When I got to "Indian," I saw that the top-rated Indian restaurant then was place called Dawat, with a food score of twenty-four out of a possible thirty. That got my attention. "Since you've come to Union Square Cafe," I said, "the restaurant hasn't received less than twenty-six for food, and for several years you've earned a twenty-seven."

Michael was listening. He was fascinated by many things Indian; he had studied spices in India; was into yoga, meditation, and Indian spirituality; and had dated Indian women. For several years now he had been cooking with Indian spices at Union Square Cafe, combining them with French and Italian techniques and ingredients from the greenmarket. By 1996, nearly 25 percent of the items on the menu at Union Square Cafe were being cooked with some type of Indian spice. "Frankly," I told Michael, "I'd just as soon see all those spices used in a new restaurant. They're delicious, but they don't even go with most of the wines in our cellar. Let's build on the success of these Indian dishes you've been cooking at Union Square Cafe and create a whole new restaurant for them. What about doing a new version of an Indian restaurant?" He put down the cookbook, looked me in the eye, and smiled broadly.

Around that time I took my daughter Hallie, now four, to a children's concert at the Metropolitan Museum of Art. The classical clarinetist Richard Stoltzman began by teaching the kids how the clarinet works and sounds by playing some well-known riffs from *Peter and the Wolf.* "Now," he said, "I want to show you how the clarinet sounds when it's played alongside another instrument." Minutes later, the curtain opened to reveal a young musician seated on the stage floor surrounded by a dozen sets of hand drums. He explained that these drums were tablas and that they are the primary percussion instrument in classical Indian music. He showed the audience how each drum had its own distinct tone and timbre. Stoltzman then came back out, and the pair teamed up to play a fusion of jazz clarinet with Indian drums. That's when it hit me: what they were doing musically was exactly what I had been envisioning culinarily for the second restaurant. I wanted to give American elements an Indian accent. It was at this moment that the second new restaurant found its name: Tabla.

MICHAEL AND I HAD been dreaming and talking openly about the Indian venture, and one day Nick Oltarsh, the head tavern room cook at Gramercy Tavern, overheard us and made an appointment to come in and see me. "I know the perfect person to be the chef at the restaurant you've been talking about. His name is Floyd Cardoz, and we cooked together at Lespinasse," Nick said. He knew that Michael never intended to abandon Union Square Cafe to become Tabla's day-to-day chef. "All I ever heard Floyd talking about was how one day he would show the world that Indians could be great cooks. What you and Michael are talking about happens to be his dream."

We learned that Floyd was a native of Bombay and had grown up in Goa, learning all his grandmother's recipes before studying classical French technique in Switzerland. That sounded too good to be true, and it got even better. Floyd Cardoz had been at Lespinasse—a four-star restaurant—for over five years and was now executive sous-chef, having convinced his chef, Gray Kunz, to greatly expand the number of aromatic Indian spices in the restaurant's pantry. We met Floyd, who confirmed that he was eager to break away and do something on his own. His dream was a perfect fit with our vision for Tabla; and after a brilliant tasting in which he cooked fifteen dishes for us that made my palate sing (and sometimes burn) with delight, we hired Floyd to be our executive chef. Later, we made him a partner at Tabla.

From the moment we had decided on the concept, I sharpened my vision for Tabla. I asked myself: "Who ever wrote the rule that if you love Indian spices and Indian breads, you should be able to enjoy them only in the context of a purely classical Indian restaurant?" I wanted Tabla to become a unique American dining experience, based on Floyd's lifelong passion for the cooking of his homeland. With Floyd's input, I asked our architects—Bentel and Bentel—to design a "spice room" in the kitchen, a laboratory of sorts where Floyd could bring a piece of fish or meat and experiment with new combinations of tastes. Together, we came up with a harmonious blend of American hospitality, French culinary technique, and expertly applied Indian spices. Soon after Tabla opened, in December 1998, it earned three stars from Ruth Reichl of the *New York Times*. She wrote, "This is American food, viewed through a kaleidoscope of Indian spices. The flavors are so powerful, original, and unexpected that they evoke intense emotions."

Next door, Eleven Madison Park had gotten off to a decent enough start. But the public knew that in just four more weeks we'd be launching a groundbreaking restaurant called Tabla, so many people saw the more classic Eleven Madison Park as the warm-up act for the main event. Eleven Madison Park would have to succeed by virtue of its architectural beauty, hospitality, and solid kitchen. Conceptually, nothing about it was breaking new ground.

In these early days, our lunch business at Eleven Madison Park was lagging far behind our optimistic projections. But rather than explaining this sluggishness as a natural challenge of building a business from scratch, we convinced ourselves that people didn't have time to leave their desks for lunch. We decided that the solution was to deliver beautifully designed box lunches to their offices. We targeted Credit Suisse First Boston in particular, since its world headquarters were upstairs at 11 Madison. We offered a choice of three exquisite sandwiches, homemade potato chips, a bottle of water, and a homemade cookie.

Unfortunately, very few people bought this concept, or the box lunches. We had made a fundamental mistake by trying to extend an original brand without having first established the core brand. It wasn't so much that people were tied to their desks; it was that they had no clear idea what Eleven Madison Park represented as a dining experience. Was it a bistro or a grand restaurant? Was it inexpensive or for special occasions? Was it French? Was it a place for sandwiches, potato chips, and cookies? Until we had answered those questions for ourselves, we couldn't avoid confusing our potential customers.

Know Thyself: Before you go to market, know what you are selling and to whom. It's a very rare business that can (or should) be all things to all people. Be the best you can be within a reasonably tight product focus. That will help you to improve yourself and help your customers to know how and when to buy your product.

Also, we hadn't done our homework: CSFB already had a first-rate, company-subsidized cafeteria for its employees, run by an outside food service. And creating the box lunches had kept chef Kerry Heffernan and the management team from focusing on what we should have been doing all along: improving the restaurant itself and doing the hard work necessary to build our lunch business one guest at a time. We abandoned the box lunch program very quickly and ended up with a costly inventory of 3,000 unused boxes. The experience was a vitally important illustration of inappropriate brand extension, wrongheaded priorities, and inadequate focus on a core product. Fortunately, by working on the basics, our lunch business doubled within six months. We had found a wonderful maître d' who was expert at recognizing guests. We worked on presenting a menu that offered enough light choices to encourage frequent dining. And we worked on speed, understanding that at lunch, time is everything.

Hybrid restaurants are challenging to imagine, and when first realized they can be confusing—both for the staff and for the customers. I've learned to live with that. I trust our ability to build a community of people who want to discover us and take an active interest in our evolution—even if it takes several visits for us all to get there.

FOR THE NEXT TWO years after we had opened Tabla and Eleven Madison Park, I was not looking for any new restaurant ventures. My plate was full and overflowing. In fact, when my cousin James Polsky asked if I might be interested in collaborating with him at 27 Standard and Jazz Standard—his restaurant and his forward-looking underground jazz club—I had to decline. James was a jazz fanatic (with an encyclopedic knowledge of the idiom), and opening the club had been a life's dream for him. The club was receiving accolades and had built a regular clientele, but his upstairs restaurant, despite a strong two-star review from the *New York Times*, was experiencing financial losses. James had considered and declined offers from high-profile restaurateurs to buy out the lease on his handsome two-level loft space on East Twenty-seventh Street; he was afraid that a new owner would immediately convert the jewel-like jazz club into a private party space.

Notwithstanding my own capacity for more work, I knew I was in no position to take on another restaurant. But ideas had not stopped bubbling up in me. For one thing, I had considered launching my own dot-com. It would be a barbecue lover's website called cue.com (or possibly Q.com). You would log on, and an animated map of America would appear onscreen. Next you'd click on a destination, and a map would generate information about traditional barbecue styles in that region, including one or two worthy local practitioners from whom we could procure barbecue for overnight delivery to your door. The idea would be to "sole-source" great barbecue, promote it, and sell it like crazy. I am reasonably confident, looking back, that cue.com would have had as tough a time succeeding as most Internet schemes did back then; and I'm happy not to have sunk even one dollar into it.

At the same time, I accepted an invitation from Rocco Landesman, a leading Broadway executive, a former St. Louisan, and a friend. He may or may not have known about my lifelong love of barbecue, but he had found an easy mark. "We know this really neat guy from southern Illinois," Rocco said, "and he is probably the greatest pitmaster I have ever met. His name is Mike Mills. What do you think about coming over for dinner one night to taste some of his ribs?"

"You're not talking about doing a barbecue restaurant, are you?" I asked him. "Because I swear I'm not opening another restaurant." My mind shouted at me, *Be careful!*

"Let's try to pick a night when the Cardinals are on TV. We'll grab some beers and get Mike to ship some of his barbecue in," Rocco replied. "I also want you to meet some people who would really like to find a way to bring his barbecue to New York. My good friend Tom Viertel—the theater producer—is in love with Mike. Tom and his partner, Pat Daley, are judges on the national barbecue circuit. You need to meet these people even if you can't do it. Maybe you can introduce them to another restaurateur who can!" That got my competitive juices flowing.

This invitation was tough to turn down, even though I now had four restaurants and knew that the last thing I needed to do was open a fifth. But these were friends; the idea involved the St. Louis Cardinals; I was a sucker for barbecue; and it struck me as an intriguing idea.

It's not what you know, it's whom you'll listen to. Sometimes— very, very occasionally—I'm presented with an idea or invitation, and I know there's a 99.9 percent probability I'm not interested in it. Yet my intuition tells me that it's worth investigating, just to see what's on the other side. I'll allow myself to be open to new ideas, particularly when they're presented by good people I know and trust. And when I hear those ideas from people I know and trust, I pay even stronger attention to my own instinct and intuition.

I wasn't attending this rib tasting with any expectation that it might lead somewhere. I was just going to discover some excellent barbecue and, I hoped, watch the Cardinals win a ball game.

But the pink-edged, dry-rubbed ribs were remarkable. And so was the moist, smoky pulled pork. The baked beans, made from four kinds of beans, stopped me in my tracks. And this stuff had been frozen, shipped, thawed, and reheated. How good might it be fresh? I suddenly began to ask myself some basic questions, such as, Why isn't there more good barbecue in a city like New York that has so much of everything, and in many cases has the very best? I convinced myself that there were environmental restrictions on producing real pit barbecue, which gives off a lot of smoke. But what if it were possible to overcome that obstacle? I knew that Virgil's Real BBQ, which was then the most commercially successful barbecue restaurant in New York, had been using some kind of smoke-eating equipment for years, just off Times Square. But I also remembered that the authentic Pearson's, in Queens, had been forced to relocate its pit to the back of a noisy, crowded sports bar after neighbors complained about smoke at the original site in Long Island City. Still, Manhattan was lacking in authentic barbecue, and Mike Mills was clearly a barbecue artist.

After the challenging twin openings of Eleven Madison Park and Tabla, perhaps it would be easier this time to do a "joint." Slowly but surely, I began to talk myself into the project. I gained confidence by visiting Mike in Murphysboro, Illinois; and subsequently in Las Vegas, where he had opened two more restaurants. Through long conversations and lots of animated dialogue about business values and barbecue, along with Richard and David, my partners, I took the measure of the man. His gift for the pit was obvious (so was his gift for fascinating gab), and a bond of trust was growing between us. One day it occurred to me that this was precisely the right fit for my cousin's restaurant space at 27 Standard and that Jazz Standard would be a natural home for good 'cue. Beginning in urban Kansas City, barbecue and jazz had long been bedfellows. Why not here in New York?

One by one, my partners gave me thumbs-up; and with their unanimous support, we made a deal for the space with my cousin James. He would stay on as an owner to help ensure the outstanding music for Jazz Standard, and we would create Blue Smoke and be responsible for the restaurant and club operations.

I WAS AMAZED TO get my first peek into the world of professional and amateur pitmasters and barbecue fanatics. These buffs, like followers of the Super Bowl or the Indy 500, will travel hundreds of miles for a main event. During twenty-four months of intense research, we became groupies ourselves; members of our Blue Smoke team collectively covered some 60,000 miles—through Missouri, Tennessee, Mississippi, North and South Carolina, upstate New York, Texas, southern Illinois, the South Side of Chicago, Boston, and Oakland, California—to research and understand barbecue's regional distinctions. Along with Mike Mills, Tom Viertel, now an investor in our forthcoming restaurant, arranged for me to attend the 2001 Memphis in May competition, the "Super Bowl of Swine," as a judge in the rib category. Mike's charismatic passion proved infectious. When I asked him what it would take for us to serve ribs on a par with those that had won him his three grand championships at Memphis in May, he said, "You'll have to figure out how to pull them from the pit at just the perfect moment. Just when the meat is relaxed enough—after six or seven hours of smoking—you baste that rack with the sauce. If you hit it perfectly—you'll see a blue smoke rise up out of those ribs." A *blue smoke*. That was that—our new restaurant had its name. We invited Mike to become our chief 'cue consultant (I called him our rib rabbi), paid him in equity, and asked him to teach us and our chef everything he had learned not only on the competitive circuit but also in his own restaurants.

We selected Kenny Callaghan, who had been a dedicated cook and sous-chef at Union Square Cafe for over eight years, to be the pitmaster and executive chef of Blue Smoke. Kenny's culinary background had little to do with barbecue: before cooking at Union Square Cafe he had worked at the Russian Tea Room. But his disciplined approach to cooking made him the perfect choice for Blue Smoke. The most successful barbecue pitmasters have a passion for doing the same things over and over, each day finding nuanced ways to improve on what they did yesterday. Barbecue is not a matter of creativity so much as a matter of dogged perseverance and execution. Kenny's no-nonsense personality, straightforward cooking style, and persistent pursuit of ways to do things better made him an ideal choice. We also chose another veteran of Union Square Cafe, Mark Maynard-Parisi, to become Blue Smoke's opening general manager. It had always been a priority of mine to develop leaders from within, both for the sake of team morale and as an assurance that we'd begin our new restaurants with as much of our preexisting DNA as possible. Letting our business grow on the shoulders of those who've gotten us there provides safety and is its own rationale for growing in the first place.

Mike gave Kenny Callaghan and Michael Romano (who was

emerging as our chief culinary sage) an intensive, hands-on course in real pit barbecue technique, teaching them in his restaurant pits, and giving them a competitive role in the famous "Apple City" barbecue contest in Murphysboro, Illinois.

There was a steep learning curve to get all the components right—selecting the best meat vendors; finding good sources for hickory and apple wood; and developing and perfecting recipes for classic barbecue "sides" like corn bread, coleslaw, pit beans, collard greens, and macaroni and cheese. There were also punishing lessons to be learned about preparing barbecue in a densely populated vertical city—where rising smoke might waft into someone's bedroom or office. One too many complaints over a flawed ventilation system, and we could be shut down irrespective of how much we'd spent to build the restaurant. And it was unnerving to present barbecue to a city that lacked its own historic barbecue tradition but that was home to more opinionated expats from classic barbecue destinations than anywhere else in the world. Mike was used to cooking on his traditional "Ole Hickory" smoker with its standard short smokestack. This was the equipment he had taught us how to use, and it was exactly what we purchased for the restaurant. But to win approval to install our pits, our smokers would need to be connected to a fifteen-story smokestack that would have to run up along the rear brick wall of the office building. It took us nearly eight months of frustratingly dry and un-smoky results before we fully understood that the powerful updraft of the skyscraper-like smokestack was acting as a high-power blow-dryer on our meats, rather than allowing the barbecue to be gently bathed by hours of smoke. First, we tried a low-tech solution to keep the meat moist, like placing a huge bowl of water in the smoker for the duration of the barbecue process. The meats turned out moister but were still not smoky enough. At last, we performed surgery on the stack, inserting a damper at the level where most smokestacks end. We had effectively tricked it into becoming the real deal. Soon thereafter, for the first time, our ribs put a smile on my face.

Perhaps because it was "just a joint," Blue Smoke was in some ways the most challenging restaurant to design. Many beloved barbecue joints around the country are on the wrong side of the tracks. And part of what people love about going to them is having to travel to a rural outpost or a down-and-out part of town to hunt down the ethereal smoked pork. The barbecue seems to taste better both because of what you have to do and because of where you have to go to get it. That's also why hot dogs taste better at the ballpark and Vernaccia di San Gimignano tastes better in Tuscany. Context is everything.

Manhattan's Park Avenue in the East Twenties is not many people's idea of the wrong side of the tracks. Once again we turned to the architects Bentel and Bentel to help us arrive at an authentic solution. The questions about design were basic but crucial. For instance, how could we blend traditional barbecue elements with what is real for a Manhattan restaurant? It was a foregone conclusion that we wouldn't resort to such clichés as bowling trophies, photographs of softball teams, or caricatures of smiling piggies. Yet such clichés are tempting because they help guests understand exactly what a restaurant is out to accomplish. People do want to feel transported when they go to a restaurant.

First, we knew we'd need booths, a common feature of barbecue restaurants. A booth can take the form of a picnic table, as is common in the Texas hill country; or it can have a Formica tabletop with hard, uncomfortable benches on either side, as in the barbecue joints of North Carolina. But we needed to have barbecue booths that made sense in New York. We chose comfortable leather cushions as upholstery, and we came up with a tabletop made of a finer laminate than cold, hard Formica.

We also made sure to have the classic black menu board with red-and-white plastic lettering hanging above our bar. But we didn't attempt authenticity by deliberately using an old Coca-Cola sponsorship sign or misspelling pork sandwiches and rib tips on the menu. There could not be even a hint of a theme park. We included a genuine New York element: an exciting, comprehensive listing of microbrew beers, bourbons, classic cocktails, and world-class wines by the glass—not your typical accompaniment to barbecue. Thoughtful design and loving cooking would go a long way toward giving the restaurant soul and authenticity. It would need to exist in harmony with its own building, its neighborhood, and the city. Once you step inside a theme park, you could be anywhere. We were determined that Blue Smoke would be an actual place.

THE GREAT MARY FRANCES KENNEDY FISHER wrote in her memoir *The Gastronomical Me,* "It seems to me that our three basic needs, for food and security and love, are so mixed and mingled and entwined that we cannot straightly think of one without the others. So it happens that when I write of hunger, I am really writing about love and the hunger for it, and warmth and the love of it and the hunger for it . . . and then the warmth and richness and fine reality of hunger satisfied . . . and it is all one."

This passage has always moved me, in part because it captures exactly what another Mary taught me. Although the gastronomical influences of my family were many, no one in my young life expressed the feeling that food is love more purely than our longtime housekeeper, Mary Francis Smith. My attachment to Mary was the steadiest, safest, and most dependable relationship I had while I was growing up. Also, she made the world's best fried chicken, macaroni and cheese, and frosted layer cakes from scratch. Mary fried her chicken in the afternoon, and she'd always sneak me a drumstick and thigh a couple of hours ahead of dinnertime. I'd eat them in my bedroom and flush the bones down the toilet so that my mom wouldn't find out that even before dinner, I had already consumed enough for dinner.

Mary had been born into a Mississippi sharecropping family, and though she was barely literate, in matters of life and love she was one of the wisest human beings I've ever met. Her husband, Charlie, was an easygoing man who drove car pool throughout the 1960s for house cleaners around St. Louis County. Mary and Charlie had not been blessed with any children of their own. We were her kids. And I was her boy. The moment I came home from the hospital after being born, my mother handed me over to Mary, saying, "Here's your boy." And Mary Smith took that to heart, all the more so since she came to view me as the underdog in the family.

Nine years later, when Charlie was killed in a hideous car accident, Mary left us for a time, devastated. It was almost as if I had lost all contact with my own mother. After I got my driver's license at the age of sixteen, I made frequent pilgrimages on Saturday afternoons to her walk-up apartment at 4726 Lee Avenue, on the western fringe of downtown St. Louis in a predominantly African-American neighborhood. She would invite me (or rather, I would invite myself) for a feast of fried chicken, deviled eggs, biscuits, macaroni and cheese, collard greens, and sweet potato pie—all things we serve on the menu at Blue Smoke.

When I opened Union Square Cafe, Mary, by then in her seventies, bought her own ticket to fly to New York to be there for me. She told me she wouldn't have missed it for the world—that "her boy" had made her proud. She managed to fly to New York one more time, for my wedding. (Mary was peerless in her human judgments, and when she had given her approval, I knew Audrey was the right choice to become my wife.) Mary died in early 2000, so she never got to know about Blue Smoke, which was the closest I could come to paying homage to her—and to the love I felt for her and my native home, St. Louis.

MY YOUTH IN ST. Louis inspired another of my restaurants: Shake Shack, the burger, hot dog, and frozen custard stand we created in 2004 for Madison Square Park. Anyone who grew up in the automobile culture in the 1950s or 1960s probably had the experience of hanging out at a local stand or shack serving this type of food. Growing up, I spent a lot of time hanging out with my family and friends at places like Schneidhorst's, the Parkmoor, Ted Drewes Frozen Custard, Fitz's Root Beer Stand, and Steak 'n' Shake. I especially loved them for their curbside service. In fact, I can't remember many weekend nights during my teenage years that didn't culminate at one of those places. And when I had lived in Chicago for two summers during and after graduating from college, I couldn't resist a more than occasional "Chicago dog" topped with its nine traditional accessories and served on a poppy seed bun. I had come to miss the drive-ins, carhops, and burger-and-shake stands of my youth, and today's version of fast food—both the sanitized experience and the production-line food—was an unacceptable substitute. As always with our new ventures, the idea was to draw on the best elements of the classic, make it authentic for its present context, and then try to execute it with excellence. There is nothing particularly innovative about any single component of Shake Shack. The key, as always, would be how we might blend all the components to make it feel original.

The inception of Shake Shack actually began with a humble hot dog cart. In the summer of 2001 our fledgling organization, the Campaign for a New Madison Square Park, persuaded Target Stores to sponsor a series of group art shows for the park, curated by the Public Art Fund and in collaboration with the New York City Department of Cultural Affairs. A Thai sculptor, Navin Rawanchaikul, created a colorful work for the show called *I* ❤ *Taxi,* which featured cartoon-like sculptures of taxicabs on stilts. The artist also designed a working hot dog cart to go with the project, since he believed that the world's two most democratic institutions were taxicabs and hot dogs. In his view, every human being on earth has either driven or ridden in a taxi and has either served or eaten a hot dog.

I ❤ *Taxi* was installed at the southern end of the park, not far from Eleven Madison Park, and when asked, we volunteered to give life to the project by actually operating the sculpture's hot dog cart.

We began by asking ourselves whether there was anything fresh we might bring to the world of hot dog carts.

Small as the project was (or seemed), I took this cart quite seriously. I was eager to use the project as a test of enlightened hospitality. I was asking myself, "Who ever wrote that rule that you can't push the envelopes of excellence and hospitality for something as ordinary as a hot dog cart? Could a hot dog cart ever be anything more than just a hot dog cart?"

My team and I decided to feature Chicago-style hot dogs (from a Chicago vendor, Vienna Beef; and boiled in water spiked with garlic, coriander, and bay leaves). We would serve the hot dogs on poppy seed buns (shipped especially from Chicago) with the requisite toppings: celery salt, onions, green peppers, tomatoes, mustard, pickles, spicy "sport peppers," cucumbers, and "neon" relish. Our menu was limited, but we would also serve bags of homemade beet-stained potato chips, fresh verbena lemonade, salty chocolate truffle cookies, and iced tea. We staffed the cart with members of Eleven Madison Park's winter coatcheck crew, providing them with summer employment; and Kerry Heffernan was our supervising chef. I assigned the project of running the cart to one of Eleven Madison Park's managers as a low-risk way to learn how to run a small business. To go with her addictive chocolate cookies, the pastry chef Nicole Kaplan also contributed refined Rice Krispy treats.

It turned out that there was some risk—by the time I ♥ *Taxi* and its hot dog stand closed in early September 2001, we had actually lost nearly $5,000 operating the cart. While demand had been high and lines were always long, we'd addressed my requirement for excellence and hospitality by hiring too many people, working in a very inefficient system.

But there was a clamor from the neighborhood for us to return with the cart in 2002 (even though that summer brought new sculpture to the park that had nothing to do with ♥ing taxis or hot dogs), and so we did. During the second summer we got a little smarter about our operations and production systems and nearly broke even, but it was 2003 that proved to be the tipping point for the profitability of the hot dog cart. Each day, beginning at eleven-thirty in the morning as many as seventy people were lining up for a Chicago dog. We could barely keep up. We needed three tables behind the cart so that the staff could assemble the hot dogs and all the assorted toppings. Throughout the day reinforcements were wheeled through the park from our kitchen at Eleven Madison Park, and some days we ran out of hot dogs well before closing hour. Before long *Newsweek, Newsday, Crain's New York Business*, CNN, and each of the big three national nightly news shows—NBC, CBS, and ABC—had done stories on our little cart. Writing for the *New York Times*, Alex Witchel helped create longer lines than ever when she called our cart the hot dog connoisseur's "equivalent of fine dining." The restaurant critics William Grimes and Eric Asimov of the *New York Times* both wrote reviews—and each had favorable things to say about the product.

We wanted our hospitality to be at the highest possible level. Without reservation lists, our staff never knew any of the guests' names, so the emphasis was on recognizing repeat customers by face and remembering their usual orders. And with nine toppings, everyone seemed to have a personal preference. We believed that a customer's desire to be recognized could just as easily be satisfied by a summer intern at our hot dog cart as by the host in the dining room of a three-star restaurant. We encouraged our young, energetic staff to create "plus ones" or "legends of hospitality"—offering those in line free samples and cookies; and spotting, say, a regular man on a park bench, making him his usual order, and bringing it to him just as he started to head for the line. Though they were spending $2.50 for a hot dog, the satisfaction and loyalty of these guests was no less important to us than that of our regulars at Gramercy Tavern or Tabla.

Our application of enlightened hospitality had proved a phenomenal success. Our staff loved the work; our patrons were captivated; the park was bustling; Vienna Beef was thrilled with the unexpected business in New York; and by the season's end we presented a check for $7,500 to the newly formed Madison Square Park Conservancy.

Around that time, the city's Department of Parks and Recreation had solicited proposals to create and operate a permanent kiosk in Madison Square Park. We were game, and we decided to expand on the hot dog cart and make our dream of a drive-in come alive for good—and for the good of the park. We submitted our proposal as operators in collaboration with the Madison Square Park Conservancy with the understanding that the kiosk itself would be built with funds raised through a philanthropic campaign (allowing us to own the business, and the conservancy and city to be our landlords) and that we would pay rent as a percentage of our sales to both the Madison Square Park Conservancy and the New York Department of Parks and Recreation.

As we imagined our new kiosk, we thought about a lot more than food. We understood that people don't go out just to eat; they also select restaurants in order to be part of a community experience. Starbucks took the notion of drinking good coffee (and standing in line to buy it) and figured out how to make the experience of drinking coffee with a community of other like-minded people become the real star of the show. The company also learned to superimpose its blueprint onto thousands of locations north, south, east, and west, while also conveying the sense that each Starbucks belonged to its particular community. It was brilliant entrepreneurship to grasp that selling excellent coffee is secondary to creating a sense of community. Coffee sells (and is habit-forming), but performing a daily ritual with a self-selected group of like-minded human beings also sells. A business that doesn't understand its raison d'être as fostering community will inevitably underperform.

My thinking about what we might add to the mission of the Madison Square Park Conservancy had been shaped largely by my experience as an active member of the board of the Union Square Partnership, responsible for the safety, development, programming, and overall welfare of Union Square. I understood that it's not enough to just restore a park: you must sustain its beauty and safety by providing good citizens with lots of reason to visit it. Otherwise, you've merely given the park a temporary face-lift. Union Square Park always relied on the greenmarket as its most powerful magnet in attracting people. Other attractions were the park's playgrounds; its dog run; and Luna Park, its summertime restaurant.

We won the city's competitive bidding process because of the strength of our overall proposal for Shake Shack, including our culinary idea; because the city had confidence in us as operators; and certainly because of the design and financing plan for the kiosk itself. It was challenging to create a model whereby the city would share the precentage rent revenue stream with the conservancy; but we made a strong case for that, and eventually the idea was embraced.

The design of Shake Shack unquestionably contributed mightily to its success. We made a fortunate choice in selecting the renowned architect James Wines of SITE Architecture (renowned for his environmentally sensitive "green" architecture) to design the twenty-by-twenty kiosk to blend in with the park's paths and foliage. It is itself, in my view, a work of art; ivy-covered, the kiosk appears to have sprouted up from the ground. Many of its design elements came from nearby landmarks; for instance, its sloping triangular roof is a nod to the nearby Flatiron Building. We certainly can't claim any credit for the design of the traditional roadside shack. But by using familiar elements of that genre and designing our kiosk for a specific environment, we allowed the Shack to become part of its neighborhood, rather than something imposed on it. (Bryan Miller had observed that my first restaurant, Union Square Cafe, had avoided feeling imposed. That comment of his once again helped me to act intentionally in an area that had previously been instinctive.)

As soon as we'd won the bid, Richard Coraine (my most enthusiastic researcher of road food) and I set off to study burger-and-shake stands all across the country. We started out, of course, at Ted Drewes and Steak 'n' Shake in St. Louis; continued on to Kansas City (Sheridan's); and individually made stops in Michigan (Culver's), Los Angeles (In-n-Out Burger), Napa (Taylor's Automatic Refresher), Chicago (Gold Coast Dogs, plus eight other establishments), and Connecticut (Super Duper Weenie, Clamps, Sycamore Drive-In)—always in search of the best of breed. Steak 'n' Shake's cooking method was my favorite for burgers. I'd always loved watching the cooks take a raw beef patty that looked like a red-and-white-flecked hockey puck, place it on the hot griddle, and then smash it down rhythmically with two heavy spatulas until it got crispy on one side. Then they'd flip it over. I trusted their motto, "In sight, it must be right."

Using the kitchen of Eleven Madison Park's private dining room as our laboratory for Shake Shack, we worked hard to come up with just the right mixture of freshly ground beef, tasting many variations until we landed upon what we thought was the perfect ratio of ground sirloin steak to brisket. The fat-to-meat blend yielded a juicy, intensely beefy result. We debated what the precise size of the burgers should be, to the half ounce. We argued over the choice of buns (soft, potato), tomatoes (plum), lettuce (Bibb), and sauce (our secret). We chose every one of our ingredients with extreme care and with an eye toward authenticity. For the Chicago dogs we decided on Plochman's mustard over French's. We opted not to serve Dijon mustard, taking the position that no "gourmet" condiments belonged at Shake Shack. We chose crinkle-cut fries (just like the ones I had grown up loving at Fitz's Root Beer Stand in St. Louis) because they deliver more crunch per bite than shoestring fries, and because they make good cheese fries. In a blind tasting, we selected Abita, a richly flavored root beer from Louisiana.

Frozen custard, as I wrote on our opening menu, is "what happens when premium ice cream shacks up with soft-serve ice cream," but with a stickier texture and an eggier taste. We worked with Nicole Kaplan, our talented pastry chef at Eleven Madison Park, to zero in on our own recipe, tasting several top custards from around the country (shipped overnight by FedEx) as the benchmarks.

Shake Shack was an instant success when it opened in July 2004. But as is often the case, the unanticipated degree of success brought new challenges. From the outset, the line was long (up to ninety people at a time). Because everyone was a first-time customer, just explaining our menu and learning to make change for each cash transaction took too much time. Because our previous experience had been serving only hot dogs, we had allocated too much space for preparing the dogs and had badly underestimated what would be needed for the overwhelmingly popular burgers and custard. We had to redo the layout of the tiny kitchen, ripping out and reconfiguring several of its stainless steel counters. That first summer saw our team struggling to assemble and serve more than 500 different items per hour at the pickup window in a nine-hour day. That's a lot of dogs, fries, floats, cups, cones, lemonade, sundaes, concretes, burgers, iced tea, soda, beer, and wine. Yes, beer and wine—building on our Blue Smoke experience, there was no way we were going to pass up the opportunity to add something to the possibilities of what one might drink with a double burger, hot dog, or bratwurst. We had passed up Dijon mustard, but that was no reason to forgo Sancerre by the glass.

We had some good fortune a few weeks after we opened, when the opening-night celebration of the sculptor Mark Di Suvero's new installations for the park was held at Shake Shack. On hand were Mayor Michael Bloomberg; Parks Commissioner Adrian Benepe; Debbie Landau, executive director of the Madison Square Park Conservancy; and Commissioner Raymond Kelly of the NYPD, among others. Photographs of the mayor sipping our vanilla shake were posted on the Internet and ran in the newspapers the next day. Before long *New York* magazine was calling Shake Shack "Burger heaven" and wrote that our Shack burger was the city's best burger ("a thing of simple beauty swaddled in a wax paper jacket").

Shake Shack became not just a huge success but also a wonderful business model. Because a percentage of every sale becomes rent, paid both to the conservancy and to the city, every hot dog, burger, frozen custard, or beverage purchased and enjoyed by a guest contributes something to the park's ongoing vitality. Shake Shack is a useful example of a for-profit entity whose success contributes monetarily and programmatically to the community. It shows that you can do well by doing good. Perhaps most important, it serves as a human-magnet, attracting all kinds of people of all ages and from all walks of life to the park. That makes them stakeholders in the park, and it increases the odds that the park will remain beautiful, safe, and enjoyed.

I never assumed that the Shack's success was going to be defined by someone saying, "This is the best hamburger I've ever had." One thing we had learned from Blue Smoke is that it's just about impossible to create the "best" version of anything when the context is comfort food. It's pretty tough to compete with the warmth of deeply emotional food memories.

But I would love it if we were fortunate enough to stay in this business long enough, and continued to execute consistently well, so that today's young people might one day be in a burger joint somewhere with *their* kids and say, "The best hamburger I ever had when I was growing up was at Shake Shack."

CHAPTER 7

The 51 Percent Solution

IT ALWAYS FEELS WONDERFUL to earn a rave from guests, and not just for the way we've nourished them. Over the years, the most consistent compliment we've received and the one I am always proudest to hear, is "I love your restaurants and the food is fantastic. But what I really love is how great your people are."

The only way a company can grow, stay true to its soul, and remain consistently successful is to attract, hire, and keep great people. It's that simple, and it's that hard. In many industries, and undeniably in ours, the competition to hire the most talented people is stiff. The stakes couldn't be higher. The human beings who animate our restaurants have far more impact on whether we succeed than any of the food ingredients we use, the décor of our dining rooms, the bottles of wine in our cellars, or even the location of the restaurants. Because hospitality is a dialogue, I have always placed the highest premium on hiring the best possible staff to engage our guests.

Fortunately, a wave of highly intelligent and creative people has swept into the hospitality business since the early 1990s. Many of them have been attracted to our restaurants for a variety of reasons:

to express a spirit of caring for others, to advance their culinary skills, to pursue a passion for wine, or to fulfill an entrepreneurial vision. Others join us for the purpose of making a living with a flexible schedule while they in fact pursue a separate career.

One reason for this surge in interest in the hospitality profession is that newspapers, television, magazines, websites, and cookbooks have made celebrities not just of chefs but also of restaurants themselves. After Eleven Madison Park was featured as a location in an episode of *Sex and the City*, hordes of people (even a bus tour) descended on the restaurant just to experience a stage set for the hit television show. Having a resumé that includes working for a celebrity restaurant or chef confers legitimacy within the industry and usually ensures at least an initial interview for a job applicant. (It also assuages the parents of a recent college graduate who's getting a first job at a restaurant to know that it's a good one.) The restaurant business has at last arrived as a legitimate, valid career choice and entrepreneurial pursuit. I believe that enlightened hospitality as a way of doing business has helped make it attractive for people to pursue careers not just in our kitchen, but also in our dining room.

In 2004, as we prepared to open one restaurant, two cafés, and a staff cafeteria at the Museum of Modern Art, and enter the off-premise catering business as well, we knew that the size of our organization was about to double to over 1,000 staff members, and it was critical to develop an even larger team of extraordinary leaders. We searched high and low for the rare employees who love teaching, know how to set priorities, work with a sense of urgency, and—most important—are comfortable with holding people accountable to high standards while letting them hold onto their own dignity. Time after time, I had noticed that great leaders tend to have a heightened sense of how to attract and hire other extraordinary people. So that we can achieve our business goals of extending warm hospitality while performing at a high level of excellence, we look intently for strong emotional and technical skills when hiring staff people. Theoretically, if the ideal candidate were to score 100 on a suitability test (something we have never administered), his or her potential for technical excellence would count for 49 percent, and innate emotional skills for hospitality would count for 51 percent.

I first learned this concept of "51 percent" from the dynamic restaurateur Rich Melman of Chicago, when I visited him in the late 1980s. Rich was an effervescent teacher and a willing mentor, and I was eager and honored to learn from him. The concept made perfect sense to me, and now it is a cornerstone of my business. Our staff performance reviews weigh both technical job performance (49 percent) and emotional job performance (51 percent)—how staff members perform their duties and how they relate to others on a personal level. In some respects this is another intentional business strategy based on instincts I developed while I was growing up. Among my friends were plenty of good athletes and talented students. But far more important to me than a friend's skills was always his or her goodness as a person.

I magine if every business were a lightbulb and that for each lightbulb the primary goal was to attract the most moths possible. Now what if you learned that 49 percent of the reason moths were attracted to a bulb was for the quality of its light (brightness being the *task* of the bulb) and that 51 percent of the attraction was to the warmth projected by the bulb (heat being connected with the *feeling* of the bulb). It's remarkable to me how many businesses shine brightly when it comes to acing the tasks but emanate all the warmth of a cool fluorescent light. That explains how a flawless four-star restaurant can actually attract far fewer loyal fans than a two- or three-star place with soul. In business, I want to be overcome with moths. Our staff must be like a scintillating string of one-hundred-watt lightbulbs, whose product is the sum of 51 percent feeling and 49 percent task.

It is my firm conviction that an executive or business owner should pack a team with 51 percenters, because training them in the technical aspects will then come far more easily. Hiring 51 percenters today will save training time and dollars tomorrow. And they are commonly the best recruiters for others with strong emotional skills. Nice people love the idea of working with other nice people.

Over time, we can almost always train for technical prowess. We can teach people how to deliver bread or olives, take orders for drinks or present menus; how to describe specials and make recommendations from the wine list; or how to explain the cheese selection. And it's straightforward to teach table numbers and seat positions to avoid asking "Who gets the chicken?" (That question sounds amateurish and makes a guest feel as if the waiter didn't pay attention to him or her in the first place.) A cook needs to know from his chef precisely what the sautéed sea bass is supposed to look like when it's sautéed properly, how it tastes when it is seasoned perfectly, and what its texture should be when it has been cooked gently and properly. We can and do train for all that. Training for emotional skills is next to impossible.

We aim to hire people who possess an emotional skill that chef Michael Romano calls the *excellence reflex*.

People duck as a natural reflex when something is hurled at them. Similarly, the excellence reflex is a natural reaction to fix something that isn't right, or to improve something that could be better. The excellence reflex is rooted in instinct and upbringing, and then constantly honed through awareness, caring, and practice. The overarching concern to do the right thing well is something we can't train for. Either it's there or it isn't. So we need to train how to *hire* for it.

We don't believe in pursuing the so-called 110 percent employee. That's about as realistic as working to achieve the twenty-six-hour day. We are hoping to develop 100 percent employees whose skills are divided 51-49 between emotional hospitality and technical excellence. As I've mentioned above, we refer to these employees as 51 percenters.

To me, a 51 percenter has five core emotional skills. I've learned that we need to hire employees with these skills if we're to be champions at the team sport of hospitality. They are:

1. Optimistic warmth (genuine kindness, thoughtfulness, and a sense that the glass is always at *least* half full)

2. Intelligence (not just "smarts" but rather an insatiable curiosity to learn for the sake of learning)

3. Work ethic (a natural tendency to do something as well as it can possibly be done)

4. Empathy (an awareness of, care for, and connection to how others feel and how your actions make others feel)

5. Self-awareness and integrity (an understanding of what makes you tick and a natural inclination to be accountable for doing the right thing with honesty and superb judgment)

I want the kind of people on my team who naturally radiate warmth, friendliness, happiness, and kindness. It feels genuinely good to be around them. There's an upbeat feeling, a twinkle in the eye, a dazzling sparkle from within. I want to employ people I'd otherwise choose to spend time with outside work. Many people spend a large percentage of their waking hours at work. From a selfish standpoint alone, if that's your choice, it pays to surround yourself with compelling human beings from whom you can learn, and with whom you can be challenged to grow.

When we look for *intelligence*, we're thinking about open-minded people with a keen curiosity to learn. Do they ask me questions during interviews? Do they display a broad knowledge about a lot of subjects, or a deep knowledge about any one subject? A hallmark of our business model is to continually be improving. I need to stock our team with people who naturally crave learning and who want to evolve—people who figure out how each new day can bring rich opportunities to do something even better. Striving for excellence, as we do every day, requires curious people who also take an active interest in what their teammates do. I appreciate it when waiters want to learn more about cooking. I love it when cooks want to learn about wine. I adore it when hosts and reservationists want to learn more about the person behind the name they are greeting on the phone or at the front door.

A strong *work ethic* is an indispensable emotional skill for any employee who is going to contribute to the excellence of our business. We want people on our team who are highly motivated, confident, and wired to do the job well. It's not hard to teach anyone the proper way to set a beautiful table. What is impossible to teach is how to care deeply about setting the table beautifully. When I walk into any one of our restaurants as its dining room is being set up for service, one of the most lovely sights to me is a waiter lifting a wineglass off the table, holding it up to the light, and checking for smudges. This is not because I'm an unreformed smudge freak, but because someone is showing care for a small detail—smaller even than what the average guest may notice. When an employee does not work out, the problem more often stems from an attitude of "I won't" rather than "I can't."

A high degree of *empathy* is crucial in delivering enlightened hospitality. Empathy is not just an awareness of what others are experiencing; it's being aware of, being sensitive to, and caring about how one's own behavior affects others. We want waiters, for example, who can approach a new table of guests and intuitively sense their needs and agenda. Have they come, for example, to celebrate or to conduct business? Are they here to experience the cuisine, or simply to connect with a colleague over a light meal? Do they want extra attention from the restaurant, or would they prefer to be left alone?

Guests may think they're dining out to feel nourished, but I've always believed that an even more primary need of diners is to be nurtured. The most direct and effective way to let our guests know that we're on their side has always been to field a team that exudes an infectious kind of empathy. No business can truly offer hospitality if the preponderance of its team members lack empathy. But when each member of the team goes to bat for the others, the mutual trust and respect engendered among them creates an infectious environment of caring for our guests.

Self-awareness and *integrity* go hand in hand. It takes integrity to be self-aware and to hold oneself accountable for doing the right thing. I want to work with people who have a handle on what makes themselves tick. Self-awareness is understanding your moods (and how they affect you and others). In a sense, it is a personal weather report. Is the mood dry or humid? Is it raining or stormy? Is it warm and sunny or chilly and cloudy? The staff members' individual and collective moods influence the customers' moods; and in the intricate, fast-paced dance between the kitchen, dining room, and guests during a meal—when hundreds of people are served—it's crucial for my staff members to be aware of and accountable for their own personal "weather reports."

No one can possibly be upbeat and happy all the time. But personal mastery demands that team members be aware of their moods and keep them in check. If a staff member is having personal trouble, and wakes up angry, nervous, depressed, or anxious, he or she needs to recognize and deal with the mood. It does not serve anyone's purposes to project that mind-set into the work environment or onto one's colleagues. We call that "skunking." A skunk may spray a predator when it feels threatened, but everyone else within two miles has to smell the spray, and these others may assume that the skunk actually had it in for them. It's not productive to work with a skunk, and it's not enjoyable to be served by one either. In a business that depends on the harmony of an ensemble, a skunk's scent is toxic.

It may seem implicit in the philosophy of enlightened hospitality that the employee is constantly setting aside personal needs and selflessly taking care of others. But the real secret of its success is to hire people to whom caring for others is, in fact, a selfish act. I call these people hospitalitarians. A special type of personality thrives on providing hospitality, and it's crucial to our success that we attract people who possess it. Their source of energy is rarely depleted. In fact, the more opportunities hospitalitarians have to care for other people, the better they feel.

No matter how focused or purposeful we are when we hire, we've still made plenty of mistakes. Most of those mistakes have occurred when we've misread an employee's emotional makeup. Technical strengths and deficiencies are relatively easy to spot. I can watch any cook sautéing a piece of fish for sixty seconds and gauge whether or not he has what it takes. I can watch a server and determine immediately if he or she has the ability to take orders gracefully. Emotional skills are harder to assess, and it's usually necessary to spend meaningful time with people—often in the work environment—to determine whether or not they're a good fit. But it's critical to begin by being explicit about which emotional skills you're seeking. Doing that—even if you do nothing else—greatly increases your odds of success.

FOR YEARS, WE'VE USED a system called "trailing" to test and hone a prospect's technical skills—the 49 percent—and to begin to assess his or her emotional skills, the 51 percent. Trailing is a combination of training and auditioning; it's rigorous and sometimes awkward. We generally keep people on probation until we've first observed their behavior within the real environment of the dining room or kitchen, and until we've assessed their overall fit with our team. We're upfront about this process, and we tell candidates that we also expect them to audition us as prospective employers. We urge those who trail to ask themselves, *Is this really the kind of place I'm going to want to spend one-third of my time? Is this place going to challenge me and make me feel fulfilled?*

Our frontline managers arrange for trails in each job category. Most prospective employees go through four, five, or six trails, during meal periods and often trail with a different waiter or cook each time. For each trail after the first, there is a specific and increasingly advanced list of what needs to be learned and accomplished during that session. Trails begin with a physical orientation to the restaurant and culminate with "taking a station" while being closely monitored by the trainer. Trailers are paid for their shifts, whether they're hired or not. In the dining room, our guests can tell who the trailers are by the fact that they are not wearing an official uniform, or by noticing that a trainer is the one standing back, observing.

Our training is designed not as a hazing, but as a healthy way to foster a stronger team. Staff members, by being directly involved in the decision making, have a good deal of influence over who is hired and thus a stake in the ongoing success of the outcome. Trailers don't advance to their second trail unless the first trainer recommends this to the manager; they don't move on to their third unless the second trainer endorses it; and so on. After five or six trails we end up with a well-trained candidate who has also been endorsed by as many as half a dozen team members. And the candidate doesn't move along unless he or she agrees that the fit seems good. By creating a built-in support system for new hires, we greatly enrich the subsequent team-building experience.

What is almost impossible to train for is the emotional stuff; identifying hospitalitarians is a tricky skill to teach. I know I have a knack for looking across a table and sensing that a person is, or is not, the right fit for us. But how do I make the subjective *objective*, and the implicit *explicit*? One effective way to articulate my gut feelings to others doing the hiring is to teach them how to listen to their own gut feelings. To do that, I ask managers (whose intuition and judgment we trust, or they wouldn't be managers) to pose themselves three fundamental hypothetical situations when they are hiring.

Situation 1: Think of someone you know well (a spouse, best friend, parent, sibling) who has an uncanny gift for judging character. If this person were on a jury, he or she could take one look at the defendant and almost always render a correct verdict. For me that someone is my wife, Audrey, who is eerily adept at reading character and integrity and who, in a flash, can almost always tell if what you see is what you get. So the first check is to imagine that you have invited the prospective employee to your home for dinner with your judge of character. The three of you discuss many things over a two-hour dinner. When the prospect leaves and the door closes behind him or her, what will be the first thing your character judge says? "What the hell are you thinking?" Or, "Hire that person immediately!" For judges of character, there is no such thing as the color gray.

Situation 2: Imagine your keenest rival in business—if you're the Yankees, say, then it's the Red Sox. Then imagine that the day you make a job offer to a prospect, he or she calls you back and says, "Thanks, but I just got a great offer from the Red Sox and I'm taking the job with them." Is your immediate reaction "Shit, we blew it!" Or, "Whew, we've dodged a bullet!" Ask yourself.

Sometimes I'll go too far down the road in a hiring situation with someone who isn't quite right for our team. I am still amazed at how often I have felt enormous relief when someone we've actively pursued ends up taking another job. This leaves me asking myself how I let the interviewing process get so far in the first place?

I'm aware that that one of my blind spots when hiring is my natural inclination to make other people feel comfortable. This impulse is so powerful that I tend to have a tough time turning it off when it's inappropriate—for example, in a job interview. It's not my job to soothe prospective employees. It's my job to assess whether they'll be a good fit for our team. That takes self-awareness. Unless we have tools like gut checks, it's very easy to get trapped into making some dangerous mistakes.

Situation 3: Most business owners or managers have a core group of customers or other people whose opinions carry special weight for them. In our industry, such a person could be a restaurant critic, who, if he or she writes for a major publication, shares those opinions with perhaps a million readers. For me personally, the person could be my mother or one of my siblings—after all these years, they know how to push my buttons (and I know how to push theirs). It could also be a frequent guest who always tells me exactly how he or she feels about a meal—and is loyal enough to return no matter how the last meal turned out. So, imagine that this person with an especially weighty opinion drops in unannounced to dine, and there is only one table left in the restaurant—a table that will be served by the person you are considering hiring. Is your reaction "Great!"—or is it "Oh, no!"

When all three situations leave you feeling positive about the prospect, you're on the right track. If any *one* of them doesn't, it's time to fold the hand. I rarely interview a candidate until two or three other managers have first had an interview with him or her. Since our restaurants thrive on a team spirit, I prefer to hire by consensus. I ask our managers to pursue a candidate's relevant job references; I ask them to take personal notes and then rank the strength of each one of the candidate's five emotional skills on a scale of zero to five; and I ask them to consider and react to the three hypothetical situations and then listen with their guts.

Finally, I ask our managers to weigh one other critical factor as they handicap the prospect. Do they believe the candidate has the capacity to become one of the top three performers on our team in his or her job category? If people cannot ever develop into one of our top three cooks, servers, managers, or maître d's, why would we hire them? How will they help us improve and become champions? It's pretty easy to spot an overwhelmingly strong candidate or even an underwhelmingly weak candidate. It's the *"whelming"* candidate you must avoid at all costs, because that's the one who can and will do your organization the most long-lasting harm. Overwhelmers earn you raves. Underwhelmers either leave on their own or are terminated. Whelmers, sadly, are like a stubborn stain you can't get out of the carpet. They infuse an organization and its staff with mediocrity; they're comfortable, and so they never leave; and, frustratingly, they never do anything that rises to the level of getting them promoted or sinks to the level of getting them fired. And because you either can't or don't fire them, you and they conspire to send a dangerous message to your staff and guests that "average" is acceptable.

There are a lot of jobs to fill in the restaurant business, and it can be frustrating, especially in a tight labor market, to impose our own stringent limitations on whom we can and can't hire. When a chef has been short a line cook for three weeks and finally finds a technically outstanding cook who isn't quite a 51 percenter, should we really pass on the candidate? Absolutely. I'm not impressed by a candidate's technical prowess if the meaningful emotional skills aren't already in place. Each of our restaurants is created with its own distinct cuisine and its own distinct décor, but caring hospitality must be a common trait that flows clearly through all of them. I tell new employees right off the bat that for their salary review, 51 percent of any raise or bonus is set by how they're faring at the emotional skills necessary to do their job well, and 49 percent is tied to technical performance. That's the perfect balance for us, and it's the currency of our company.

IN THE EARLY DAYS at Union Square Cafe, long before I had codified any of this for my managers, I knew instinctively what kind of employee I wanted. I had a simple formula: I knew I would be spending many, many hours working in the restaurant business, so I'd need to surround myself with employees who were fun, smart, and interested in learning, not to mention dedicated to excellence and eager to play on a winning team. I grew foolishly confident that I could recognize a good hire in a roomful of applicants even without an interview. (Back when I was dating, that may have been an OK strategy at a bar, but it was sorely defective as a way to make meaningful hires.) In building my first team for Union Square Cafe in 1985, I also did something that now sounds insane: I decided not to hire anyone from New York City. I applied affirmative action to anyone who hadn't grown up in the city, believing that any native of New York would bring a New York attitude to the place. Of course, back then, I viewed New York as a scary, crime-ridden city, and its population as cynical, unfriendly, and tough. Today, I understand that my opening strategy was remarkably ignorant and narrow-minded. But it was motivated by my wish to hire only nice, optimistic people to help me create a restaurant with a fresh feeling.

My biased perception of New York has long since disappeared, and some of our greatest servers and cooks have been from the city. Yet today whenever I ask at the monthly meeting I conduct for new hires how many of them were born in New York, no more than 10 percent raise their hands. We have hired a lot of people who, at the time, were also pursuing careers in fields like writing, theater, art, comedy, jazz, and even midwifery. But the common thread is that most 51 percenters, regardless of their birthplace, are driven by a personal pursuit of being the best they can be in whichever field they choose.

My hiring methods began to evolve by necessity, shortly before Gramercy Tavern opened in 1994. Following the recession of 1991–1992, a new bull market led to a spike in restaurant openings throughout New York City. Until then, we could run a single ad in the *Village Voice* and count on attracting so many applicants that there would be a long line outside the door for just two waiter positions. But suddenly we were no longer just in the business of competing to serve the best food; we were engaged in the blood sport of competing to hire the strongest staff. The real battle among restaurants in New York was taking place not in dining rooms but rather in the classified section of the Sunday *New York Times*. In restaurants, as in any other business, you stand a much better chance of ending up with the most customers when first you have the best employees.

Through the years I have thought a lot about where to place want ads and have honed my ability to write them. I was clearly no longer free to hire people simply because I imagined we would have been good friends had we met while I was growing up in St. Louis. I had gotten by to some extent by relying on that instinct, but it was becoming irresponsible and self-limiting. I had to adapt to a fast-changing industry.

However, classified ads are expensive, and one tough year, after several had yielded no returns, I resorted to some unorthodox approaches. I asked readers of Union Square Cafe's newsletter—among them hundreds of guests who had written to praise our staff—to act as recruiters for us. If they ever came across people at other restaurants whom they'd love to see serve them at Union Square Cafe, I wrote, "I would really appreciate if you would refer them to us." (I usually offered a free meal or a bottle of wine for successful referrals.) We were able to hire a few cooks and waiters, and even a top manager with that method. But it wasn't all smooth sailing. I did incur the wrath of at least one restaurateur who had read the newsletter and called to cry foul and accuse me of poaching, even though we hadn't hired or even met anyone from his restaurant. The classified "fishing hole" was drying up, and I was just tying a different piece of bait on my line, and casting it into a new pond.

I also ran ads in San Francisco, Chicago, and Los Angeles (all great restaurant towns); in Atlanta (a big restaurant city during the heady buildup to the 1996 Olympics); and in Boston and Washington, D.C. (easy cities from which to transfer to New York). I figured that at any given time there were at least fifty people in the restaurant business in those cities considering a move to New York. If just two of those fifty were terrific, why wouldn't they want to come work for us if they knew we had an opening? During this lean, competitive period, I also learned what a powerful recruiting tool the *Zagat Survey* could be. When a restaurant ranks among Zagat's top-forty or top-fifty most popular places, diners aren't the only people who notice. Restaurant employees looking for work immediately read through the top-ranked places and check them off one by one while job hunting. Zagat's top-rated restaurants tend to be the busiest, and that's exactly what top job candidates want.

Our ability to remain as good as we have been has always depended on our ability to attract great people. To the degree that we can do this a "virtuous cycle" of hiring spins on. Sustaining peak performance helps us to attract other highly talented people, who in turn help keep our performance at a peak. Earning high rankings from critical sources, such as the *New York Times* and the *Zagat Survey*, not only increases business; it improves our chance of fielding better and better teams. These teams further perpetuate our ability to perform with excellence and they polish our public image.

But I always caution against complacency. I instruct our managers to recruit new staff "blood" as if we're behind. In fact, we'll even create a job that wouldn't otherwise exist when we meet someone we just know belongs on our team.

In addition to instituting an athletic hiring strategy, it's critical to be a champion at retaining top staff members. A business owner can too easily squander the winning edge that comes from fielding a great team by not treating its members with respect and trust, teaching them new skills, and offering clear challenges. Part of what I'm doing when I make my rounds visiting our restaurants is tuning in to my team to feel, see, and hear what's truly going on. I'm watching to gauge their approach to their work, and I want to see 49 percent technical prowess and feel 51 percent emotional mastery. The ability to derive enjoyment from the pursuit of excellence is the best way to measure the team's 51-49 ratio, and it allows me to feel assured that we're doing our job as well as we can.

A good sense of humor—about oneself, one's business, and life in general—goes a long way toward fostering good feelings to accompany excellent performance. Somehow in our society a mind-set took hold many years ago, whereby the only way for a restaurant (or any business, for that matter) to be taken seriously was to act serious. But if you go to many fancy restaurants you'll sense that something's missing. There's a facade of refinement—guests are leaning forward while speaking in hushed tones; tuxedoed servers are calling a woman *madame* and a man *monsieur* when everyone knows they're both American. Everything is delivered perfectly, cleared perfectly, decanted perfectly, and yet it's not fun. It's not sincere. There's no soul. It's a perfectly executed but imperfect experience.

I encourage my staff to express and reveal their humanness, learn from their mistakes, lighten up, and relax. This is a contribution to the dialogue on hospitality that we work at quite consciously. But it, too, requires the optimal 51-49 mix. The idea is to attain a balance: hiring people who are naturally upbeat and genuine but who are also high-level achievers capable of delivering excellence.

We make it clear to our employees that we're going to give them a great troupe of positive, hopeful colleagues to work with, with whom they can feel mutual respect and trust, and with whom they will be asked to achieve lofty goals.

We are not a constellation of individual "star" employees: that idea would work against my core belief that hospitality is a team sport.

I had a challenging experience early on in my career that served as a cautionary tale about how individual ambition can threaten team-building. In 1987, less than two years after Union Square Cafe had opened, an organization called the Society for American Cuisine, based in Louisville, sponsored a nationwide competition to promote and celebrate the newly recognized importance of service as a component of dining in America. Entrants were asked to write an essay in which they defined the virtues of the perfect waiter. The grand prize would be an all-expenses-paid trip to dine at the best "new American" restaurants, in Los Angeles, San Francisco, Santa Fe, Chicago, and several other cities. Participating in this competition struck me as an interesting way to build pride among my servers and foster a sense that what they did day in and day out not only was valid but demonstrated their gift for caring. Back then, I had always noticed how many servers seemed to apologize for their work, with remarks like: "I'm actually an actor. I'm just waiting tables until I land a real job." I knew that instilling pride in our service staff was a monumentally important concern if we were ever to take steps toward excellence. That would be impossible if the people executing our service felt in any way ashamed about being in the restaurant business.

I was still in my twenties, and this was years before I had begun to think about enlightened hospitality as a coherent management philosophy. In fact, my style of managing back then had barely evolved since my sophomore year at Trinity College, when I was the news director for WRTC, the campus FM radio station. I gave people the schedules they wanted, subbed for them myself if they couldn't make a shift, and wrote all the news copy rather than asking anyone for help. I had an overdeveloped desire to please, and to have everybody like me. Now, as a young restaurateur, I would clear and reset tables, check coats, mop up spills, pick up olive pits off the floor, and reset tables along with everyone else. To this day, I can't and won't walk past something dropped on the floor without picking it up. I wanted people to know that this job was neither beneath them nor beneath me. I also wanted to embody the same team spirit and caring for others that I expected from the staff.

To encourage interest in the national contest, I offered $50 to anyone who wrote an essay of at least 1,000 words—no matter how good or poor it was. I offered $100 to the writers of the five essays I felt were our strongest. And I'd pay $250 to the writer of the essay I thought was the best. A dozen wonderful pieces were submitted, and I had each writer read his or her essay aloud. This process alone was effective team-building, and it sent a powerful message that waiting tables need not be something to be ashamed of. Remarkably, the waitress who won our own contest at Union Square Cafe (and the top cash prize) also went on to win the grand prize in the national competition. Her recipe for the perfect waitress was, "two parts Walter Cronkite to one part Mae West, carefully blended with a cup of Mikhail Baryshnikov and a liberal sprinkling of Mother Teresa."

But my experiment soon began to backfire. Our winning waitress began dubbing herself "waitress of the year," and our staff snidely began calling her "WOTY." She had confused winning this writing contest with being the nation's leading waitress. She then made a remarkable request of me. "I really think you should pay me extra money," she told me, "for all the publicity I'm going to generate for Union Square Cafe when I go on the national tour." I was stunned, and told her that she should just enjoy her trip and needn't conduct any interviews or mention Union Square Cafe the entire time.

Before long, the food writer Marian Burros of the *New York Times* picked up on WOTY story and wrote a "De Gustibus" column for the paper on September 26, 1987, titled, "Aspiring Actress Finds Stardom Waiting on Tables." This put the whole situation over the top. Marian had come for lunch and, without identifying herself, asked to be seated in WOTY's station. The next day she called to interview WOTY. The piece was accompanied by a staged and undignified photograph of WOTY holding a stack of eight dirty plates in each hand. That is certainly one aspect of waiting tables, but it was not the image I had intended to convey, and it did not suggest that waiting tables was an enriching way to bestow hospitality. Waitress of the Year looked more like Bus Girl of the Month. Understandably, the photo and the story's unfortunate spin left WOTY feeling embarrassed and angry.

That fueled even more resentment, which was directed toward me, and I began to wonder how I had somehow created this monster. I was tormented because what had initially seemed like such an uplifting idea was backfiring. The story took on an even more bizarre turn when the grand prize trip was delayed, then postponed indefinitely, purportedly for scheduling reasons, but actually because the organizers had gone bankrupt. Just when it appeared that WOTY would never get the trip she had earned, the society found a way to make good on its obligation. WOTY returned from her trip not enormously impressed with what she had seen or tasted, and soon thereafter gave her notice at Union Square Cafe. Some eight or nine years later, when I had practically expunged the anguishing episode from my mind, out of nowhere, I received a long, beautifully hand-written letter from her, in which she apologized for her behavior during what she described as an enormously trying personal episode. Above all, she had felt guilty about her behavior's impact on her colleagues. It was a brave thing for her to do, and it reaffirmed my belief in the power of the team over that of the individual. I also learned how critical it is to manage expectations—and to plan for success, not just for failure. Too often, we've made mistakes by not anticipating what the consequences would be if we were to win.

I have no problem if employees use the fame of our restaurants to advance their careers. For example, celebrity chefs, who add as much to a restaurant's renown as it adds to theirs, are clearly here to stay, and that's not a bad thing for our industry. But individual victories have to register for the whole team or they can be more disruptive than helpful.

Indeed, many exciting career opportunities have derived from team-building leaders. Our chefs have all been invited to perform cooking demonstrations, appear on television, cook for charity benefits, and conduct interviews in the media. Several of them have written cookbooks. As of May 8, 2006, our team members had collectively won sixteen awards from the James Beard Foundation, the "Oscars" of our industry. I have a gut-wrenching concern only when any employee, no matter why or how they've been recognized, feels entitled to special privileges and opportunities and forgets that we are all servers who come to work for the simple purpose of creating pleasure for others. On occasion, we've hired someone who is more interested in currying favor with a certain regular guest (sometimes to land another job) than in the overall welfare of the team. Similarly, a "star" chef who has already launched a line of brand-name food might well turn out to be a poor fit for us. Promoting his or her own "brand" would probably be more important than promoting ours.

The team can be weakened or divided by conflicting loyalties if any one member feels or acts more important than everybody else. I have found that the people most likely to thrive in our organization are individuals who also enjoy playing team sports. And that's true for any organization in which people depend on others for their ability to succeed.

Punctuality is nonnegotiable. Yet any number of people seem to have a habit of using a broken alarm clock; they're chronically late for their shifts, and it's always seemingly due to some extenuating circumstance. They're the ones stuck on a "late" subway or bus even though everyone else managed to commute to work on time. The first time someone on our staff is late, we'll make a charitable assumption that maybe there was a foul-up on the subway. The second time we might start to wonder. The third time we'll realize that our colleague may just have a poor work ethic. Chronic lateness (whether it's showing up late for appointments or not returning phone calls or e-mails promptly) is a form of arrogance—"I'm important enough to make others wait for me"—and it puts other team members in a bind because they have to cover for the tardy person or just wonder what's going on. We're looking for the kind of people whose internal alarm clock is always working and who always make adjustments for occasions when subway and bus lines don't roll on schedule.

Ever since my first experience as a boss, when I worked for John Anderson's presidential campaign in 1980, I have continued to view people who work for me as volunteers. It isn't that they've agreed to work without pay. "I'm aware that you're all here, on the most basic level, to pay the rent," I tell new hires. "Just as you need a job, I need people to take orders accurately, and to cook wonderful food."

Then I remind them that if they're as talented at what they do as we believe they are, they could have gotten a job at any of 200 other very good restaurants for the same pay. "You could all be doing what you do anywhere else," I say. "But you chose to be with us. You have volunteered to be on our team, and we owe it to you to provide you with much more than just a paycheck in return. We want you to feel certain you have made a wise choice in joining our company." It's a chance to work at a company where respect and trust are mutual between management and workers, where you can enjoy working alongside and learning from excellent colleagues, and where you can know that your contributions can make every day truly matter.

Meeting with all our new hires—as I continue to do once every four weeks—often makes me think of the way champagne houses make nonvintage, or multivintage, champagne. All the major houses strive to produce a very good nonvintage champagne that tastes virtually the same every single year. They know exactly what the taste profile is and how to achieve it. They also know that the grapes vary from year to year—each vintage produces grapes with varying degrees of acid, alcohol, or fruit—and so they keep aside wine from previous vintages, so that in successive years wine makers can blend together various vintages until all the elements balance perfectly and they've achieved the same consistent flavor they had the year before. That's called house style.

Building our team is not unlike creating nonvintage champagne. Hundreds of employees have worked at our restaurants over the course of many years. And yet our guests, like expert wine tasters, should be able to identify a sense of continuity in the way they feel and experience our dining rooms. This continuity is based on our own carefully selected blend of the most caring, intelligent, and talented people in the hospitality business. That's our house style.

CHAPTER 8

———— I ————

Broadcasting the Message, Tuning in the Feedback

T HE FOUNDER OF ANY new business has an opportunity to initiate the first expression of that business's point of view through a compendium of aesthetic and philosophical choices. The minute the business hangs its shingle on the door it is not only open for business, but open to public feedback and scrutiny. Effective businesses remain true to their core, but also know how to hear, respond, and adjust to constructive feedback. In my business, much of this input comes from restaurant critics and journalists.

The press loves covering restaurants, and with each year its voracious appetite continues to grow, in response, I assume, to the public's own insatiable interest in consuming and devouring information about dining out. On our best days, the media can be extremely helpful to our business. When we err, or are perceived to have fallen short of someone's mark, or simply fall out of favor, negative press can set back our business. Imagine that I'm standing on the shores of Manhattan and I am required to cross the Atlantic to France. The catch is that to get there, I have only two options: I can either swim or ride there on the back of a shark. Swimming is obviously out of the question. I'll tire, freeze, and soon drown. My only choice then, is to hop on the back of the shark and ride with exceptional care and skill, or I'm lunch.

The shark, you see, is the press, and it needs to keep swimming or it dies. I can benefit from acting very carefully with that knowledge. If my riding technique is expert, the shark can be my vehicle to deliver me safely to my destination. In my experience of riding sharks, I've been tossed off, nipped at, and even bitten—but not, so far, devoured. And I've always managed to reach my destination. Sometimes I've even enjoyed the ride.

Like most business owners and CEOs, I am responsible for articulating to the public the core principles and values for which we want our business known. I always try to use media interviews to elaborate on those business concepts, and that's when the ride begins. It's a high-risk game: play it well and you will fill seats, build the top line, and attract new employees; make a mistake and the penalties can be stiff, either for your business, for staff morale, or for your hard-earned reputation. With the exception of late-breaking news, most journalists' stories, even those based on fresh interviews, tend to rehash material from previous stories, accurate or not. You hope the good messages get repeated by other journalists and work hard to make sure the bad ones are snuffed out quietly, or at least live a very short life.

In the summer of 2004 our business—and almost every restaurateur's business—suffered during the Republican National Convention. It was just before the Labor Day weekend, and the city felt desolate. Many families were away on vacation, and thousands of other New Yorkers simply chose to flee the city to avoid the influx of conventioneers or from fear that the convention might once again make the city the target of a terrorist attack. Mayor Michael Bloomberg had optimistically touted the convention as a boon for business.

Perhaps it was in the long term, but for that week, business was dead.

In an interview, Randy Garutti, who was then the general manager of Union Square Cafe, candidly acknowledged to a reporter from the *New York Post* that the restaurant's business was off 25 percent, which was true. (I have always encouraged our managers and chefs to speak openly and directly to the media, and to make other efforts to connect with the public beyond the walls of our restaurants by teaching classes, joining community organizations, conducting cooking demonstrations, and serving food at fund-raising events where food and wine aficionados gather.) But the paper mistakenly quoted Randy as saying that our business was off by 75 percent. That "news" made other news—and the *Post's* error was picked up as fact and subsequently reported on by everyone from Fox News to David Letterman. Union Square Cafe unwittingly became a prominent symbol of business losses during convention week. This incident was far from fatal, but it was nonetheless an irritating shark bite.

Fortunately, the vast majority of the actual reviews that our restaurants have received from critics have been quite positive. With each review, I always have two primary concerns: how might it affect the restaurant's business, and how might it affect the collective morale and individual egos of the hardworking members of our team? I'm thankful that, thus far, not one review has put our business in peril. On the other hand, I have felt bruised—both personally and on behalf of our team—when a critic takes what I consider a painful swipe, particularly after we've just opened a restaurant.

In New York, being first on the scene is a journalist's rite and right. There is a large subsection of the New York dining public, too, who will descend on a new restaurant just after it opens simply to fulfill a need to boast about the hottest new place: "Been there, done that, and I got there first." But savvy diners know that it takes a fair amount of time for a staff, no matter how talented, to learn to work together smoothly. A restaurant can take months to understand which of its dishes work and which don't; the fine-tuning of the menu can easily take up to a year. In fact, it generally takes two to three years for our new restaurants to even approach their ultimate potential for excellence. And this is because it takes that long for a restaurant's soul to emerge. I tend to hold my nose for the first three months, and I don't begin to have any real fun for six months. It's usually a full year after one of my restaurants has been open before I begin to feel truly proud.

By the time I feel confident, however, the critics and the people who simply do not share our chemistry—those who never will enjoy our restaurant, no matter how much it eventually improves—have already moved on to the next new restaurant.

To be sure, a restaurant is fair game for a critic the moment it starts charging patrons. Both the public and the new restaurant can actually be shortchanged by the very early reviews, because these snapshots rarely provide an accurate preview of what that restaurant will eventually become.

Am I suggesting that critics or the dining public just stay away from a new restaurant? Of course not. It's useful to know how a restaurant tastes and works when it first opens, but it's also helpful to understand what to expect down the road. If I buy a case of a newly released wine, I'll usually drink a bottle right off the bat—even if I know it's too young—just to have a point of comparison as I follow its development. That's not a bad thing to do with a new restaurant, as long as you trust that the restaurant will continue to grow and evolve. Indeed, opening a restaurant is a little like making wine. The wine is often clumsy or "dumb" when it's initially bottled, but wines with a solid pedigree almost always improve over time. I'm a hedonist. I drink wine to enjoy it when it's at its best, once the components have settled into delicious harmony. Similarly, I go to a restaurant to enjoy it at its best. (We're fortunate in New York, and indeed across the country, to have an abundance of evolving and evolved restaurants. This means that I have the luxury of patiently waiting before trying a new restaurant—I don't have to try it before it's at its best.)

We're constantly on the lookout for guests who appear to have a natural affinity for our product—the food, staff, and design—even when it is new, flawed, and rapidly evolving. On such a foundation of trust, respect, and enjoyment, we can get their reactions and begin to develop a meaningful dialogue, especially early on, when there is so much—almost too much—feedback from the general public. For instance, when Tabla opened in 1998, a frequent criticism from some early guests was that Indian food would never succeed in a sensual, fine-dining guise. We listened, but that input was not particularly helpful. Another criticism was that, good as Tabla was, it was just too loud. That was more constructive. In fact, we'd anticipated before opening that noise might be a problem. I had insisted on using a beautiful, rich wood called padauk for the floor. The restaurant's ceilings were untouchable because of the requirement to restore and preserve their historic ornamentation, so sound-absorbent tiles were out. Tabla was loud, and a chorus of complaints led to several subtle fixes that greatly lowered the noise level. We hung plush curtains, stuffed balls of fabric underneath our tabletops to capture noise bouncing off the floors, and upholstered the seat backs of our chairs. One lesson we learned from the experience is that every little thing you do to mitigate noise helps a lot. This is because when a restaurant is noisy, a cumulative effect occurs: each guest has to speak a little more loudly to be heard over the ever-increasing din.

When we have failed to tune in to our guests who let us know where we have a real problem, we've risked hearing about it from someone with a megaphone. This happened with our most popular dessert at Tabla—*kulfi*, an extremely dense, decadently rich, cone-shaped ice cream. After observing guests early on struggling to cut this very hard frozen dessert, I told Tabla's general manager that we needed to provide an easier way to eat *kulfi*: serve it with a serrated grapefruit spoon. "Great idea," he said.

Months went by and somehow my reminders were not working. People kept ordering *kulfi*; it was still frozen solid; and the restaurant still hadn't found the right spoons. A restaurant critic beat us to the punch: "The *kulfi*'s delicious once you get it in your mouth," he wrote in his newspaper, "but it slid halfway across the table when I tried to cut into it with my spoon."

Reading that was exasperating for me, an unnecessary, public black eye for the restaurant, and an undeserved slight for the pastry chef. This delicious dessert need not have been panned. In fact, within one day the manager had found serrated spoons for it. The experience taught me yet another lesson about trusting my instincts and holding others accountable.

For the first two years at Tabla and at its less expensive downstairs café, called Bread Bar, we had another unusual problem. Most of our early guests had never before experienced Indian spices paired with local, seasonal ingredients, hip cocktails, sexy music, and modern art; and the curiosity generated by Ruth Reichl's three-star review in the *New York Times* kept Tabla packed for the entire first year. But then in the second year business tailed off a little, and our performance in the third year was flat (it was especially hurt by the 9/11 attacks). This was the first time one of our restaurants had failed to post consistent, steady, year-over-year growth.

But we hadn't built Tabla to be a flash in the pan. So I did something different. I ran some focus groups with a few loyal guests and included chef Floyd Cardoz, our general manager, Randy Garutti, and our director of operations, Richard Coraine. We consistently heard two distinct observations, seemingly at odds: "I would dine at Tabla far more often if it were more Indian," and "I would go to Tabla far more often if it were a little less Indian." So we hit on a solution. We would emphasize the bold-flavored Indian food downstairs in the Bread Bar and emphasize refined, gently spiced food upstairs in Tabla's main dining room. We believed that this would satisfy both constituencies. And we had the input from our guests to thank for making those changes. Almost immediately, the food critic Eric Asimov of the *New York Times* noticed the new format. He gave the newly Indianized

Bread Bar a rave in his column "$25 and Under" that instantly recharged the restaurant and returned it to its earlier business levels.

We made a different kind of adjustment at Eleven Madison Park not long after it opened, also thanks in part to feedback from our guests. I arrived at the conclusion that my original concept for this restaurant had been flawed, and that the guests were picking up on it. Eleven Madison Park looked and felt far more like a grand, gorgeous restaurant than the breezy brasserie we had envisioned. As a consequence, rather than exceeding the guests' expectations for a brasserie, we were falling short of their expectations for a grand restaurant. The food was indeed better than that of a typical brasserie, but not as refined as one might expect from the restaurant's majestic, urbane décor. This seemed to be a two-pronged challenge. We had to find a way to muss up our hair a little—to make the restaurant a lot more fun—and to meaningfully improve the quality of the dining experience at the same time.

When it opened, Eleven Madison Park had received a handful of very good (but not excellent) reviews, much to my dismay. (In fairness, though, it did earn four stars from the *Daily News,* a James Beard nomination for best new restaurant in America, and a coveted place on *Esquire* magazine's annual list of America's best new restaurants. Also, the intense anticipation surrounding its sassier next-door sibling, Tabla, which was opening a month later, didn't help.) Part of the problem, we figured out, was that people weren't having enough fun at Eleven Madison Park. The restaurant is a breathtaking, soaring space in a monumental, marble-filled historic art deco building. No matter how we accessorized the place to make it look like a brasserie, its elegant bones were not going to change. It looked like a special-occasion restaurant, and that was that. Richard Coraine urged me to consider one straightforward solution: we needed to book more large parties. On opening, we had decided to limit tables to six or eight. That, we had believed, would give the kitchen an advantage—cooking better food for fewer people. "People are constantly calling us, wanting to use this restaurant for a big party," Richard said.

We began pushing tables together in nearly every possible configuration and started welcoming parties of eight, twelve, and even eighteen. Next, we expanded our wine list, adding California wines to a list that had been exclusively French—a narrow approach that had been part of my hubris at the beginning. Now, each evening, animated mini-parties sprouted up all around the dining room, and suddenly Eleven Madison Park became a bustling, lively restaurant. We hired a dynamic maître d', Derek Watkins, who seemed to remember every customer—Richard described him as a front door "smoochie." Later we added Stephen Beckta, another thoroughbred dining room and wine manager, who lit up the room like a swank circus master. The menu was rethought and refined; and within six months, Eleven Madison Park made the cover of *Wine Spectator* as one of New York's best new restaurants for wine lovers. It soon earned a James Beard Award of Excellence for its service; and it has landed a spot in *Zagat's* top twenty most popular restaurants almost every year since. In 2006 we made another bold move by bringing in an immensely talented, young Swiss-born chef, Daniel Humm, whose very refined cooking style would trump any last vestiges of brasserie feeling at Eleven Madison Park. The restaurant's design had convinced our guests, and us, that it was meant to be a great, grand restaurant.

The opening problems at Blue Smoke weren't so easily fixed, though we considered just about every shred of the tons of feedback we were getting from the people who ate there in our early days.

To begin with, we were totally unprepared for the mobs of people who came to sample our barbecue restaurant almost from the first night. We had never quite believed that so many suave New Yorkers would be willing to loosen their ties and pick up bones with their fingers. Would-be patrons could not get through on the phones to make reservations. Tables were overbooked and double-booked because of our own inadequate preparation, frustrating and angering the very people we most needed to have on our side. One night that spring of 2002, during the annual meeting of the American Booksell-

I've tried to pick our media moments carefully. *Yes* to Julia Child's visiting my home kitchen on *Good Morning America* in 1990. *Yes* to profiles in *People, Town and Country, CBS Sunday Morning,* and the *New York Times. Yes* to a national ad campaign for American Express (more on that later). *Yes* to a segment with Martha Stewart learning to cook barbecue from the pitmaster Kenny Callaghan in the kitchen of Blue Smoke, or playfully apprenticing herself at Shake Shack. *No* to my own national talk show on Lifetime. *No* to national advertising campaigns for a fragrance and a line of menswear. *No* to a story in the *New York Times* about why I think Union Square Cafe deserved a Michelin star. (If I were Bibendum, the Michelin man, I'd have a comment.) And *no* to *The Apprentice.*

The first time I chose to participate in a high-profile media opportunity was in 1992, when I was invited to appear in a radio campaign and, later, a national television campaign for American Express. It became one of the first examples of a national cause-related marketing campaign by a global corporation. I had agreed to do the spots, which were filmed at Union Square Cafe, on the condition that their focus be on American Express's efforts to help fight hunger. Those ads dramatically elevated the profile and positioning of Union Square Cafe. They were also the seeds of what would become a multiyear, $20 million "Charge Against Hunger" program waged by American Express and Share Our Strength, the exceptional organization founded by Billy Shore to relieve hunger and poverty. I'm more proud of that than almost anything else I've accomplished in my career, but not because it put me on television screens and in Sunday newspaper magazines across the country. That fame was fleeting. What endured was the impact on real kids who for the first time got school breakfasts, or who were enrolled in failure-to-thrive clinics, or whose parents learned how to stretch their food dollars and to buy and cook nutritious meals. All thanks to American Express's funding of Share Our Strength programs, and all because of the early positive consumer feedback generated by those ads.

ers Association, we inadvertently booked two parties on the same balcony, which has room for only one group. These weren't just any parties, either. One host was an important editor, publisher, and friend; the other was also a celebrated publisher, introducing the latest book from Steven Raichlen, the country's top-selling barbecue author. This incident required us to eat crow, and it still makes me shudder. Each party insisted that they'd be happy only on the balcony, until I got involved and persuaded one to switch to our more spacious rear dining room. Then all I had to do was answer to the forty or so guests who had made regular reservations for tables in the rear dining room. It was embarrassing, chaotic, and costly.

Part of the explanation for this mistake and many others was that we had deliberately hired a younger, far less seasoned staff than we usually would have for an opening team. My initial idea was that Blue Smoke would become our organization's "farm system" for talent. We would be able to hire 51 percenters whose technical skills might not yet be refined enough for a job at Union Square Cafe, Tabla, Gramercy Tavern, or Eleven Madison Park. I reasoned that they wouldn't need those more advanced restaurant skills in a barbecue joint; but if and when they acquired enough ability to earn a promotion to one of our other restaurants, we would be ready with a job. And we would nurture "green" managers in precisely the same way.

This scheme proved to be a serious miscalculation. I learned that no matter what our concept is, people expect three specific things of our brand: culinary excellence, knowledgeable service, and gracious hospitality. At any price point and for any kind of food—barbecue or black truffles—our guests expected excellence and hospitality, and we were falling short. And my idea of Blue Smoke as "farm system" was also offensive to high-quality employees who may have been qualified for a job at one of our more "refined" restaurants, but who simply preferred the relaxed, fun atmosphere of Blue Smoke.

By heeding our guests' constructive criticisms right away, we were able to make crucial adjustments and begin to solve some of our most daunting problems. First, we removed one-fourth of the seats in our dining room—a costly change, but one that we hoped would allow us to take charge of the place. Next, we increased the number of dining room and kitchen managers by half, transferring some very talented managers to Blue Smoke from a couple of our other restaurants.

To help deal with late-seated reservations and to take care of people who made a spur-of-the moment decision to drop in for some barbecue, Richard Coraine urged that we set aside as much as 50 percent of the business each night for walk-ins. This strategy was effective in two ways. First, we regained control over how busy we would be on any given evening, since once we had seated the guests to whom we had promised tables, we still had discretionary control over whether or not to seat the other half of the dining room. Second, since we knew that aficionados are not used to planning—or interested in planning—four weeks in advance to go to a barbecue joint, we were able to satisfy their desire to enjoy barbecue on the spur of the moment.

Encouraging walk-ins also attracted a whole new population to our business: barbecue lovers who wanted to drop in for some ribs and a couple of pints of beer, hang out with friends, and hear some great live music downstairs or on the jukebox upstairs. They weren't inveterate foodies surfing the Internet for reviews and wondering what the food bloggers were chatting about. By eliminating the requirement to reserve in advance, we had removed the "special-occasionness" of Blue Smoke, and almost instantly we encouraged and attracted hundreds of new patrons who packed the bar four and five deep, actually enjoying the experience of waiting as much as an hour for a table to free up. Of course, the most important adjustments would be those we made as we persevered in our quest to serve top-quality barbecue.

WE'RE CONSTANTLY SEEKING TO increase the mind share each of our restaurants enjoys with the public. It's crucial that our establishments remain on the tip of people's tongues, because we have hundreds of seats to fill every day and night in a city that offers the public thousands of options for dining. I am also well aware that people are pummeled with more information each day than our ancestors received in an entire lifetime. Therefore, our messages have to be useful and have to be sticky if we are to stand any chance of earning a piece of your mind share. And they must be presented in a context that supports our larger business point of view, or they will be confusing at best and damaging at worst.

One winning idea was a wonderful segment on the *Today Show* featuring chef Kerry Heffernan. In addition to being an avid fly fisherman, Kerry is an expert on anything that breathes through gills. The segment showed him on a boat catching a fish, cleaning it, and then cooking it in the studio. It sent the message that the chef of Eleven Madison Park is authentically knowledgeable about fish, cares for the environment, and is also a nice guy. It generated not only a lot of business for the restaurant but excellent feedback for Kerry as well.

This was a great fit, but an appearance on Donald Trump's show *The Apprentice* would not have been—no matter how colossally successful the show was. The producers called one day and asked me to be part of a competition. As I understood it, the plot was that two restaurateurs would each be challenged to create, build, and open a new restaurant, within a week. Then the *Zagat Survey* would send in its troops to vote on which one was better. At the time, *The Apprentice* had some of television's loftiest ratings, but I knew it was not for us. People told me I was crazy, that it would be great for the company to appear on a show that everyone in America was watching. What I saw instead was a high-profile opportunity to become distracted from our business, and perhaps to send conflicting messages about our seriousness as a company that exists to develop enduring restaurants with soul.

But there was an underbelly to this story. In the aftermath of the very successful Amex campaign of 1992, I was in Washington, D.C., at Red Sage, Mark Miller's red-hot new restaurant, to attend a meeting of the board of directors of Share Our Strength. Just as we were about to break for lunch, a host beckoned me to the restaurant's crowded maître d' stand to pick up the telephone. One of my managers at Union Square Cafe was on the line, calling to tell me that our restaurant was at that moment being marched on by a group of gay and lesbian activists under the banner "New York Boycott Colorado." They had formed a picket line blocking the front door of Union Square Cafe to protest my agreeing to travel to Colorado to host a seminar on Italian wines at the upcoming *Food and Wine* Classic, the magazine's annual event in Aspen, which I had been attending as a speaker since 1987. I was dumbfounded.

I could understand why the group was incensed about Colorado's forthcoming vote on a state constitutional amendment that would effectively abridge civil rights for gays and lesbians. But I was baffled by its strategy of picking me as a linchpin for the protest. The only way the activists even knew about my participation on the wine panel was that *Food and Wine*, owned by American Express, had capitalized on my exposure through the recent ads, and had promoted my participation as a speaker in Aspen. I had read about the proposed amendment and happened to agree with the protesters' position on it. But I was stunned to have become a target. A picket line in front of the Union Square Cafe? I found that incomprehensible. The boycotters' thinking seemed to be: "If we can pressure Danny Meyer to pull out of Aspen, that will help convince voters to support us." But there was no connection between my wine class and the disputed amendment. I knew that my decision whether or not to participate would have no impact on how any citizen of Colorado might decide to vote.

For days I felt trapped in this situation, which was growing worse by the minute. I was being inundated with absurd, angry faxes accusing me of homophobia and threatening to hurt my business. Some of the writers maintained that if the amendment had been relevant to a Jewish issue, I would long ago have refused to go to Aspen. The restaurant's office floor was covered with such a mess of thermal fax paper that it looked as if the Torah itself had scrolled from our fax machines. Exasperated, I contacted friends at American Express and *Food and Wine*, and we all agreed that despite my intention to follow through on my commitment to speak, it would be best if I stayed home.

I had studied and worked in politics, and I understood that activists need traction—and a good target. But this protest had become a perversion of what was originally a positive media effort by American Express (and me) to relieve hunger. The experience left me profoundly wary of the potential downside of media exposure.

A dozen years later, something similar happened. Toward the end of summer 2004, the Missouri delegation to the Republican National Convention rented Blue Smoke to throw itself a party. We had booked the business not only because it was highly profitable for us to do so during a week when business in New York was quite slow, but also because the "Missouri connection" was a great fit for the restaurant, given my roots in St. Louis. Then, just days before the convention, Missouri passed a new amendment to its state constitution, banning same-sex marriage. When word got out that the state's delegation had selected Blue Smoke for its party, gay and lesbian activists arrived at the front door of our barbecue joint ahead of time and gave a special welcome to the "Show Me" state. The protestors pelted the delegates' buses with eggs and yelled at the delegates as they entered the restaurant. I missed the action, having been inside the restaurant to greet the Republican guests, including Senator Kit Bond. (Not wanting to broach politics at this particular party, I steered the conversation toward things we had in common, like barbecue and the St. Louis Cardinals.) As soon as I had made my rounds, I left the party. As I walked out the door, the protesters began chanting at me: "Shame! Shame! Shame!"

Astounded, I looked at them and asked, "Me?"

"You!" someone roared back. And then they began chanting, "You, you, you!"

A reporter bounded out of the pack and asked me to state my position on the amendment. "I'm against it," I said bluntly. "There's no story here."

More recently, in 2005, activists advocating a ban on foie gras began protesting and handing out gruesomely illustrated fliers every few nights on the sidewalk outside both Union Square Cafe and The Modern. (Those protests didn't dissuade more than a few people from entering our restaurants, and to date, sales of foie gras remain where they have been for the past few years.) Our restaurants are among hundreds in America that serve foie gras, but once again, we seemed to be an attractive target for activists. That's way beyond anything I'd imagined when I first got into the restaurant business. It's an odd aspect of success and one of the ironies and risks of having a public profile. Still, there's value in being the target of a protest: it certainly opens the door to learning more about a controversial subject. To think that, back in 1985, people laughed at me when I said I'd be parlaying a political science degree into a career as a restaurateur!

SUCH EXPERIENCES HAVE CONDITIONED me to try to fly under the radar as much as possible when I'm opening a new restaurant. There have been two times in the course of my career as a restaurateur when I found myself and one of my restaurants at the center of a feeding frenzy by the media. The first was upon opening Gramercy Tavern on July 21, 1994.

What set the craziness in motion was an unprecedented cover story by Peter Kaminsky in *New York* magazine, which hit the newsstands the day the restaurant opened. The cover was simple enough: a photograph of a box of Gramercy Tavern matches, underscored with four gold stars, and the cover line: "The Next Great Restaurant?"

We hadn't known about the cover in advance, but to a lot of New

Yorkers it smacked of blatant self-promotion, as if we were boasting about the new restaurant, presenting ourselves with four stars, and calling ourselves the next great restaurant. Target practice commenced, with Gramercy Tavern in the crosshairs of practically every restaurant critic in New York. Most business owners, especially restaurateurs in a media capital like New York, would kill for the kind of buzz generated by an appearance on the cover of *New York*. You can't buy that kind of advertising. But whatever interest it generated, the open invitation to eviscerate the new restaurant was even greater.

Just one week before the story appeared, I found myself in the absurd position of being the first to inform the magazine's food critic, Gael Greene, that Gramercy Tavern was going to be the subject of a feature story. She'd called me to find out when the restaurant was to debut so that she could include a short blurb in "Cue," her restaurant listings at the back of the magazine. I was faced with a difficult choice: inform her for the first time that we were to be the subject of a major feature (this was before I knew we'd be on the cover) and incur her anger over not having been told, or withhold the information and invite even more wrath for being disingenuous. When I told her about the forthcoming feature story, she blurted, *"What?"* and then uttered bitter invectives against her own editor for not having communicated the information to her. I didn't blame her for being outraged, but I knew we were in for trouble. Before it had served its first meal, Gramercy Tavern found itself in the doghouse with one of the most influential food critics in New York.

Predictably, Gael did launch an assault on the restaurant in her review; she was responding as much to her own magazine's hype as she was to her sense of the restaurant itself. That her editors had shown disrespect for her by not telling her about the cover story certainly added to her distaste for Gramercy Tavern.

In case we wondered about its impact, the cover of *New York* was referred to in subsequent reviews of Gramercy Tavern by other critics. For example, Ruth Reichl in the *New York Times* cited it in her reviews. If the restaurant's aspiration is four stars, the critics seemed to be saying, I'll tell you what I think! Gramercy Tavern remained busy throughout the torrent of reviews, but they were a painful distraction from making the kind of improvements that would eventually allow it to evolve into a great restaurant. The story ratcheted up expectations and made it almost inevitable that we would fail to meet them.

But the opening reviews of Gramercy Tavern paled in comparison with what was written about Blue Smoke eight years later. The initial scorching reviews for Blue Smoke tested the limits of our customers' loyalty and our employees' morale.

For the first time in my career the criticism felt personal and mean-spirited. One Wednesday in March 2002, I was on my way to Chicago for an early morning business meeting with family members. My grandfather was in failing health, and there were important matters to discuss concerning his philanthropic activities. Knowing that the *New York Post*'s review of Blue Smoke was running that day, I picked up a copy of the paper just before boarding the plane. Flipping to the food page, I turned pale as I saw the headline, "Smoke Blows It." The critic declared, "I know barbecue and this ain't it." There wasn't much in that criticism we could use to improve our performance. I could only feel bad, and I did. Then I picked up that same morning's *Daily News* and read an article about how the Internet was becoming a popular place to post anonymous musings about restaurants. Blue Smoke, the article noted, had already attracted more than sixty postings on one site, many of them scathing. A barrage of negative, often hostile reviews followed, creating the impression that by its very existence, Blue Smoke was committing a capital offense—and that it would probably not survive. The subtext of a lot of the press was: "Who the hell is Danny Meyer to be opening a barbecue restaurant? What could he know about it? See? Aha! Blue Smoke will be his Waterloo!" I wondered if there had ever been a more intensely scrutinized barbecue restaurant than Blue Smoke. In most parts of the country, when a barbecue joint opens, the world takes scant notice.

I tried hard to see beyond every pronouncement to find something constructive. I knew Blue Smoke was not performing anywhere near its potential. In fact, the ribs were not as good as they should have been, and not nearly as good as they would eventually be after we figured out how to make necessary adjustments to our smokestack. But the critics weren't taking on just the ribs, pulled pork, and brisket: they seemed to be assailing my credibility, and my justification for opening a barbecue place in New York. The *Post* pounded away with a vengeance. In one piece, one of their writers called our opening night "the worst" he'd ever experienced. A week later, in its review, the *Post* gave us zero stars. Its gossip column "Page Six" piled on by noting that Al Roker of the *Today Show* had thrown his book party at the "critically panned" Blue Smoke.

I was feeling raw, reading nothing but scarring reviews—yet somehow we remained packed every night. Either the public wasn't reading the reviews, or people just didn't care what the critics said. Or perhaps people were taking a grisly interest in witnessing and even getting a taste of a train wreck in progress.

New York magazine was up next. When our fourth child, Peyton, was about to begin nursery school, the school asked Audrey (who was by now the mom of three young alumni of the school—Hallie, Gretchen, and Charles) if she would help welcome new parents of the kids who would be in Peyton's class. Coincidentally, one of those new parents was Adam Platt, now *New York*'s lead food critic. At the open house for new families, Adam was introduced to Audrey. I was unable to attend, and the next day Audrey debated whether or not to share with me what he had told her: "I don't know if your husband is going to like the review of Blue Smoke that's going to run Monday" he had said. "But I do like his other restaurants."

I was sleepless all weekend, anxiously waiting for a damaging review. By Monday morning, I understood why Adam had warned Audrey. He'd found Blue Smoke's pit barbecue so-so and noted that while he loved the salmon we were serving, a friend he'd brought along who was a barbecue connoisseur refused to even try it. "Salmon does not belong on a real barbecue menu," the friend had told Adam.

Much of our early guest feedback felt like what we'd heard at Tabla: half the people would go to Blue Smoke more often if only our barbecue were more authentic, and the other half would go more frequently if only it were less of a barbecue restaurant.

New York struck again, when Gael Greene, still writing for the magazine's listings section, suggested that the ribs were "wimpy," and that I had never been in front of a pit in my life. That did it. I had to respond. I wrote Sally and Nardie Stein, the longtime owners of Camp Nebagamon, and asked if they could unearth any photograph showing me as a fourteen-year-old in front of the fire the night I was declared the cowinner of the Chef's Cap outdoor cooking contest. Inveterate archivists, they managed to find it, and sent a copy to Gael Greene along with a good-natured letter about my early prowess as an outdoor cook.

One important lesson I learned while doing research for Blue Smoke, traveling through North Carolina, Texas, Tennessee, Alabama, Illinois, Mississippi, and Missouri, is that people love to discover barbecue places off the beaten path—and that there's a correlation between one's affection for barbecue and the adventure of the road trip itself. I began to understand that opening a barbecue place in the middle of Manhattan denied 'cue seekers the thrill of trekking to, or happening upon, something obscure and fabulous. If the same restaurant, even with all of Blue Smoke's early flaws, had been opened by an upstart restaurateur in a remote part of Brooklyn or the Bronx, its arrival—no, its discovery by the press—would have been heralded all over town: "Finally, we have great barbecue in New York!"

Blue Smoke seemed to turn everyone into an instant expert on barbecue. Self-proclaimed connoisseurs suddenly bombarded me with their prized techniques for smoking, their secret family recipes for sauce, and their preferred regional styles. People sent me their ribs to try, and I also received pints of coleslaw, barbecue sauce, cheese crackers, and potato salad from well-meaning patrons who thought their recipes could help. Everyone felt entitled to judge barbecue because it's an essentially American product with a common point of reference. Nobody had ever gone to Tabla and asked, "Didn't Grandma make a much better pulled lamb and mustard-mashed potato sandwich on toasted naan drizzled with fresh lime juice and chilies?"

For months, Blue Smoke remained a big, juicy target. The *New Yorker,* which had rarely published negative restaurant reviews, wrote in its column "Table for Two" that Blue Smoke belonged "in a strip mall in Disney World." After the *New Yorker* piece I called Eric Asimov of the *New York Times.* One week after we opened, he had written a long feature on Blue Smoke's novel fifteen-story smokestack, and his piece had helped create an inordinate amount of early interest and hype (and subsequent antipathy). I began by asking him, "You're not going to be reviewing us, are you?" Eric's weekly review "$25 and Under" never assigned stars to a restaurant—unlike the featured weekly review written by William Grimes.

Eric said, "No. I wish I were, but Blue Smoke is high-profile, so Biff Grimes really wants to do it."

"Tell me, is Blue Smoke really as bad as everything they're writing?" I asked.

"Well, there are things you need to work on," he said cryptically, "but you're on the right track." He didn't elaborate.

All that was left for would-be patrons who had read the reviews was the rather perverse pleasure of finding out for themselves what was wrong with the place. And then something odd happened. Some of our colleagues actually rallied on our behalf. Tracy and Drew Nieporent, of Myriad Restaurant Group (Montrachet, Tribeca Grill) went out on a limb to defend us on the website Citysearch, writing, "Look, we are competitors with these guys but I have to tell you—Blue Smoke is and will be a great restaurant. You don't understand what goes on there." It was an amazing and welcome gesture of loyalty and friendship.

Not long after this, Eric Asimov called me. "I've got two things that will surprise you," he said. "I am, in fact, writing the main review for Blue Smoke. I also want you to know that it's running tomorrow as the starred review, and not in '$25 and Under.'" He explained that the newspaper's regular critic, William Grimes, was unexpectedly taking a leave of absence and that the *Times* had asked him to be the interim critic. Eric had been given only one week's lead time; and after having just spent the week visiting a restaurant called Smith and writing its review he had just learned that it was closing. "Somehow, I've got to get a review in tomorrow," he said, "and Blue Smoke is the only other restaurant I have eaten in three times."

In fact, he had been to the restaurant two times during the first days we had opened and had been in for a third visit the night before he called me. I had seen him that night and said hi—although it hadn't crossed my mind that this might be *it*. I had urged him to try our collard greens and for dessert, our special: a green tomato pie.

I sat there at the phone silently wringing my hands, thinking, *The restaurant has already improved so much since our first week—why can't we have just one more month before the* Times *weighs in?*

Eric gave Blue Smoke one star ("good"), and his review marked a powerful turning point for two reasons: one, it contained none of the vitriol and anger present in so many of the earlier reviews; and two, it was balanced, constructive, and fair. He wrote about Blue Smoke's trajectory, describing the opening of a barbecue restaurant in Manhattan as a formidable and, some might say, crazy task. He observed that it had started off awkwardly but that improvement had been dramatic and that this restaurant and its mission to bring real pit barbecue to New York deserved to be supported. The last three words of his review were encouraging: "Go, baby, go!"

Eric also made a television appearance on the local cable news channel New York 1 in conjunction with the review. He put things in perspective on television, "This is the first time the *New York Times* has ever given even one star to a barbecue restaurant."

Sometimes the critics do come back for a second look, as Bryan Miller did in first promoting Union Square Cafe to three stars back in 1989, and as Ruth Reichl did when she upgraded Gramercy Tavern to its third star in 1996. At the end of 2002, Adam Platt became the first critic to return to Blue Smoke for an update and to write enthusiastically about its vast improvement. His decisive reversal helped make it safe for others to reexamine their early pronouncements as well. By 2003, *New York* was declaring Blue Smoke's brisket "the best barbecue in New York."

Previous success in any field invites high expectations and scrutiny the next time around. People are less forgiving when a winner falters than they are when an up-and-comer stumbles. But a mark of a champion is to welcome scrutiny, persevere, perform beyond expectations, and provide an exceptional product—for which forgiveness is not necessary.

IT WOULD BE FASCINATING to look up all fifty-two weekly restaurant reviews in the *New York Times* over the last ten years, or compile the *Zagat Survey's* "Top Five Newcomers" each year, and count how many establishments are still in business. My guess is that it would be shocking to see how much ink gets wasted on places that start out hyped and hot but eventually don't go anywhere. Restaurant criticism tends to be an ephemeral snapshot of an opening, providing little to no perspective on where the restaurant might end up.

I've observed that, with a small group of critics, the outcome of a review can be positively influenced by a free meal. One writer for an important paper wrote harshly about Blue Smoke during our opening. He was probably correct in his judgment, but a less naive approach on our part might have persuaded him not to share that observation with his many readers.

He had dined that evening with a well-connected publicist whose clients included an A-list of New York restaurants. We queried the publicist after reading the pan and said, "Gee, we must have really screwed up in a big way with you guys that night. What happened?"

The reply left no room for misunderstanding: It didn't help that we had charged them for their meal, especially since they were sure they had seen other guests throughout the dining room being "comped." That was true. It was one of our first nights, and in lieu of throwing an opening party, we had opted to invite a few friends to sit down at some of our tables as our guests. They did see Tom Brokaw and Brokaw's wife, Meredith, longtime regulars and friends; and yes, we were hosting them that night. James Carville, another loyal friend, was dining with our compliments at another table. Seeing this, plus being charged after having been on the receiving end of painfully slow service, understandably infuriated the writer. Clearly, I had played this one wrong.

One critic who had given Tabla a no-star rating when it opened was about to review Blue Smoke. He wrote for another influential publication in New York, and I understood through the restaurateur grapevine that he welcomed being "hosted." I had also heard that whether or not he was hosted might even affect the tone of his review. When one of my managers spotted this critic in Blue Smoke one night, she let me know. To that point, I had never comped a critic before in my entire career. I had learned that most newspapers and magazines prohibited their writers from accepting freebies in order to avoid any conflict of interest. But after weeks of watching the restaurant take a public beating, I decided to experiment. With the miserable reviews we were getting, there was nothing to lose. And since critics aren't public officials, I reasoned that hosting them wasn't illegal. As instructed, the manager went to the critic's table and said: "Danny is honored that you're dining with us tonight and he wants very much to welcome you as our guest for your first visit." That one visit was enough to produce a glowing two-star review, one of the very best we got early on. The strategy had worked so well that I tried it again, this time with a freelance reviewer doing a piece for a downtown magazine. Another shining review: two for two. In seventeen years I had never tried to stage a comeback by hosting critics. Choosing to do so in those circumstances was testimony to the pain from the scar tissue that had been forming on my rear end.

SOME RESTAURANT REVIEWS DEFY explanation. One of these ran in the *New York Times* in late February 2005, just shortly after The Modern had opened, and it blindsided us. Unexpectedly, it was not a review of our new restaurant—The Modern—but rather a rereview of six-year-old Eleven Madison Park. I had actually hoped for some time that we'd get another look from the *New York Times*. Ruth Reichl had given the restaurant a "very good" two-star rating three months after we opened (to the dismay of the staff and chef, who had been hoping for three stars and were actually in tears on receiving the news). After six years of continual evolving and improving, I felt that we were very close to deserving a third star.

The first half of the review, by Frank Bruni, now the *Times's* lead reviewer, read like a valentine: "If anyone has cracked the code for high-end restaurants in this fickle city," it began, "it is Danny Meyer." Our way of nourishing and nurturing guests had, Bruni wrote, transformed them into "besotted loyalists," while enabling us to "achieve sophistication without self-consciousness, polish without pretension." He also took note of the smile in the reservationists' voices on the phone, the smile at the front door, the smile on the waiters' faces. I was loving it—at least until I continued on to the next column.

Abruptly, his tone veered sharply from a valentine to damning with faint praise to outright scolding. True, the roasted lobster with lemongrass velouté was "unforgettable," but the zinfandel-marinated beef cheeks tasted like "day-old pot roast," the chicken was "overcooked," and the sweetbreads were "dry." Only the pastry chef Nicole Kaplan's desserts—"pure pleasure"—survived unscathed. By the time Bruni was done dissecting our offerings, he reversed course. He had initially praised our hospitality but now he issued the cynical suggestion that the welcome was all a facade. "Although the dining room is flooded with those smiling servers," he observed, "their dance is less a ballet than a military drill, glaringly mechanized."

The last line was painful to staff members at Eleven Madison Park, and to me. The restaurant retained its two stars, but this was not, in the end, just a review of Eleven Madison Park. It felt like a sweeping judgment about the genuineness of our hospitality. I couldn't find a scintilla of usefulness in being told by a critic that our hospitality was not sincere, or that it was executed by rote—especially when his experiences with us, detailed earlier in the review, seemed to imply caring treatment by warm human beings.

I had no clue as to what Bruni's motivation was in admonishing Eleven Madison Park. He summarized his review as less a "complaint" than a "rumination on the limitations of all formulas, even Mr. Meyer's." I was anguished about his observations and pained to see them shared with hundreds of thousands of readers. Believe me, if someone has that big and loud a megaphone, I'd much rather it was one of our "besotted loyalists."

Frank Bruni had been right about those loyalists; in fact, he had stirred them to action. Clearly, a three-star review would have put the wind at our backs by generating more first-time guests; but no review could have produced as strong—as protective—a reaction from our enormous following as this one had. We got many dozens of letters as well as e-mails and visits from people who found his comments off base and contrary to their own experience. I was stopped at my sons' school the next morning by a mother. "This just makes us want to come to the restaurant all the more," she said indignantly.

I felt a need to address our staff at the restaurant. I immediately reminded them that I'm the first one to welcome and reflect on constructive criticism. If the beef cheeks at Eleven Madison Park are too dry, or the service is too slow, we have a responsibility to fix the problem. And in a long e-mail to my chefs and general managers, who then forwarded it to their teams, I let everyone know exactly how I was feeling. "It was truly disturbing that Mr. Bruni chose to use Eleven Madison Park as a vehicle to analyze the success of each of our restaurants," I wrote. "In applying his judgment that our hospitality is on 'autopilot,' he also implied that the welcome we give is in some way disingenuous or rote. It's almost as if Mr. Bruni wanted to try to explain the very experience that our guests most cherish, and then knock us for it. There is no way that our team has been so capable of winning the hearts of thousands of jaded New Yorkers with insincere smiles and robotic service."

I ended the memo by quoting something my late grandfather, Irving Harris, always used to remind me. "People will say a lot of great things about your business, and a lot of nasty things as well. Just remember: you're never as good as the best things they'll say, and never as bad as the negative ones. Just keep centered, know what you stand for, strive for new goals, and always be decent."

That's what I hope our restaurants will always work toward—just as we have done since day one.

CHAPTER 9

Constant, Gentle Pressure

THREE HALLMARKS OF EFFECTIVE leadership are to provide a clear vision for your business so that your employees know where you're taking them; to hold people accountable for consistent standards of excellence; and to communicate a well-defined set of cultural priorities and nonnegotiable values. Perhaps most important, true leaders hold themselves accountable for conducting business in the same manner in which they've asked their team to perform.

I struggled mightily with the emotional and technical skills required for that kind of leadership as a twenty-seven-year-old first-time leader of my own company. As Union Square Cafe grew up, I realized that I too would have to develop new skills just to keep pace with my own restaurant and its staff.

During one of his uncannily well-timed, impromptu visits to Union Square Cafe when I was still in my twenties, Pat Cetta sat down at a table with me and indulged my need to fret about the travails of managing my staff. I bemoaned the fact that I was failing to get any kind of consistent message across to my staff members regarding standards of excellence. Waiters and managers (at least half of whom were older than I) were continually testing me and pushing the limits, and this was driving me crazy.

"If you choose to get upset about this, you are missing the boat, luvah," Pat said with reassuring calm, in his indelible New York accent. Then he gave me a demonstration that has become integral to the way I view management. Pat Cetta's simple lesson has helped me navigate through years of challenging moments as I've worked to encourage our team to build and sustain standards of excellence, especially while we're growing.

Pat pointed to the set table next to us. "First," he said, "I want you to take everything off that table except for the saltshaker. Go ahead! Get rid of the plates, the silverware, the napkins, even the pepper mill. I just want you to leave the saltshaker by itself in the middle." I did as he said, and he asked, "Where is the saltshaker now?"

"Right where you told me, in the center of the table."

"Are you sure that's where you want it?" I looked closely. The shaker was actually about a quarter of an inch off center. "Go ahead. Put it where you really want it," he said. I moved it very slightly to what looked to be smack-dab in the center. As soon as I removed my hand, Pat pushed the saltshaker three inches off center.

"Now put it back where you want it," he said. I returned it to dead center. This time he moved the shaker another six inches off center, again asking, "Now where do you want it?"

I slid it back. Then he explained his point. "Listen, luvah. Your staff and your guests are always moving your saltshaker off center. That's their job. It is the job of life. It's the law of entropy! Until you understand that, you're going to get pissed off every time someone moves the saltshaker off center. It is not your job to get upset. You just need to understand: that's what they do. Your job is just to move the shaker back each time and let them know exactly what you stand for. Let them know what excellence looks like to you. And if you're ever willing to let them decide where the center is, then I want you to give them the keys to the store. Just give away the fuckin' restaurant!"

Wherever your center lies, know it, name it, stick to it, and believe in it. Everyone who works with you will know what matters to you and will respect and appreciate your unwavering values. Your inner beliefs about business will guide you through the tough times. It's good to be open to fresh approaches to solving problems. But, when you cede your core values to someone else, it's time to quit.

That center point of the table, Pat was saying, represented my core of excellence. Every other point on the table was, to some degree, a measure of mediocrity, or even failure. But his powerful lesson also taught me to preserve my energy and not waste it getting upset about a basic, ongoing fact of life: "Shit happens, luvah!"

Understanding the "saltshaker theory" has helped me develop and teach a managerial style I call *constant, gentle pressure*. It's the way I return the saltshaker to the center each time life moves it. A restaurant is like the stage for a modern dance ensemble, designed with props and animated by an intricate choreography from the front podium through the dining room, into the kitchen, and back to the dining room again. It doesn't take much to move our saltshaker off center. All it takes is for one guest to be late, having taken longer than expected to send that last e-mail from the office, to kiss the kids good night, or to finally get a taxi in the rain or cold. One party's tardiness may cause us to be as much as twenty minutes behind for the next reservation. If two or more tables are running late, we may end up with a pileup at the front door—causing our standards to appear less than excellent. Our job is to adjust to circumstances, and keep the dance flowing with technical precision and artful grace.

It's my job, and consequently the job of every other leader in my company, to teach everyone who works for us to distinguish center from off center and always to set things right. I send my managers an unequivocal message: I'm going to be extremely specific as to where every component on that tabletop belongs. I anticipate that outside forces, including you, will always conspire to change the table setting. Every time that happens, I'm going to move everything right back to the way it should be. And so should you! That's the *constant* aspect. I'll never recenter the saltshaker in a way that denies you your dignity. That's the *gentle* aspect. But standards are standards, and I'm constantly watching every table and pushing back on every saltshaker that's moved, because excellent performance is paramount. That's the *pressure*.

Constant, gentle pressure is my preferred technique for leadership, guidance, and coaching. It's the job of any business owner to be very clear as to the company's nonnegotiable core values. They're the riverbanks that help guide us as we refine and improve on performance and excellence. A lack of riverbanks creates estuaries and cloudy waters that are confusing to navigate. I want a crystal-clear, swiftly flowing stream. Riverbanks need not hinder creativity, and in fact I leave plenty of room between the riverbanks for individual expression and personal style.

Every business needs a core strategy to be what I call *always on the improve,* and for us it's constant, gentle pressure. The name for this management style came to me from another restaurateur, who was using it to describe his view of our company. I was in Aspen for one of my annual summer appearances as a speaker at the *Food and Wine* Classic. My partner at Union Square Cafe, Paul Bolles-Beaven, and I had returned to town following an appearance on *Good Morning America* at the crack of dawn, and we dropped in to the Ajax Tavern in search of a cup of coffee. We got to talking with Michael Chiarello, who was then the chef and coowner, and who was holding court at the bar. This was in June 1998, a few months before we were to double the size of our company by launching Eleven Madison Park and Tabla, and we were looking for all the strategic advice we could get. Michael was in a growth mode himself, with restaurants in California and Colorado, and a big idea for a mail-order company to be called Napa Style. We asked him a lot of questions about how he managed his time with so many businesses to run, how he delegated, and to whom. After sharing a number of valuable insights, he said, "There are some things I could learn from you guys as well."

"Like what?" I asked.

"Well, the word on the street is that you've got the single best management style of any restaurant company."

"It's nice of you to say that," I said. "But what do you mean?"

"I'd call it constant, gentle pressure," Michael said, and then described precisely what we had been doing.

That morning was the first time I ever stopped to really think about this important aspect of my own business style, which so far had been intuitive. Michael Chiarello had given us a great gift by providing language that would allow us to share and teach a business philosophy. It helped me understand that we needed all three words—*constant, gentle, pressure*—working at once to push our business forward. This is one aspect of business where batting .667 isn't a winning average. Leave any one element out, and management is far less effective. If you are *constantly gentle* but fail to apply pressure when needed, your business won't grow or improve: your team will lack the drive and passion for excellence. If you exert *gentle pressure* but not constantly, both your staff and your guests will get a mixed message depending on what day it is, and probably won't believe that excellence truly matters to you. If you exert *constant pressure* that isn't gentle, employees may burn out, quit, or lose their graciousness—and you will probably cease to attract good employees. Leaders must identify which of the three elements (*constant*, *gentle*, or *pressure*) plays to their greatest natural strengths and, when necessary, they must compensate for their natural weaknesses. For example, over the years I've learned that *constant* and *gentle* are my natural instincts, and so I've had to focus on developing ease at applying *pressure*. My friend Robert Chadderdon has his own variation on this management style: "Spread some sunshine, kick 'em in the ass, and always remember who loves you! (And hope you'll wake up tomorrow to do it again!)"

ULTIMATELY, THE MOST SUCCESSFUL business is not the one that eliminates the most problems. It's the one that becomes most expert at finding imaginative solutions to address those problems. And lasting solutions rely on giving appropriate team members a voice, as well as responsibility for making decisions. There is definitely an art to this inclusive type of leadership. It can take a lot more time than leadership based on "my way or the highway." It demands dialogue, compromise, and a willingness to share power. Two keys to building consensus for problem solving are coaching and communication. Coaching is correction with dignity. It's helping people refine skills, showing how to get the job done, and truly wanting employees to reach their peak potential.

Communication is at the root of all business strengths—and weaknesses. When things go wrong and employees become upset, whether at a restaurant, a law firm, a hardware store, a university, or a major corporation, nine times out of ten the justifiable complaint is, "We need to communicate more effectively." I admit that for many years, I didn't really know what this meant. I had no problem standing up in front of a group to give a talk. I thought I was a pretty good communicator, but then it dawned on me: communicating has as much to do with context as it does content. That's called setting the table. Understanding *who* needs to know *what*, *when* people need to know it, and *why*, and then presenting that information in an entirely comprehensible way is a sine qua non of great leadership. Clear, timely communication is the key to applying constant, gentle pressure. To illustrate the point, I teach our managers about the "lily pad" theory.

Imagine a pond filled with lily pads and a frog perched serenely atop each one. For the fun of it, a little boy tosses a small pebble into the water, which breaks the surface of the pond but causes just a tiny ripple. The frogs barely notice, and don't budge. Enjoying himself, the boy next tosses a larger stone into the center of the pond, sending stronger ripples that cause all of the lily pads to rock and tilt. Some frogs jump off their lily pads, while others cling to avoid falling off. But the ripples affect them all. Not content, the boy then hurls a huge rock, which creates a wave that knocks each and every frog into the water. Some frogs are frightened. All are angry (assuming that frogs get angry). If only the frogs had had some warning about the impending rock toss, each one could have timed its jump so that the wave would have had no serious impact.

Grasping the lily pad theory and training yourself and your managers to implement it prevents many, if not all, communication problems.

People who aren't alerted in advance about a decision that will affect them may become angry and hurt. They're confused, out of the loop; they feel as though they've been knocked off their lily pads. When team members complain about poor communication, they're essentially saying, "You did not give me advance warning or input about that decision you made. By the time I learned about it, the decision had already happened to me, and I was unprepared." Team members will generally go with the flow and be willing to hop over the ripples, so long as they know in advance that you are going to toss the rock, when you'll be tossing it, how big it is, and—mostly—why you're choosing to toss it in the first place. The key is to anticipate the ripple effects of any decision before you implement it, gauging whom it will affect, and to what degree. Poor communication is generally not a matter of miscommunication. More often, it involves taking away people's feeling of control. Change works only when people believe it is happening for them, not to them. And there's not much in between. Good communication is always a factor of good hospitality.

In the fall of 2004 I was invited to appear on the *Today Show* with Terry Miller, a gourmet sausage specialist from Colorado, to do a segment on pairing hot dogs and wine. This was based on a popular seminar we had conducted together the previous summer at the *Food and Wine* Classic. The jovial Miller, a self-described redneck, was in New York to help us with our inaugural Shacktoberfest at Shake Shack. On the segment with Al Roker and Ann Curry, Terry mentioned some of the specialty bratwursts (jalapeño-elk, smoked buffalo, pheasant-and-mushroom) that we'd be serving at Shake Shack throughout our Shacktoberfest festival. He got a whoop from the studio audience when he asked Ann Curry to kiss the colorful, life-size smiling hot dog he had tattooed on his calf.

I am not naturally inclined to send out a lot of e-mails whenever I'm going to be on television. (To her chagrin, I usually don't even remember to tell my mother.) But by not forewarning anyone that day, I tossed a rock and failed to give my team adequate warning of some wave-like ripple effects. The seven-minute segment on *Today* caused the day's lunch business at Shake Shack to soar, and our staff had no idea what had hit them, what had caused it, or how to prepare for it. Their lily pads were pounded, turning what should have been a public relations triumph into a fiasco. The cooks couldn't keep up with the unanticipated demand for bratwursts, guests waited far too long for their orders, and we quickly ran out of food. Any company that thrives on a steady flow of creative ideas needs correspondingly strong communications. Ideas at their best happen *for* people. At their worst they happen *to* people. Had the staff members known in advance about the *Today Show*, they probably would have brought in an extra cook and additional product, and we would have had a lot more fun serving a lot more bratwursts.

IN THE BIMONTHLY TRAINING sessions I conduct with all our new managers, most of whom have just recently taken on the big new responsibility of becoming someone else's boss, I stress how fundamentally different their new job is from their old one. As "line" employees (cooks, waiters, hosts) their first concern was to achieve win–win transactions for guests. As managers, their primary job is to help make other people on our team successful. I urge them to use their position to maximize the positive impact they can have on and for our team. By what they embody and the spirit in which they embody it, good managers can have a multiplier effect and add significantly to the company's excellence. Poor managers have the power to do just the opposite.

The moment people become managers for the first time, it will be as if the following three things have happened:

- An imaginary megaphone has been stitched to their lips, so that everything they say can now be heard by twenty times more people than before.

- The other staff members have been provided with a pair of binoculars, which they keep trained on the new managers at all times, guaranteeing that everything a manager does will be watched and seen by more people than ever.

- The new managers have received the gift of "fire," a kind of power that must be used responsibly, appropriately, and consistently.

The imaginary "megaphone" is to let our managers know that we place so much value on what comes out of their mouths that we want to make sure everyone hears it. The "binoculars" are to convey that we expect each of our employees—as well as our guests—to watch them as they exemplify the values and goals of our restaurants. The megaphone and the binoculars place a weighty responsibility on the shoulders of the managers. What they say and embody matters and will be heard, seen, and scrutinized by all. If we were a copy machine, managers would be the documents we'd want to replicate. We are very careful about which documents we feed into that machine.

"Fire" is the most important element in management's application of constant, gentle pressure. During my early, inexperienced years as a boss when I first got into business, it was far more important for me to please people and be liked than to be respected. By abandoning my fire, our excellence suffered. The biggest mistake managers can make is neglecting to set high standards and hold others accountable. This denies employees the chance to learn and excel. Employees do not want to be told, "Let me make your life easier by enabling you not to learn and not to achieve anything new."

I'm a bottom-up manager who subscribes to the concept of "servant leadership," as articulated by the late Robert Greenleaf. He believed that organizations are at their most effective when leaders encourage collaboration, trust, foresight, listening, and empowerment. In any hierarchy, it's clear that the ultimate boss (in my case, me) holds the most power. But a wonderful thing happens when you flip the traditional organizational chart upside down so that it looks like a V with the boss on the bottom. My job is to serve and support the next layer "above" me so that the people on that layer can then serve and support the next layer "above" them, and so on. Ultimately, our cooks, servers, reservationists, coat checkers, and dishwashers are then in the best possible position to serve our guests. A balanced combination of uncompromising standards and confidence-building reassurance sends a very clear and consistent message to your team: "I believe in you and I want you to win as much as I want to win." You cannot have a dynamic organization unless you are constantly encouraging people to improve, and believing that they can do it.

For years I didn't believe that power was a positive force, or anything to strive for. I grew up in the 1960s, and 1970s, when many young people saw business as about taking, not about creating value for the world as you profited.

When I first went into business in 1985, I was determined not to display power overtly. I thought I could be a business owner and a manager without using my own fire. I was entirely wrong, and for years I unwittingly sent mixed messages, befriending staff members rather than leading them. So I now tell new managers: "Fire is power. We are giving you the gift of this fire. Use it responsibly, appropriately, and consistently. People need it, want it, crave it, and expect it. Use it wisely, and you will become the greatest leader your team ever had. Use it abusively, and you will lose your fire." Don't be afraid to lead and to teach. As it does in cooking, fire adds heat, clarifies, and distills the ideas that drive your business to solid results.

Most managerial problems stem from an irresponsible, inappropriate, or inconsistent use of fire. It takes time to learn, but until managers understand all the different ways they can—and must—use their fire, depending on the circumstances, they cannot reach their own greatest potential or help others reach theirs. Managers can use their fire as a *torch*: a light for guidance and teaching, and for leading and showing the way. They can use their fire to offer warmth and empathy, to make employees feel safe. A manager's fire can be used as a *campfire*, to form collegial bonds with employees, and to inspire others and help them grow. A fire can also be a *bonfire* to rally the troops, to foster team folklore, to get the group motivated, and to bring people together in a unified pursuit of a common goal. Managers who inspire high levels of performance in their employees know how to produce magical results that leave people in awe. Managers must be wizards—the way they *"breathe fire"* is a source of motivation that impels employees to imitate them, and to grow. And managers must learn to use the *fire in their own bellies* as a way to fuel and refuel their own ongoing passion for this business. If leaders lack fire, why would anyone want to follow them?

When managers use their fire improperly, employees will always figure out ways to snuff it out. If a manager builds too many camp-fires (suspending his or her power and authority and spending too much time relating to certain employees as close friends), power may be compromised, causing the line between manager and employee to dissolve. And others may resent feeling left out. Even the most com-passionate manager must sometimes use *fire to singe or scorch* someone who is dishonest, or disrespectful to a teammate, a guest, the commu-nity, a supplier, or the restaurant itself. An organization puts itself in grave danger when it permits integrity to be compromised.

The development and training of managers and the articulation of a cohesive and consistent management model are crucial for any company, especially a company that is experiencing rapid growth. With each year I've spent as a leader, I've grown more and more con-vinced that my team—any team—thirsts for someone with authority, and power, to tell them consistently where they're going, how they're doing, and how they could do their job even better. And all the team asks is that the same rules apply to everyone.

BY 2004, AS WE prepared to open the complex of dining opera-tions for the Museum of Modern Art (MoMA) that now together serve up to 2,000 people each day, I realized that we had been making an error that left us ill prepared for success. However well we had hired and trained line employees, we had done only a middling job of developing managers who had the requisite skills to open and oper-ate a high-volume, high-level restaurant. There wasn't enough depth on our team to transfer managers to the MoMA complex without also stripping away talent we needed at our existing restaurants. For me this was a troubling, slap-in-the-forehead moment. I asked myself, How could we have been in denial all this time? As our company grew, virtually overnight, from about 650 employees to over 1,000, we needed to focus even more intently on strengthening operating and accounting systems, human resources, and technology. It's delusional to think that the day-to-day performance of your business is anything other than a reflection of how motivated (or unmotivated) your managers make your line employees feel. It was suddenly imperative for us to give priority to the development, education, and coaching of managers. This part of our infrastructure was all but nonexistent. It was as if we had been basing my approach to readying managers on the tenuous assumption that anyone we hired as a manager already "got it," knew the system, and could articulate and pass along the values and methods that define the company. Not only was I wrong; this sweeping assumption—"just add water"—was grossly unfair to the managers and the people they led. We were at a turning point.

THE BIGGEST CHANGE IN our industry over the past twenty years has been the emergence of "fine-dining" restaurant groups. They didn't exist when I got into the business. In those days, you encountered either a single-unit fine restaurant—like Lutèce, where the peerless chef and owner, André Soltner, was always present and actually lived upstairs—or multiunit restaurant chains like T.G.I. Fridays. There was a widespread belief that one could own only a single fine-dining establishment, because it was mandatory to be on site all the time, greeting every guest, watching every employee, and personally inspecting every plate that left the kitchen.

That all changed in the 1990s, when the restaurant business at last came to be viewed as a valid entrepreneurial pursuit, and consequently began to attract more and more people who, in addition to their culinary and hospitality skills, had a solid education and impressive business acumen. As a way to provide growth opportunities for outstanding employees so that I wouldn't keep losing them to restaurateurs who could provide "next-level" jobs, I gradually found myself with four, then five, and then six restaurants. And of course, when I was in one of them, I was *not* in any of the others.

For the first time, it hit me—although I had tried hard to deny it— that I was no longer purely a restaurateur. Rather, I had become the CEO of a growing restaurant company. That was a huge pill to swallow. My passion and professional identity had been based on the pure pleasure I derived from greeting guests at the front door and in the dining room, as well as working closely with our restaurant staffs. But now my responsibilities had become far broader. For years, I had been afraid of overexpanding as my father had done; and I had contended with this fear by simply pretending that our organization was in fact not expanding. Turning a blind eye to reality was handicapping me and my company.

When we launch a new restaurant, I am still intently focused on the entire opening process and on trying to help the venture become as good as possible as quickly as possible. It's demanding to be in that mode and also to play the role of CEO and do "big picture" things like formulating and presenting our five- or ten-year strategic plan. Consciously or not, I'd created a new challenge for myself by reinventing my own job description. Nothing about being the CEO at a restaurant company had diminished my yearning to be in my restaurants all the time. The only way I can be effective is to remain a high-touch leader and stay involved with our staff, our guests, and our product. It's rare that I'm in my office more than 25 percent of my day. Yet as recently as 2003 I was actually trying to operate five restaurants, a jazz club, and a hot dog cart out of my basement office at Gramercy Tavern without any type of corporate structure at all. My philosophy back then was that supposedly smart organizations (where there was a corporate chef and pastry chef, a corporate wine buyer, a corporate *everything* dictating to managers how to toe the company line) led to dumb—or at best average—restaurants. Wherever I saw the word *corporate* applied to restaurants, I saw cookie-cutter or at least derivative establishments with little soul.

I've always strived to create and develop distinct restaurants that each bear, over time, the handcrafted feel of a mom-and-pop venture. But our growing pains were making it clear to me that we needed to figure out how to remain soulful *and* become a lot more sophisticated. I was now sharing my basement office with David Swinghamer, my CFO and partner in business development. Another partner, our director of operations, Richard Coraine, worked out of an office four blocks to the north at Eleven Madison Park. We had no public relations, marketing, IT, human resources, or any other infrastructure. I wanted us to become a group of intelligent restaurants served by an intelligent organization, but I just didn't think it was possible. I honestly believed that to sustain smart restaurants, we would need to have a "dumb" organization. And that's exactly what we got.

I admired some excellent restaurant companies in New York and across the country. But those large groups seemed more effective at building systems, "stores," and "concepts" than they were at taking the time to develop the personal, groundbreaking, soulful restaurants I was interested in.

Not surprisingly, thanks to my own mixed feelings about expanding, our undeniable business growth had at last butted up against my skittishness and inertia. Standing in place had become unacceptable and risky. I had to figure out some way to have both smart restaurants and a smart organization. Finally, I listened to my partners, and bit the bullet. Taking the lead, David Swinghamer persuaded me to join him in searching our neighborhood for office space. We looked throughout a long, hot summer, and eventually we found a bare-basics office overlooking Union Square, which had been vacated by a failed dot.com. In 2003, almost twenty years after I'd opened my first restaurant in New York, I finally admitted to myself that I needed to change my career and become chief executive officer of Union Square Hospitality Group, or USHG.

At first, "USHG" had simply been my way to name the family of restaurants of which I was the founding and principal owner. Each restaurant began as a separate company with, in some cases, separate outside investors. That would still be the case. But now USHG would also need to evolve into a management company on its own—to provide coherent direction and support for each of the restaurants in whose success I and others had such a large stake. My goal was to extend my reach over many restaurants by surrounding myself with a team of people who were more talented at any given specialty than I had ever been on my own. I wanted a capable team that would act for me as "owner's representatives," applying their respective talents to my style of doing business. In my first decade as a restaurateur at Union Square Cafe, I was solely responsible for the kinds of things I would now need an entire team to accomplish:

1. Human resources—making sure we get the best (and right) people on our team, training them to succeed, and ensuring the kind of healthy culture and environment in which they can thrive.

2. Operations—making sure that people and things work as excellently as possible and that we are executing to our fullest potential.

3. Accounting and finance—making sure we have a constant stream of timely, accurate information that reflects our past performance, and helping us make good, informed choices about our future through a culture of planning, budgeting, and analysis.

4. Public relations and marketing—making sure we are telling the stories about our business and its employees that will keep our restaurants on the tip of people's tongues, whether they be journalists, prospective guests, or employees; and building relationships with other like-minded companies with whom we can forge the kind of business partnerships where $1+1=3$.

5. Information technology (IT)—making sure we have the most effective software and hardware to allow us to communicate

internally and externally, and to assess and improve our performance as a company.

6. Business development—making sure we're not leaving money on the table with existing businesses, and analyzing and negotiating potential new business ideas to keep our employees and company vital and moving forward.

7. Community investment—making sure our company and its employees are finding and taking ample opportunities to play an active role in helping our communities fulfill their greatest potential.

At last I realized that the dynamics of company and restaurant need not be either dumb-smart or smart-dumb. We had to make the dynamics *smart-smart*. Like any business owner, entrepreneur, or corporate executive, I had to figure out how to put winning systems in place, clarify for others all the things that I do and all the things that I expected everybody else to do, while repeatedly asking myself one essential question: How many of these things could be done at least as well or better by somebody else if only I were willing to let go and allow that to happen? I was suddenly faced with a mandate to grow personally. An extra year to prepare me for becoming a CEO would have been wonderful. But I hadn't given myself that luxury. This was a deeply disconcerting time of organizational change and self-redefinition—it felt like trying to change the wheels on a high-speed train while the train was roaring down the track. This hugely challenging period taught me critical lessons about how to lead a business. Often, I wanted to throw in the towel, and I fantasized about traveling back to 1985 and finding myself welcoming guests for lunch at Union Square Cafe's front door. But I had chosen the appropriate path, and I knew there was no going back.

Until now, our restaurants had been determinedly individual and therefore inconsistent in the way they did just about everything: promoting themselves; recruiting, hiring, orienting, coaching, reviewing, disciplining, and "transitioning" employees; and establishing vacation policy. Dissatisfied staff members had no systematic way to air grievances beyond speaking with their general manager or chef. But what if they needed advice on how to solve a problem that *involved* their general manager or chef? Their issues would come to our attention—sometimes in unhealthy ways, such as anonymous letters, Internet posts, or even via a legal complaint. We lost some good people along the way. We found ourselves handling an increasingly large number of HR issues from a reactive posture.

One of the first things I did as CEO was to promote my longtime colleague Paul Bolles-Beaven from managing partner of Union Square Cafe to director of human resources for all of USHG. I wanted to bottle his exceptional judgment, wisdom, and sensibility about working effectively with people and sprinkle it liberally over my entire organization. Paul's efforts in human resources swiftly provided inputs and outlets for people where previously there were none. He'd host "roundtables" and other forums where employees felt safe about providing feedback. At the outset the process uncovered some unpalatable realities—some areas of discontent that we hadn't previously known about. But the openness was a breath of fresh air and allowed us to address the preexisting issues as we learned of them. More dialogues began flowing among team members. Instead of chronically internalizing their anger and frustration, people now had far healthier ways to express their feelings about problems that arose with colleagues or management.

As we had learned to do many years ago with our guests, we were now giving our staff a lot more opportunities to feel heard. My mentor (and our longtime consultant) Erika Andersen gave me a gift when she taught me that for most people it's far more important to feel heard than to be agreed with.

You can get the best productivity from your employees only when they believe that their leadership is open-minded, is accessible, and welcomes input. Managers who give only lip service to an open-door policy effectively shut the door by being defensive, by not holding themselves accountable when they make a mistake, and mostly by not actively looking for ways to make their employees feel heard. We apply constant, gentle pressure to our leaders to stay tuned in to the aspirations and frustrations of staff members. We want the leaders not just to keep the door open but to walk out that door and actively beckon people to come in.

HIRING MANAGERS

I have yet to find any skills more pivotal to success than effective recruiting and hiring. And the most important hires are the managers, who are themselves responsible for hiring and setting the tone for the business. Like it or not, it's their performance that represents the highest excellence and hospitality you can expect from your staff. At any given time, approximately 15 percent of our employees are managers. Since I believe that as our management team goes, so goes our staff, Paul Bolles-Beaven and his HR staff created a list of nine specific traits that define the mind-set and the character traits we look for when making a decision about hiring a manager.

1. *Infectious Attitude*

Does this person have the type of attitude I would want to have spread around? Would I want my staff to be imbued with it? If the answer is yes, I continue on.

2. *Self-Awareness*

When I scan their resumés, I often tell management candidates that their career story is like an autobiography they have been writing for many years: "You've made a lot of interesting choices. I'm very curious about why a job with us strikes you as the logical next 'chapter' in the book of your life." I also want to know why they feel they have finished the most recent chapter: "Why does this particular twist in the plot make perfect sense to you right now?" Candidates may convey a straightforward desire to move on to a better place. They may express resentment about the managers they have been working for. If a person shares details that are none of my business, that can reveal something about his or her discretion, or lack thereof. Sometimes candidates indicate that they have simply maxed out on their present employer's career curve, and are determined to make a wise next choice. I am also quite interested in people who have shown enough enterprise and curiosity to have learned something about our restaurants. I'm most impressed when they apply what they know about themselves and about us to what they know they want for their career.

3. Charitable Assumption

Enlightened hospitality is a philosophy that works best with optimistic, hopeful, open-minded people at the helm. It tends not to work when the leaders are skeptics who think they already have all the answers. Those people are a finished product in their own minds, and so is everyone else they work with. A charitable mind-set assumes the best in other people. Mind-sets tend to become self-fulfilling prophecies. When you assume that people's stumbles are honest mistakes that come from a good place, you get farther with them during their victories. When you assume the worst of people, you get the worst from people. It's important that our managers maintain a charitable assumption about the people with whom they work and about the guests we serve. Doing so even when a mistake has been made gives employees the chance to react with integrity and to be accountable for their actions.

I expect our managers to have the same mind-set with regard to our guests. I've been to many restaurants where management be-rates guests for being twenty minutes late for a reservation—when there may well have been a good reason for their tardiness. It's hard to justify being ungracious to anyone who wants to spend money at your restaurant. A charitable assumption might be, "You must have had a tough time getting here. We're delighted that you made it!" I am going to get the most out of my relationship with every guest, including repeat business, when I base the relationship on optimism and trust. Hospitality is hopeful; it's confident, thoughtful, optimistic, generous, and openhearted.

To be sure, there are other ways to run an organization. Many people have grown very successful by managing the downside. They're nobody's fool, and they'll be damned if they're going to be taken to the cleaners. That's a valid attitude. But skeptics tend not to thrive in our organization, because their values are the antithesis of the business and personal principles that guide every decision we make, as well as the way I choose to connect with people. My way is certainly not the only right way, but it is *my* only right way.

4. Long-Term View of Success

If you have a philosophy that puts employees first, guests second, community third, suppliers fourth, and investors fifth, you implicitly have a long-term perspective—at least as long as your lease. We create restaurants for the long haul, and we make decisions based on that commitment. Every time I'm faced with a decision that involves an investment of money, I analyze the potential return by asking, "Will this yield *today* dollars, *tomorrow* dollars, or *never* dollars?" Only the third alternative—never dollars—is unattractive to me.

For example, if you come to one of our restaurants and the waiter accidentally breaks the cork on your bottle of wine, everyone is uncomfortable. The waiter is embarrassed, and you might be wondering if that means the wine itself is bad. At this point I would want the waiter to be candid: "I'm sorry I broke the cork. I assume the wine is still fine but if for any reason it's not, please let me know and we'll gladly replace the bottle for you." If the wine is good, we'll get our *today* dollars. If it's not, we're still in the running for *tomorrow* dollars, because we've established goodwill with our guest.

This approach also gives the guest a stress-free opportunity to be right (in the event that the wine turns out to be "off") and removes the onus on them to challenge us.

There's practically no downside to a hospitable, charitable assumption. Experience has shown me that 90 percent of the time the bottle of wine whose cork broke is going to be good. If the guest rejects it and I still believe it's good, I can always sell the wine by the glass at the bar. And if the bottle's not good, it's far better for me to have been gracious about the transaction in the first place. That's a long-term view, and it's one that sees an investment in a guest's continuing loyalty as being far more valuable than almost anything else.

5. Sense of Abundance

One of the toughest disciplines in every business is to measure and predict cash flow—the volume of money available after all expenses have been paid. In very lean times (such as we've experienced during serious recessions or in the weeks and months following 9/11) effective managers and owners need to develop the ability to squeeze olive oil from a stone. In our restaurant culture that tightfisted approach can put the optimistic principles underlying our business style to the test. This approach makes it much more difficult to be generous to staff members, guests, and the community. In hard times, it can be enormously challenging to be generous with suppliers, and next to impossible to be generous with investors. But counterintuitively, we've also learned that it is sometimes possible to recharge and stimulate the top line of a business by instilling a generous and confident sense of abundance.

Just after September 11, 2001, the revenue at each of our restaurants dropped precipitously. The number of guests reserving was also way down. For about two months following the attacks on the

World Trade Center, the entire downtown restaurant and business sector suffered. Of our restaurants, Tabla suffered most and had the toughest time recovering. One reason was that Tabla (like Eleven Madison Park) is housed on the ground floor of the investment bank Credit Suisse, whose own business suffered dramatically following 9/11, and whose bankers cut back on their business entertaining. A further reason was that Tabla, being associated with Indian culture, was unfortunately an object of the early backlash after 9/11. Some Americans were prejudiced against any person who looked like what ignorance and fear imagined a terrorist to be, or toward any business staffed by such people. Bangladeshi and Indian taxi drivers in New York were affected by this ill-informed wariness, and so was Tabla.

We tried hard to not lay anyone off, but to make ends meet we did have to shorten the hours many of our staff members were scheduled to work. We looked at the menu and asked ourselves whether we really needed to use expensive ingredients like lobster. Did we really need twelve entrees if ten would save money by ending each night with less waste?

We also analyzed the menu to see if it might be possible to eliminate a cook through attrition. The fewer menu items, the fewer hands we'd need. It occurred to me that starving our way out of this predicament might protect our business; but for me, playing defensively was an unnatural approach to the underlying problem of too few guests and too little revenue. I hated doing business that way.

So I made a decision that taught me a lasting business lesson: rather than apply a sense of scarcity and uncertainty to Tabla, I applied a sense of abundance. Hand-wringing over low covers and low revenue was getting us nowhere. I truly believed that a sense of abundance would create more business. Though it made little apparent budgetary sense, we began participating in charity fund-raisers and offering gift certificates for dinners at Tabla as auction prizes—far more generously than ever before. It was a very effective way to target our marketing to people who tended to care about our favorite causes, and who also might take an interest in Tabla. If an occasional guest at Tabla happened to attend a charity fund-raiser and noticed that we were a sponsor of the charity, he or she would probably feel a sense of affiliation with our restaurants. And anyone who would compete to make the highest bid on an auction item for our restaurants is a fan or a potential fan. By giving more, we'd end up getting more. If you want to be busy, especially in times of scarcity and uncertainty, you cannot accept diminished standards of excellence in even one area. You do everything you possibly can afford to show your staff and guests that you care deeply about improving. That's acting from a positive and hopeful place, rather than from fear that can ultimately be self-fulfilling. The mind-set "We're just hanging on" perpetuates scarcity. Investing money, imagination, and hard work to create a mind-set of abundance achieves abundance.

Not long ago we donated dinner for four at six of our restaurants to the Brady Center for Handgun Safety, which would auction off the dinners. The winning bid for the twenty-four dinners was $12,000. We helped a cause that mattered to us, created an opportunity for like-minded guests to affiliate with us, and effectively advertised all our restaurants to an ideal audience.

Since 1992, we have applied our philosophy on abundance most effectively during New York City's annual Restaurant Week. More than 150 participating restaurants throughout the city have offered a three-course lunch for about $20. (The price began at $19.92; then it rose to $19.93, $19.94, and so on.) Most restaurants are packed during Restaurant Week as guests flock in to experience new restaurants as well as old favorites. The value is unbeatable, and people feel good about doing something collectively with so many other New Yorkers. Some restaurants, unfortunately, offer inexpensive fare and propose very limited menu options as a way to manage costs and do a bit better than break even on a three-course meal. We take the opposite approach. I am convinced that if you're going to offer a gift, it's important to give it graciously. We approach Restaurant Week by offering a generous number of choices for the appetizer, main course, and dessert, representing considerably more than $20 worth of food and quality. The point is to make people feel a sense of abundance and value.

In several of our restaurants, we go a step further. As the already-low check is dropped, each guest at the table is presented with a thank-you note as well as a gift certificate to welcome him or her back for lunch at another time. (In 2005, for example, we presented each guest with a "come back" lunch certificate for $20.05.) At this point, guests are thinking, "They've already offered an outstanding lunch for $20.05, and now they're giving me a $20.05 gift certificate to return!" And return they do.

Countless times, this has proved that the more we give the more we get back. Generosity is clearly in our self-interest. We get two things out of the deal. We gain a means of reaching new guests and remaining in touch with them, because the only way guests can redeem their certificate is first to provide us with their name and contact information. And when they return, we've gained a crucial second opportunity to create regulars. In fact, a returning guest may bring, say, three new guests with him or her, having told them how generous we were during Restaurant Week. So, for example, four gift certificates worth $80 can have a multiplier effect and produce as many as twelve additional new guests at full price. Roughly 80 percent of the certificates are redeemed at lunch in the season following Restaurant Week, and lunch business in each of our restaurants has consistently grown each year.

As I always point out to managers and staff members, the single most powerful key to long-term success is cultivating repeat business, and ultimately regular guests. I don't believe you even enter the competition for regulars until you get people to try your product for at least a third time. Restaurant Week provides us with a perfect opportunity to do that.

Although this event—organized by NYC and Company—is certainly a bargain and a huge promotional occasion for New York City, it pays its largest dividends to restaurants by generating goodwill—and, eventually, revenue (tomorrow dollars). Some of our managers have asked me whether all this largesse is worth it. I remind them that after each year's Restaurant Week, our restaurants have grown more popular and more profitable. No amount of generosity has so far succeeded in putting us out of business!

6. Trust

It's extremely difficult for a manager to motivate people if he or she tends not to trust others. Similarly, it's extremely difficult for employees to trust or want to follow the lead of a manager who doesn't trust them. It's hard to do your best for an extended period of time when your primary motivation is to avoid disapproval. We look for people who are naturally trusting. True, it's necessary for a manager to have a modicum of healthy cynicism in order to identify team members who act out of self-interest or who work the system to their advantage. But it is never useful to cause paranoia in everybody else by having a mind-set of mistrust and fear.

Most human beings are motivated far more by the desire to please other people than by the desire to stay out of trouble. Mistrust tends to breed more mistrust and ultimately dishonesty. If your bosses do not trust you to begin with, they unwittingly set up a game, or a trap: the employee is challenged to figure out ways to beat "the system." If I can't please you by just being good and honest, and I can't advance at work by performing admirably, I may as well play a game in which I can win by giving you what you're expecting from me: mistrust. Trust and mistrust are also mind-sets that become self-fulfilling.

Some bosses and managers rule by constantly threatening disapproval or, as is often worse, by giving no feedback whatsoever. Being nonresponsive keeps employees on edge, off-balance, feeling vulnerable and divided. For many insecure managers, that's the point. It's not an oversight; it's a strategy—or it's insecurity about confronting conflict. Either way, it's counterproductive. It will not sustain a healthy workplace.

Our managers need to understand the dramatic distinction between fear-based and trust-based control. Analyzing this distinction helps us to sharpen the managerial skills needed to define excellence and failure in our model of enlightened hospitality.

FEAR VERSUS TRUST

Fear: them against us	*Trust: us as a team, together and united*
tyranny	collaboration
ruling	empowering
fleeting	enduring
selfish	giving
scarcity	abundance
closed	expressive
telling	listening
knowing	learning
cynical	hopeful
gatekeeper	agent

In the divisive fear-based system, employees miss out on the true joys of sustained satisfaction, the satisfaction that comes from achieving for the sake of the pleasure that achievement itself affords. They also miss out on the pleasure of being part of a unified ensemble that achieves great things together. Fear-based management fosters a corrosive, dim-witted business culture where huge amounts of energy are squandered by bosses who fear employees, and by employees who fear bosses. There's a steep price to pay for an organization when a staff member feels confused or intimidated. Prospective leaders often opt to leave before they can become great managers; and good employees quit because they know they can never thrive in such a negative climate. That leaves the kind of employees whose emotional needs are met by autocratic, non-empowering bosses. And those are not always the world's brightest, happiest, or healthiest employees. And so goes the business.

The good news, for us, is that there are enough bosses out there who rule by fear that they actually make hiring well-trained, motivated managers much easier. It often happens that bosses who rule through fear are actually very good at teaching skills. You never need to wonder what's expected of you when you work for an ironfisted boss. When they drive people with excellent skills out the door, some of those talented people find a haven working for a company that welcomes them and encourages them to contribute and thrive. Happily, they often come to us.

7. Approving Patience and Tough Love

Tough love is another term for frank, "I'm on your side" honesty. It's saying, "I care enough about you to tell you the truth, even if the truth is tough to hear." Patience with tough love sends a clear message to your staff that you're on their side. We also put a premium on outward and unequivocal messages of approval. It is absolutely incumbent on managers to praise employees for good work. As I once read in Kenneth Blanchard's *One Minute Manager*, it's the managers' job to "catch people in the act of doing things right." I subscribe to that and take it one step further. When managers catch somebody on their staff doing something right in a consistent or remarkable way, I encourage those managers to let me know about it first so that I can learn, and also so that I can connect with employees and tell them that their boss told me what a great job they've been doing, with specifics. This allows the employees to feel seen and appreciated by both their boss and me. It feels especially good and is a powerful motivator when your boss's boss catches you doing something right.

Our former chef at Eleven Madison Park, Kerry Heffernan, once told me that since a dishwasher named Juan had been on the dish station, 50 percent fewer forks and knives were being lost by getting carelessly thrown into the trash. Juan was helping to sort through dirty plates that hurried waiters and busboys were bringing back to the kitchen after clearing tables in the dining room. Such savings add up. I found out when Juan, who had been with us for many years, was working his next shift, and I was there that day to catch him in the act of doing something right. "Chef Kerry has told me that you are doing an amazing job saving our silverware, and I want you to know how much I appreciate that," I told him. "Your work means a lot to the restaurant." He learned that his boss had noticed what a terrific job he was doing, and that Kerry was so pleased that he had chosen to tell his own boss—me—about it. I hope the experience made Juan feel good about the value of his work and proud that his contribution was appreciated by somebody he didn't even know was paying attention.

Feeling seen and acknowledged is a powerful human need. Paul Bolles-Beaven taught me that a traditional greeting among South Africans is *umbuntu*. It is not traditional there to salute people by saying "Hi," "How are you?" or "What's new?" *Umbuntu* is an expression of humanness, which conveys "I see you." That simply and effectively addresses the core human need to be seen and to feel seen. It's hard to imagine that it wouldn't also apply to an employee, a customer, or a manager of a company. The number one reason guests cite for wanting to return to a restaurant is that when they go there, they feel seen and recognized. Imagine if our hosts consistently conveyed, "I see you!" I'm fairly certain that's precisely what most people want.

8. *Not Feeling Threatened by Others*

I would not want to follow a paranoid leader who is always looking over his shoulder, fearing that someone was trying to put out his or her fire. I'd want to follow a leader who is secure, firmly in control of that fire to illuminate the way for me, to keep me enlightened; teach me; keep me warm, motivated, awed, and inspired. Under those circumstances I'd be delighted to follow my leader and, occasionally, even lead my leader.

But I would certainly not be at my best as an employee if I were constantly enabling my leader's insecurities. Show me a defensive boss and I'll show you a team desperate for new leadership. Great bosses own up to their mistakes, insist on learning from them, thank others for pointing them out, and move on.

9. *Character*

For our managers to become great leaders, we identify and assess a number of crucial character traits that are a subset of the five core emotional skills—optimistic warmth, intelligence, work ethic, empathy, integrity, and self-awareness—that make a "51 percenter." Those traits include *honor, discipline, consistency, clear communication, courage, wisdom, compassion, flexibility, ability to love* (and be loved) *humility, confidence* (to possess it and to inspire it in team members), *passion for the work and for excellence,* and *a positive self-image.* These traits may mean something slightly different to different people, but in the aggregate they are the ideal characteristics of a highly effective leader, no matter what business he or she is in. You cannot be a great leader unless a critical mass of people are attracted to following your lead.

Overall, integrity and self-awareness are the most important core emotional skills for managers. You must be self-aware enough to know what makes you tick. You have to understand your own strengths, weaknesses, and blind spots. You need to surround yourself with a team of people who will mirror your integrity but complement and compensate for your strengths and weaknesses. That's critical. There is absolutely an art to surrounding yourself with great advisers and effective auxilliary sets of eyes and ears. These are the leaders on whom you must rely to present you with timely, accurate, balanced information and to apply constant, gentle pressure on your team so that you can move your company decisively forward.

A leader can be charismatic and lack integrity. A leader can be charismatic and have no compassion or empathy. A great leader must repeatedly ask himself or herself this tough question: "*Why would anyone want to be led by me?*" And there had better be a good number of compelling reasons.

I believe that leadership is not measured just by what you've accomplished, but rather by how other people you depend on *feel* in the process of accomplishing things. Frequently, the people who tend to get tripped up in our company at higher levels have a tough time plugging into how other people feel. It's not that they don't care about others. They just lack a strong natural sense of empathy. We do the best we can to coach them and to show them where they are missing the boat. Some are able to rise to this challenge; many aren't.

The air grows increasingly thin the higher up the ranks of leadership a manager moves. The more powerful people become in an organization, the more emotionally intelligent their management skills must become. We've had many, many people who have succeeded as dining room managers and even in the next position up, such as assistant general manager. But they've subsequently fallen short as general managers, and we've had to part ways. This has also been true of some cooks who became sous-chefs and ultimately executive sous-chefs, the rank just below chef. Many excellent cooks have become sous-chefs after technical cooking prowess won them the respect of the staff. But when they next became executive sous-chefs, their emotional skills were no longer adequate for this higher level of authority and power, and the staff withdrew its support—making it clear that we should do the same.

For some reason, when certain people gain more authority and power, they tend to demand respect from those who work for them. But what got them their promotion in the first place was their natural ability to *command* respect. Demanding respect creates tension that can make it very tough to lead, and very uncomfortable to follow.

Strong technical skills are usually the reason most people get their first or second promotion. But the higher you climb the ladder of power, the less technical skills count and the more significant emotional skills become. Employees are expert boss-watchers who instinctively focus their "binoculars" on the bosses with the most power. If they see weaknesses in character traits and ideals, they can and often do strive to put out the boss's fire in a hurry. Sometimes we have terminated managers not because I decided unilaterally to fire them, but because over time the staff came to a collective decision that they were lacking in some of these character ideals.

Managers have a power over employees that creates a distinct imbalance in their relationship, and that power must be consistently and fairly imposed for the good of the restaurant and the way we do business. And team members are fully entitled to hold management to even higher standards, particularly in a company that embraces for itself the same character ideals that it demands of others.

This becomes a "virtuous cycle." People who get promotions should earn them not just because they're ambitious, but primarily because they embody the company's character traits in abundance. And since they are willing to do everything it takes to perpetuate those ideals, we function as a "hospitalitocracy," with the entire team reciprocally bound by the same underlying culture of enlightened hospitality.

CHAPTER 10

———— ⌐ ————

The Road to Success Is Paved
with Mistakes Well Handled

IN SEPTEMBER 1994, I traveled to Dallas, Texas, to begin a tour
promoting *The Union Square Cafe Cookbook*. During a dinner hosted
on my behalf by the owner of San Saba Vineyards, Dr. Mark Lemmon,
at the Mansion at Turtle Creek, I had a chance to sit next to Stanley
Marcus, the department store mogul, whose family had founded the
luxury department store Neiman Marcus in Dallas in 1907. Marcus
was then nearly ninety, and for more than half a century he had used
his genius as a marketer and retailer to expand the Neiman Marcus
chain and burnish its reputation for extraordinary service. It turned
out that he was interested in meeting me too; although he had dined
at Union Square Cafe through the years, we had never had a chance
to connect one-on-one.

It should have been a wonderful evening—here I was, seated
next to a legendary figure whose company I admired greatly. But I
was preoccupied. Gramercy Tavern had just opened, in late July, and
in part because of all the early media hype, it was getting knocked

around in the press. I was deeply troubled by this, and also by Union Square Cafe's performance, which was wobbly. Union Square Cafe wasn't used to operating without me at the helm every minute of the day. I had betrayed my own commitment to expand only if I was certain I could do so without compromising quality there. I confessed all this to Stanley and told him that I felt guilty for traveling out of town so soon after opening Gramercy Tavern.

"Opening this new restaurant," I said, "might be the worst mistake I've ever made." Stanley set his martini down, looked me in the eye, and said, "So you made a mistake. You need to understand something important. And listen to me carefully: *The road to success is paved with mistakes well handled.*"

His words remained with me through the night. I repeated them over and over to myself, and it led to a turning point in the way I approached business. The problem wasn't that I naively believed in perfection. Perfection is impossible in business. As a company policy, the notion of perfection can be dangerous, and the folly of pursuing it can stunt your team's willingness to take intelligent risks. How could I expect my staff to create "legends of hospitality" if they were playing it safe by trying to avoid mistakes? Stanley's lesson reminded me of something my grandfather Irving Harris had always told me: "The definition of business is *problems.*" His philosophy came down to a simple fact of business life: success lies not in the elimination of problems but in the art of creative, profitable problem solving. The best companies are those that distinguish themselves by solving problems most effectively.

Indeed, *business is problem solving.* As human beings, we are all fallible. You've got to welcome the inevitability of mistakes if you want to succeed in the restaurant business—or in any business. It's critical for us to accept and embrace our ongoing mistakes as opportunities to learn, grow, and profit. Baseball's top hitters can make seven mistakes out of every ten at-bats, and still ride a .300 lifetime batting average into the Hall of Fame.

We also need to expect the unexpected. We never know in advance if the next pitch will sail up and in or down and away. Will it be a fastball, a forkball, or a knuckleball? For us, the secret of the game is anticipating mistakes, harnessing them, and addressing them in constructive ways so that we end up in a better spot than if we had never made them in the first place.

I like to think of our staff members not as servers, but as surfers. Surfing is an arduous sport, and no one pursues it involuntarily. No one forces you to become a surfer, but if you choose to do it, there's no point in wasting energy trying to tame the ocean of its waves. Waves are like mistakes. You can count on the fact that there will always be another wave, so your choice is to get back on the surfboard and anticipate it. The degree to which you ride it with better form than the next guy is how you improve and distinguish yourself.

The style with which a company rides the tough waves and addresses mistakes can define its heart, soul, and talent. Otherwise, there is no art to doing business. Our company is populated with surfers—fortunately, since in the restaurant business you can always count on another wave.

In our restaurants, we've experienced all kinds of mistakes, mishaps, and adversity. Once a large dried floral arrangement caught fire in the dining room, with flames shooting ten feet high. We've survived electrical failures and flooding; we've called EMS units after guests have passed out in the middle of the dining room. We've seen a mouse once run across a guest's white tablecloth, and a beetle turn up in someone's salad. Back when we permitted smoking, a two-inch cigar ash was flicked from the upstairs balcony down into someone's bowl of risotto at Union Square Cafe. A drunk man took his pants down and mooned our guests through the outside window of our front dining room. We've sent out our share of garments for quick dry cleaning when servers have accidentally spilled soup or drizzled olive oil on designer scarves hanging over the backs of chairs. But the worst mistake is not to figure out some way to end up in a better place after having made a mistake. We call that "writing a great last chapter." Whatever mistake happened, *happened*. And the person on the receiving end will naturally want to tell anyone who's interested all about it. That's to be expected. While we can't erase what happened, we *do* have the power to write one last episode so that at least the story ends the way we want. If we write a great one, we will earn a comeback victory with the guest. Also, the guest will have no choice but to focus on how well we responded to the mistake when telling anyone we made it. We can, then, turn a mistake into something positive. To be effective, the last chapter must be written imaginatively, graciously, generously, and sincerely. And sometimes we even write a great last chapter when it was the guest, not us, who made the mistake. If someone spills his or her glass at the bar, we pour another round, period. A child once spilled a glass of Sprite at his table, so we bought all six members of his family a round of what they were drinking. If a guest doesn't like his or her dish, it is to be removed from the bill.

I have found that when you acknowledge a mistake and genuinely express your regret at having made it, guests will almost always give you a chance to earn back their favor. Take, for example, a mistake as simple as a dropped plate of food. If a waiter who is heading for a table of six accidentally drops a plate on the way there, five people in the party will have hot food but a sixth guest will be left with nothing to eat. Do we make all six people wait? Do we leave one person feeling awkward while the other five eat? We deliver the five ready dishes, and, checking to see what the sixth guest has already eaten, we come up with a quick (and complimentary) midcourse—a small soup or salad—for him or her to enjoy while we remake and replate the missing dish.

THE FIVE A'S FOR EFFECTIVELY ADDRESSING MISTAKES

- **Awareness**—Many mistakes go unaddressed because no one is even aware they have happened. If you're not aware, you're nowhere.

- **Acknowledgement**—"Our server had an accident, and we are going to prepare a new plate for you as quickly as possible."

- **Apology**—"I am so sorry this happened to you." Alibis are *not* one of the Five A's. It is not appropriate or useful to make excuses ("We're short-staffed.")

- **Action**—"Please enjoy this for now. We'll have your fresh order out in just a few minutes." Say what you are going to do to make amends then follow through.

- **Additional generosity**—Unless the mistake had to do with slow timing, I would instruct my staff to send out something additional (a complimentary dessert or dessert wine) to thank the guests for having been good sports. Some more serious mistakes warrant a complimentary dish or meal.

Unless something truly grave has occurred (food poisoning, someone slipping in a pool of olive oil), it's sometimes helpful, when appropriate, to inject a little humor into the "great last chapter." I was

at Eleven Madison Park during lunch one day when the former senator Bob Kerrey of Nebraska, a regular at our restaurants since becoming president of the New School, came in. When he greeted me, he
asked, "Did you hear what happened last night at Gramercy Tavern?
We had a dinner party in your private dining room."

I had not heard about it, and that embarrassed me. I should have
been given a heads-up by my staff.

"So how was it?" I asked

"Well, it was good except for the beetle in my friend's salad," he
said.

"Oh, my God. I feel horrible," I said. "I apologize. I hope my team
handled it well. Did you bring it to their attention?"

"Oh, yeah," the senator said. "[The person] was a bit upset, but
your people handled it incredibly well." I walked away, shaking my
head. What a business.

After seating Senator Kerrey, I spoke to our manager at Eleven
Madison Park. "There was a mistake with a salad last night at Gramercy
Tavern. We've got to figure out how to write a great last chapter here,"
I said. I gave her the background, adding, "Whether or not Senator
Kerrey or his guest orders a salad during his lunch, I want you to deliver a beautiful salad and garnish it with a small piece of paper. On
that piece of paper I want you to write the word RINGO, and when
you deliver it, you can tell them, 'Danny wanted to make sure you
knew that Gramercy Tavern wasn't the only one of his restaurants
that's willing to garnish your salad with a beatle."

Fortunately, the mistake hadn't been very serious; no one had
gotten sick or been hurt. But it was now impossible for Senator
Kerrey to tell anyone the story about the beetle in the salad without
also mentioning the "last chapter" we wrote the following day.

Most mistakes, like this one, are simple enough to fix. But when
we receive complaints of any type, our mission is twofold: first, to
learn from the mistake and to profit from what we've learned; and
second, to write a great last chapter that allows us to end up in a

better place with the guest than if we had never made the mistake in the first place.

The time frame for addressing mistakes is crucial. When something goes wrong, it is essential for the manager on whose watch the mistake occurred to make every effort to connect with the guest within twenty-four hours. Meanwhile, we immediately review and analyze our own performance to determine exactly what happened. (When a baseball pitcher hangs a curveball that gets whacked out of the park for a home run, you can bet he reviews the videotapes the next day to avoid making the same mistake again.) No matter how much you may try to erase what's happened, you cannot. Why wait for a second or third letter from somebody who has now cc'd his report of your fallibility and culpability to the Chamber of Commerce, the restaurant critic of the *New York Times*, and the *Zagat Survey*? Instead, take the initiative:

1. Respond graciously, and do so at once. You know you're going to resolve the mistake eventually. It's always a lot less costly to resolve the matter at the outset.

2. Err on the side of generosity. Apologize and make sure the value of the redemption is worth more than the cost of the initial mistake.

3. Always write a great last chapter. People love to share stories of adversity. Use this powerful force to your advantage by writing the closing statement the way *you* want it told. Use all your imagination and creativity in thinking about your response.

4. Learn from the mistake. Use every new mistake as a teaching tool with your employees. Unless the mistake involved a lack of integrity, the person who made it has actually helped your team by providing you with new opportunities to improve.

5. Make new mistakes every day. Don't waste time repeating the old ones.

When we do learn about a mishap in one of our restaurants, I always want to hear the staff member's side of the story before I connect with the guest, since our first responsibility in the culture of enlightened hospitality is to be on the side of our team. If a complaint involves a server's "bad attitude," we will find out exactly what took place and then use that knowledge to help the staff member learn from what happened. (Sometimes we learn that guests brought in their own bad attitude. In that case, there's still an opportunity to learn about how to respond more effectively to a guest's challenging mood.) If a server repeats the same mistakes—a second or third spill, a pattern of complaints about his or her attitude—then we may need to address that person's overall ability to excel or comply with our priorities.

SOMETIMES IT IS OUR job to go the extra mile for guests to solve problems not of our making. One day at Tabla a woman walked in for lunch and realized that she had left her wallet in the taxi. A summer intern from Cornell was working at the front desk that day and did his best to comfort the shaken woman, reassuring her that we'd of course extend her credit, and urging her to relax and enjoy lunch. That was good, but I thought we could do even better. I got Tabla's general manager, Randy Garutti, involved. "Randy," I said, "this woman is going to tell the whole world that she left her wallet in a taxi while she was on her way to Tabla. I know we can create a legend out of this somehow."

I didn't give Randy a script to follow. But he knew exactly what I meant by creating a legend. He spoke to the woman and learned that she had also left her cell phone in the cab. He immediately had a staff member start calling her cell phone number. Meanwhile, the woman was seated, her friend arrived, and they ordered lunch. After half an hour of persistent redials, a man's voice finally answered her phone. It was the taxi driver, who was by now way up in the Bronx. He confirmed that he had the wallet in his car too.

Unbeknownst to the woman, we sent a staff member uptown to meet the driver and retrieve the wallet and cell phone, both of which were in her hands before the check for lunch was on the table. She was amazed and obviously delighted. We had turned a nightmare into a legend of hospitality. Our round-trip taxi ride had cost $31. I'd be surprised if the woman hasn't already given Tabla 100 times that value in positive word-of-mouth.

One night a few years ago at Eleven Madison Park, a couple came in to celebrate their anniversary with us. Our maître d' congratulated them and offered them each a complimentary glass of champagne. They were quite pleased. Then the man asked, "Do you know much about wine?"

"I know a lot about our wine list," the maître d' said. "Do you need some help selecting a great wine for your dinner?"

"No," the man said, "I have a technical question. We have a very special bottle of champagne at home to celebrate with after dinner. But the bottle was warm, so before we came here tonight I put it in the freezer. Is that bottle going to explode?"

"Yes, it's going to explode," the maître d' said. The man stood up in a panic and said to his wife, "Oh, my God, honey, I've got to go home and deal with this before that bottle explodes."

The maître d' saw a great last chapter taking shape. "Listen," he said, "you're here for your anniversary, and we want you to have a great night. If you'll give me your address, I'll gladly go over to your apartment and take the champagne out of the freezer."

"All right, you're on," the man said. He called to alert his doorman, and our maître d' took a cab to their address where he transferred the champagne from the freezer to the refrigerator. And next to the bottle, he set some dessert chocolates from the restaurant and a small tin of caviar along with a note that read, "Happy Anniversary from Eleven Madison Park." These folks became dedicated regulars.

In handling mistakes, our goal is always to alter course to create a positive outcome and an experience that ends up being memorable for the right reasons. Sometimes that has required an athletic effort—literally and figuratively. One night when we'd closed Tabla for a private party, a couple walked in for dinner. "What do you mean, you're closed?" the man asked Richard Coraine, who was then acting as Tabla's general manager. "Then why did one of your people take our reservation for tonight?" To make matters much worse, they had driven 250 miles from New Hampshire just to eat at Tabla. Richard was in a tough spot. Obviously, he couldn't seat them. Frustrated and angry, the couple stormed out and headed uptown along Madison Avenue.

For one very long minute, Richard and his maître d' sat mortified and wondered what they should do. Suddenly, they had a solution. They bolted out of the restaurant and sprinted up Madison Avenue, catching up with the couple a few blocks away. "We're so sorry about the situation at Tabla," Richard told them. "We want you to come back soon." He gave them a gift certificate for a future dinner at Tabla. He next called Gramercy Tavern on his cell phone to make sure there was a table available immediately, and he offered to buy them their dinner that night. They accepted, and the maître d' walked them to the restaurant on East Twentieth Street and made sure that they would be very well cared for.

Later Richard handwrote them a note in which he reiterated his apology. The couple kept up a correspondence with him and eventually became regulars at Tabla, making the 500 mile round-trip nearly every month for dinner.

We're most interested in developing a good relationship that results from the way people feel about how we've overcome a mistake. Just before lunch on a sweltering summer day, the air compressor at Eleven Madison Park broke down. More than 100 people had reservations. The ambient temperature was in the mid–eighties and rising as noon approached. For one of our managers, this crisis became an opportunity to write a great last chapter.

First, he ran out and bought two oscillating fans for the two perspiring reservationists, who were stuck in a small, hot office fielding calls. He instinctively understood that it was crucial for the people on our front line in offering hospitality to remain comfortable while they were taking care of callers seeking reservations two and three weeks ahead. Next, he went to a nearby Woolworth's and purchased every small battery-operated mini-fan in the store's entire inventory.

On entering the sauna (aka Eleven Madison Park), each guest received not just a deep apology about our air-conditioning failure, but a gift of one of the fans. The mood in the dining room was actually festive, not hostile. New Yorkers often take adversity and crises in stride, and the guests that day seemed to be enjoying the novelty of the tiny fans on each table.

One of the most challenging days of my professional life was the result of another heat wave. It was April 2002, just a few weeks after Blue Smoke opened, and because the temperature was freakishly high for spring—in the high nineties—we had a brownout in the restaurant. I was out of New York on business when I got a cell phone call with the news that our electrical system had failed. Both Blue Smoke and Jazz Standard were completely booked and scheduled to open in half an hour.

Between the restaurant and the jazz club, we had taken some 500 reservations that we were now unable to honor. I called my senior management team and instructed them to reach (or leave messages for) as many as possible of the people who had made reservations . We needed to let them know that because of our brownout we couldn't open that night, but also to assure them that we would gladly rearrange dinner at their convenience.

We decided that every guest who did show up—and nearly 200 did—would receive not only an apology but also a Blue Smoke to-go bag filled with barbecue sauce, Magic Dust seasoning, and a $50 gift certificate to the restaurant. We also made reservations for the guests, wherever they chose to dine that evening. We sent seventy-five people to Eleven Madison Park and bought their dinners. (That we went so far overboard with our apology is an apt illustration of how defensive we felt about our performance in those very early days at Blue Smoke.)

Eventually the electricians and engineers jerry-rigged a system to pump just enough air-conditioning into the dining room to let us seat about two dozen hardy guests. Even without kitchen exhaust fans, the staff followed through professionally and fed all those people, a display of remarkable grace under sweltering and smoky pressure.

RUNNING (AND WORKING FOR) a company whose restaurants are known for their hospitality and superior service can sometimes be a double-edged sword. I'll bet we get at least as many letters of complaint from guests as other restaurants do precisely because we set the bar for excellence so high. The great majority of objections follow the same format: whatever has gone wrong always comes as a "complete letdown" because the guests had arrived with such high expectations, and we've let them down. They're correct to let us know.

During lunch service one day in 1995, in the very early months at Gramercy Tavern, the hostess of a party of six told her server that she didn't care for her salmon and asked for something else. A manager on duty was alerted and told the server to leave the salmon on the woman's bill, since there was nothing wrong with it and she had eaten more than half of it. As the host of a business meeting, she did not contest the bill, understandably wanting to avoid an awkward scene. Then, on her way out, the woman was handed a doggie bag containing the uneaten balance of her salmon. There was no confusion; this was done by design. The guest wrote to me: "I can't believe how insulting and passive-aggressive that was, and it's not what I would expect at one of your restaurants." She was spot on, and I was mortified when I learned what had happened.

This incident led to a pivotal moment in my career. Until then, hospitality had been no more than a personal instinct. I hadn't articulated to myself what hospitality meant—or, for that matter, what the absence of hospitality meant. How could I possibly have been explicit about it to anyone else? These were the initial days of my becoming a two-restaurant restaurateur, and for the first nine years of Union Square Cafe's existence, I had always been on hand to see and fix things as they were happening—demonstrating what to do rather than teaching others how or why to do it. I had never had to codify how particular mistakes or crises should be addressed.

At the weekly management meeting immediately after this incident, it became clear to me that a number of others on our team would have done exactly what the manager did. Why remove the salmon from her bill when it was perfectly good and she had eaten most if it? Contrary to my belief that you get more by giving more, they were concerned about how to get screwed less by protecting yourself more. That's a valid model for some people—including many across the entire spectrum of businesses—but it's one with which I'm completely uncomfortable. I don't believe that the principle of erring on the side of generosity is inherently superior to the principle of fiercely protecting yourself in order to make as much money as possible. But generosity is the way I choose to do business in my restaurants, and so far it has always contributed mightily to our success.

I   Are you in it for keeps? It's almost always worth bearing a higher short-term cost if you want to win in the long run. I'm convinced that you get what you give, and you get more by first giving more. Generosity of spirit and a gracious approach to problem solving are, with few exceptions, the most effective way I know to earn lasting goodwill for your business.

I realized that a critically important role for me, as the leader of the company, was to define upfront what was nonnegotiable. That way, if employees were not comfortable, they could choose to walk. More than any other previous mistake had done, the incident of the doggie bag taught me that it was more imperative than ever for me to articulate my core values and vision.

Our training has evolved and improved dramatically through the years. I'm quite explicit now in setting the table for our staff. I make it absolutely clear that if guests don't like something they've ordered, it is removed from the check, period. It's the server's job to sense that guests are unhappy before they have to tell you. (As for the manager, we parted ways, as it became increasingly clear that we just saw business differently.)

Though lapses in hospitality, fortunately, don't happen every day, we have had plenty of other examples from which we've been able to learn. In the early days of Tabla, chef Floyd Cardoz felt strongly that he and his staff could never do a superior job of cooking for tables larger than a party of eight. Floyd had come from the old, rigid French school of kitchen management, having been sous-chef for seven years at the very refined Lespinasse.

I understood his fear, though not his position. When a table of eight or two parties of six arrive all at once, their orders can clog up the restaurant's flow and wreak havoc. Trying to cook for and coordinate the timing of too many large parties can be very challenging. It demands precise alignment among the various stations in the kitchen and the dining room—and meanwhile, service for the smaller tables can grind to a halt.

We managed to get along with Floyd's party-size limitation until a night when one of our most loyal customers, having made a reservation for eight, arrived with an unexpected ninth guest in tow. Floyd absolutely refused to let the maître d' seat them, giving the entire party of nine no choice but to leave Tabla.

This shouldn't have happened to anybody, but it turned out that the host of the party was Fern Mallis, who, while heading the influential Council of Fashion Designers of America for more than a decade, conducted the "Seventh on Sixth" fashion shows in Bryant Park and was a friend and a frequent guest at our restaurants. Fern was disappointed and justifiably furious.

When I heard about this, I immediately met with Floyd. My message was stern and clear: *Policies are nothing more than guidelines to be broken for the benefit of our guests. We're here to give the guests what they want, period.* Floyd was initially stubborn in arguing his point; but to his credit, he listened, understood the impact his inhospitable reaction had made on our guests, and changed his approach dramatically. Tabla has since found ways to seat parties of nine, ten, twelve, and even sixteen without compromising quality; and Floyd's adaptivity has been an important source of hospitality and profitability for the restaurant. Still, it's a shame that a loyal guest was offended before we learned the lesson that took our restaurant to a much better place than before.

As for Fern, I acknowledged, apologized, and acted on our mistake. "I am embarrassed and I feel terrible," I told her. "We absolutely made the wrong decision, and I'd hate for you to never come back as a result of that one incident. Next time, it's my treat." I wouldn't blame anyone who had received that kind of non-welcome for choosing to never return.

An even worse kind of mistake is one that involves a lapse in character—theft, deception, or disrespect. In the fall of 2000, in an article in *Gourmet* magazine, an unnamed maître d' at Union Square Cafe was alleged to have accepted a $50 bribe (palmed in a handshake) from a walk-in guest who had just been told there were no tables available without a reservation. The guest was actually the reporter, who had gone undercover at a number of top restaurants to learn at which ones a table might be bought.

Reading the piece was deeply disturbing to me. Union Square Cafe had been publicly humiliated, and we had no idea who on our team had been involved. It put us in a position where we had to ask our entire front-door staff if this could be true (no one confessed), and the questioning alone hurt the team's morale. I refused to go on a witch hunt. Instead, I wanted to turn the incident into a group learning experience. I wasted no time writing a great last chapter: in this case, an actual letter to the editor, which was published in the next issue of *Gourmet*. Despite what I called *Gourmet*'s "successful sting operation," I wrote: "[It] is *absolutely* against the policy of Union Square Cafe for anyone on our staff to accept a tip as an inducement to provide a last-minute table. We are deeply embarrassed that one member of our staff violated our standards . . . and, above all, apologize to the hundreds of thousands of Union Square Cafe patrons who have made their reservations the fair way throughout the 15 years we've been in business." The story had a very happy ending when I got to know the author of the article, Bruce Feiler. He ended up featuring Union Square Cafe in another article in *Gourmet,* for which he infiltrated the ranks of our staff to understand the secret behind the restaurant's "hospitality culture." He won a James Beard Award for that piece. Not a bad last chapter.

I find it enormously instructive to observe how other companies handle their mistakes. I was in Bloomingdale's department store on the Upper East Side to stock our home kitchen, and I bought several items, including an electric hand mixer. Several weeks went by before my wife needed the mixer to make a cake. When she opened the box for the first time, she found that there were no blades inside.

Audrey didn't get around to bringing the mixer back to Bloomingdale's until several months later, after the kids were back in school. When she found a saleswoman in the housewares department, she opened the box and began explaining: "I feel so bad, I was out of town for the summer, I can't find the receipt, and this is the first chance I've had to come back . . ."

The woman interrupted Audrey with one of the greatest hospitality responses I've ever heard. "Say no more! You didn't even have to bring the box in. You could have just called. Now let me get two replacement blades for you right away."

Audrey was so impressed that she ended up buying five more things in housewares—and Bloomingdale's ended up in a much better place with her than if those blades had come with the mixer in the first place. The story gets even better. When the sales clerk saw Audrey eyeing a set of barbecue tongs and spatula for the pit, she said, "That's on sale today. Do you have one of our coupons?" Audrey said no. "Too bad," the saleswoman said. "It's thirty percent off today. Hold on—I'm going to go find you a coupon in the back office." On her way there, she stopped to pull the two mixer blades from the demo model on the floor, and then returned with the coupons.

Say no more! There's always a solution if you're open to finding one.

Another example of a company that knows how to overcome a mistake is JetBlue. Not long after the airline had started up, Richard Coraine booked a flight to Florida to visit his parents. The day before he was to depart, he received a phone call and an e-mail asking him to call JetBlue immediately. First, the airline confirmed his reservation. Then, it admitted making a mistake. "We overbooked that flight," the agent told him. She gave Richard a choice: travel the next day as planned, or give up his seat on that flight in exchange for a later trip, free, to Palm Beach.

Typically, most airlines don't address their overbookings until just before, or sometimes even after, everyone has boarded the plane. This was the first time, Richard said, that an airline had ever reached out twenty-four hours ahead of time to give him such a choice. Richard chose to give up his seat, got a free trip, and had hardly any disruption of his plans: he was able to depart just two hours after his original flight.

Bloomingdale's and JetBlue, their five A's soundly in place, wrote great last chapters with Audrey and Richard, and won loyal customers and enthusiastic apostles for their businesses. Richard's experience also helped encourage our company to want to build a strong business relationship with JetBlue. The airline now sponsors our Big Apple Barbecue Block Party as well as our annual Autumn Harvest dinner and auction at Eleven Madison Park to benefit the hunger relief organization Share Our Strength.

Stanley Marcus was absolutely right. By viewing mistakes as opportunities to repair and strengthen relationships, rather than letting them destroy relationships, a business is paving its own road to success and good fortune. And mistakes are the best form of job security I know of. Just as with waves in the ocean, you can bet your bottom dollar that there's always another mistake behind the one you're confronting at any time. So long as you're determined to distinguish yourself and your company by how well you approach mistakes, you'll always have steady work.

CHAPTER 11

The Virtuous Cycle of Enlightened Hospitality

THERE ARE FIVE PRIMARY stakeholders to whom we express our most caring hospitality, and in whom we take the greatest interest. Prioritizing those people in the following order is the guiding principal for practically every decision we make, and it has made the single greatest contribution to the ongoing success of our company:

1. Our employees
2. Our guests
3. Our community
4. Our suppliers
5. Our investors

As any rational businessman would, I'd like our restaurants to earn a handsome profit and ultimately create a sustainable return for our investors. In the model of enlightened hospitality, only after you have first taken good care of your top four stakeholders will you be able to take care of your fifth group—your investors—and provide them with a sound and enduring return on their investment. To prioritize differently breaks the virtuous cycle of enlightened hospitality and seriously compromises the chances that your business will achieve excellence, success, good will, and soul.

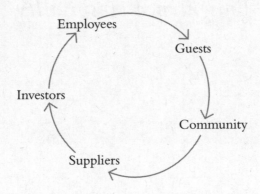

Why do we care for our stakeholders in this particular order? The interests of our own employees must be placed directly ahead of those of our guests because the only way we can consistently earn raves, win repeat business, and develop bonds of loyalty with our guests is first to ensure that our own team members feel jazzed about coming to work. Being jazzed is a combination of feeling motivated, enthusiastic, confident, proud, and at peace with the choice to work on our team. I place the interests of our investors fifth, but *not* because I don't want to earn a lot of money. On the contrary, I staunchly believe that standing conventional business priorities on their head ultimately leads to even greater, more enduring financial success. And, just as important, it's the kind of success that adds tangible value to the lives of a wide range of stakeholders. As business or organizational logic, enlightened hospitality can be applied far beyond the restaurant industry.

Suppose that you care for your investors' interests first. You can then potentially make a speedier financial hit for them, but it's not as likely to sustain itself over time. There will inevitably be a revolving door of staff members who, finding themselves in a business culture that does not place their own or the customers' interests ahead of the other key stakeholders, will quickly cease to feel particularly proud, motivated, or enthusiastic about coming to work. By contrast, prioritizing our way has enabled us to offer investors an opportunity to affiliate with a business known for outstanding employees, warm hospitality, strong ties with exceptional suppliers, and a solid commitment to playing an active, valuable role in its community. And we believe those investors are also delighted to be affiliated with the consequent quality of our restaurants, themselves.

Our investors (as well as our other four stakeholders) also trust that I am not going to affiliate any of our restaurants with any other brand that would diminish ours. For example, it was a simple decision for us when we had a chance to affiliate with a company like Timberland. That is an exceptional organization whose products exemplify enduring quality, whose employees are outstanding, and whose community-building culture is impressive and inspiring. It was natural to choose Timberland as the supplier for Blue Smoke's staff uniforms as well as the merchandise we sell, like Blue Smoke baseball caps and T-shirts.

We don't have many outside investors in our restaurants—most of the investors have been family members, close friends, or colleagues. We've been fortunate that those we have attracted are stimulating people who bring broad experience, fascinating perspectives, and strength of character to the table—all with a supportive mind-set.

We're blessed to have such investors, who take a genuine interest in sharing the financial risk upfront while offering their abundant wisdom through the duration of their investment. Few things make me prouder than when a restaurant begins to make profit distributions to its investors.

I make sure that every investor knows going in that enlightened hospitality is a business model designed for long-term, sustained profitability. It's not a recipe for overnight distributions or instant riches. It is inherently expensive to design high-quality restaurants that are built to become institutions, and then to operate them with a long view. While our investors are willing to be patient upfront, they do rightfully expect a healthy long-term return on their investment and we feel a solemn responsibility to deliver it. And since I personally invest in each one of our businesses, all of our interests are aligned.

In a private entrepreneurial (and nonliquid) investment—unlike a typical stock market play—investors aren't simply looking for a strong return; they're also making a bet on an affiliation with the overall principles of the company.

By prioritizing our five stakeholder groups in this way, we have been able to build loyalty where it most counts. The long-term success of our business is determined by, and intrinsically linked to, the degree to which we excel at taking care of these stakeholders' respective interests.

The Five Stakeholders in Enlightened Hospitality

1. Employees

When I first walk into any restaurant or any business, I can immediately guess what type of experience I'm in for by sensing whether the staff members appear to be focused on their work, supportive of one another, and enjoying one another's company. If they are out to help one another succeed, I know I stand an excellent chance of having an excellent experience accompanied by a feeling of welcome. From any business, what better outcome is there than that? People who like to please others tend to do so with many, if not all, constituencies.

Well before our staff members can extend any kind of meaningful hospitality to our guests, they need to first understand the primary importance of being on each other's side. Mutual respect and trust are the most powerful tools for building an energetic, motivated, winning team in any field. And the most talented employees are often those attracted to companies that can provide them with the most important job benefit of all: other great people with whom to work.

Considering that most of us spend about one-third of our lives at work, it is the value of the human experience we have with our colleagues—what we learn from one another, how much fun we have working together, and how much mutual respect and trust we share—that has the greatest influence on job satisfaction.

When I talk about the staff caring for each other, I stress that it's incumbent upon all members of our team to be citizens of our company and to come to work looking for opportunities to be on one another's side.

The restaurant business can be grueling. When you are the expediter in the kitchen, you may have thirty-five "dupes" (guest checks) staring you in the face, each of which needs to be cooked "on the fly." That means trying to send appetizers out to thirty-five tables, coordinating dishes from the sauté station, the pasta station, the grill station, and the salad station. Waiters are running in and out of the kitchen asking for an update on table 26's food and telling you that table 28 needs its main courses in order to make a theater curtain. And the kitchen is hot, with up to thirty people racing around while performing tough tasks in tight quarters. It's tense.

Under those circumstances our people need to remember that the best, most efficient way to work through all the dupes is first to take care of one another and work together as a team. Does working together take more effort than screaming and yelling—a more common practice in restaurant kitchens? Not especially. But the results of respectful collaboration build long-term success and prevent the same problems from recurring every day. I love to hear waiters asking one another, "Is there anything I can do to help you with table 41? Can I help carry any of these plates out?" When there is abundant mutual respect and trust, and people are continually looking for opportunities to help one another, that infectious spirit becomes the culture. That reciprocally uplifting feeling then translates into a better product because managers help waiters, waiters help cooks, cooks help waiters, and cooks help cooks. If a waiter is "in the weeds" (restaurant-speak for "up shit creek"), there is invariably a waitress one or two stations away who is for the moment in control of her station, and able to offer help. What I never want to see is a cook getting short with the expediter, or the expediter getting short with a waiter, or any other such combination. Guests can definitely pick up on and, I think, even taste discord among employees, even if it's taking place offstage, in the kitchen.

Yet our employees don't come to work just because our "culture of hospitality" resonates with them and feels good. They have to pay the rent, too. It is critical to me that our wage scales be competitive with those of other restaurants, and that we provide the finest benefits we can afford, including medical and dental insurance for all our full-time employees.

The primary reason we have such a loyal and dedicated staff (in a fickle industry notorious for high turnover), is that we understand what people want most from their workplace is to respect and be respected. And it certainly helps to know that their honest day's work— mistakes and all—is appreciated. We try to find opportunities to express our respect in many ways.

Just as we invite our customers to give us feedback on comment cards, we also conduct periodic roundtable discussions with each restaurant's staff, during which we invite employees to provide honest feedback about how they feel our business is performing.

We also conduct a monthly dining-voucher program for all staff members with at least three months' tenure that allows them to dine at any of our restaurants using a credit. The catch is that in exchange for the credit, employees must answer a detailed questionnaire about their dining experience. Why do we prize—even need—the input of our own employees? Better than almost anyone else, they understand the mission of our restaurants, and they are in the best position to react to and measure our actual performance against our ideal outcome. They are expert at observing their colleagues in the dining room, tasting the food they know so well, and assessing the restaurant's overall performance. They get to observe and be on the receiving end of the consistent, unifying power of hospitality throughout all our restaurants. They see that each sibling restaurant is staffed by "51 percenters" who have the same excellent technical and emotional skills for which they themselves were hired.

It's especially useful for us to hear and read where improvement is needed, from insiders who are on our side. This is certainly preferable to first learning about a problem from a critic whose megaphone reaches an enormous audience. Above all, the program sends our own team a crucial message: "We respect, trust, and care enough about you to actively seek and value your input." And we put our dining dollars where our mouths are.

We've also asked our staff members to periodically participate in a questionnaire created by our human resources department: our "Walk the Talk Survey." This offers them a chance to tell us how we're doing as leaders and managers. It's a remarkably instructive report card that provides illuminating, challenging, uplifting, and occasionally discouraging results. When you take the risk of telling your staff what your company stands for and what's nonnegotiable, and then give them a mirror to hold up, they are delighted to reflect an accurate picture. For example, we've learned about managers who weren't effective listeners or who didn't seem to consistently inspire standards of excellence. We've heard that a restaurant's management has fallen behind on repairs and maintenance, sending out a message that perhaps we don't take enough pride in the facility. And we've also picked up clues that the degree to which a restaurant is subscribing to the tenets of enlightened hospitality is flagging. That encourages me to take an even closer look at how well management is or isn't investing in our staff.

2. Guests

Hospitality starts with the genuine enjoyment of doing something well for the purpose of bringing pleasure to other people. Whether that's an attitude, a behavior, or an innate trait, it should become a primary motivation for coming to work every day. We strive to treat our guests the way we would want to be treated. The golden rule remains as fresh and meaningful as ever; and beyond how well it serves people in their lives, it may also be the most potent business strategy ever devised. In business, as in life, you get what you give. We try to apply a humanitarian viewpoint to every business challenge, to find creative, gracious solutions and reassure our guests that we are solidly on their side.

Our front line in delivering on our promise of hospitality is our team of telephone reservationists. I consider the initial dialogue so crucial to our business that for years the path to becoming a manager at Union Square Cafe began with being a reservationist. Answering our reservation telephone lines remains an excellent proving ground for this business: when a reservationist can maintain composure under the non-stop volume of calls taking place on the telephone and still be an agent of hospitality—all without the benefit of eye contact or smiles—that's a strong indicator that he or she has the right stuff to advance in the hospitality profession.

In the course of their calls, our reservationists must continuously listen to themselves and ask: am I being perceived by this caller as an *agent* or a *gatekeeper*? An agent makes things happen for others. A gatekeeper sets up barriers to keep people out. We're looking for agents.

In every business, there are employees who are the first point of contact with the customers (attendants at airport gates, receptionists at doctors' offices, bank tellers, executive assistants). Those people can come across either as agents or as gatekeepers. An agent makes things happen *for* others. A gatekeeper sets up barriers to keep people out. We're looking for agents, and our staff members are responsible for monitoring their own performance: *In that transaction, did I present myself as an agent or a gatekeeper?* In the world of hospitality, there's rarely anything in between.

It's not an easy job. At most of our restaurants, as many as four out of five callers on any given day don't end up with the exact time they initially wanted for a reservation. Whether a reservationist is in an office or at the host's desk, most calls present opportunities to make callers feel that we genuinely care about them—or that we don't. This exchange also gives callers, free of charge, an excellent preview of how they might expect to be treated at our restaurants. Reservationists are under heavy pressure because they can't control how many people call; but they're trained to maintain a hospitable composure no matter how many calls come in and no matter how quickly the calls come. The true test of a win–win dialogue with an agent is that somebody who does *not* get the exact time or date he or she wanted nevertheless leaves the call convinced that we tried. One year, among its highly complimentary comments about Union Square Cafe, the *Zagat Survey* quoted a participant: "The reservationists even feel badly when they can't accommodate you." That made me very proud.

Gatekeepers for very busy restaurants often say things like, "We're fully committed," or, "All we have is six or ten o'clock in the evening," without expressing genuine regret or suggesting an option like placing the person's name on an active waiting list. The hospitality door is slammed shut. Many callers, conditioned to expect such experiences, assume we're all gatekeepers who are somehow bent on keeping them out. As a result, they have learned that the best way to get what they want is to be pushy and nasty from the get-go. That has never been an effective strategy, since someone who is impolite on the phone will likely treat our staff members the same way once he or she is in the restaurant. We don't play those games. I'm convinced that nice gets nice.

Inside our dining rooms, one basic way we take care of our guests is by providing an atmosphere of comfort and welcome. Controlling noise and designing a thoughtful seating arrangement are effective tools to help us do that. I hear noise the way a good chef tastes salt: too much is overbearing; too little can be stifling. Guests are equally uncomfortable whether they have to shout to be heard or are required to speak in self-concious, hushed tones in order not to have their conversation heard by other tables. With just the right noise level, each table has the luxury of becoming enveloped by its own invisible veil of privacy, allowing animated conversation to flow within that discreet container. Too much noise, on the other hand, aggressively invades the space and interferes with the guests' ability to engage with one another. It's annoying, stressful, and inhospitable.

With regard to music, we can control what's playing and at what volume. We also put a lot of effort into dampening ambient noise with acoustical treatments (for example, hanging draperies, and stapling sound-absorbing fabric to the backs of chairs and to the undersides of tables). We've placed acoustic tiles behind walls of wine bottles and applied ceiling and wall treatments wherever they made sense. Because a carpet feels institutional, picks up smells, and is hard to maintain, I am not a fan of most restaurant carpeting. An absorbent floor treatment would solve a lot of noise issues, but purely as a matter of my own taste, our floors are almost always hardwood or terrazzo.

A restaurant's seating arrangement also contributes mightily to how guests are made to feel throughout their meal and is a potent opportunity to create a social environment. In the design of each of our restaurants we've been quite conscious about dividing seating plans as if we were forming several smaller communities within a larger zip code. Walk into any of our restaurants, and you'll see a series of different dining areas that are meant to make a larger space feel more intimate and more human. That format and scale allows our guests to feel anchored, and it encourages genuine connections between the staff and guests as well as between guests and other guests. After all, beyond cooking your food and doing the dishes, a restaurant must provide a public social environment that distinguishes it from the experience of eating at home.

I'm not pleased when tables are so close together that it's impossible to have any kind of private conversation with your companions. That's one of the most inhospitable things a restaurant can do to its guests. It immediately breaks down the imaginary wall of intimacy between tables. For example, when you see a restaurant with banquettes against a long wall, it's often a design strategy for fitting more people in as efficiently as possible. And to shoehorn in the maximum number of tables, most restaurants choose the narrowest possible tables to line up along the banquette. But in order for all the food (plus bread and butter, wine bottle, flowers, and salt and pepper) to fit on these very narrow tables, they are often designed to be both very narrow and very long. That puts a guest twice as far from the face of the person he or she came to dine with and twice as close to the ears of strangers at the tables on either side. It's almost impossible to be intimate with anyone other than the people on either side of you. That's inhospitable.

With its classic brasserie-like volume of space, we conceived Eleven Madison Park to be a restaurant filled with banquettes. In deciding on table sizes, I asked our architects, Bentel and Bentel, to design every one of the tables along our banquette walls two inches shallower than the standard table (allowing closer, more intimate face-to-face communication), and also to make the tables a bit wider than the standard. The spatial effect is subtle, but significant: in a very grand space that could feel imposing and make our guests feel remote and small, they instead are seated slightly closer than usual to their dining companions and a little farther from their neighbors on either side. That strategy also has the effect of controlling noise throughout the restaurant. In such an arrangement, there is no need to yell to be heard.

A lot of people enjoy being seated at a corner table, so in each restaurant we try to design as many corner tables as possible. Rather than designing a restaurant as one big room, creating subcommunities within each space has the advantage of giving us more corners to work with. For example, Gramercy Tavern has three dining rooms with twelve corner tables. At Eleven Madison Park there are three dining areas with sixteen corner tables. That's actually a lot of corner tables. Another design goal is to avoid having any "bad" tables. We try to anchor every "deuce" (table for two) to a wall or to a window, and rarely, if ever, float a deuce out in the middle of the dining room. Most deuces are interested in intimacy. A table of five to eight is most often positioned in the center, exerting its gravitational pull on the rest of the dining room. The people at that table have one another as anchors, and are less sensitive about precisely where their table is placed.

The genuine welcome with which we make our first impression while greeting guests is a simple but extremely powerful statement about our care for them. For any guest, the greeting should provide an immediate affirmative answer to the question: "Are they happy to see me or not?" Guests know when a host is insincere, harried, or just going through the motions in greeting and seating them. It's not genuine hospitality when the host fails to make eye contact, fails to smile, or fails to thank the guests for coming. It's also inhospitable when a host rushes ahead of you while showing you to your table, making you feel like a dog being yanked along on a leash. You try to keep up, but inevitably end up trailing several paces behind. It's all function, with no emotional connection between the host and the guests. Eye contact tells a guest, "I see you." A smile is an assurance that you are happy to see the guest. Each is a simple but crucially important non-verbal expression at the very beginning of a dining experience.

It's a wonderful thing to be in the presence of a host who knows how to establish a warm welcome and natural rapport. The image I have of a guest's ideal experience with our host is an ongoing sentence that begins with the host's genuine welcome; continues with the host's reassuring visit to the table at some point during the meal to let guests know he or she is there if they need anything; and is completed with the punctuation mark of gratitude and an invitation to return to end the sentence as the guest is leaving. If our staff is on its game, guests cannot help feeling that they matter, and that we have taken a true interest in them.

A close examination of our reservation sheets and of our detailed "guest notes" provides our floor managers and hosts with a significant edge in conveying a warm welcome and good-bye. The host may have collected some dots for an effective initial point of contact, such as, "I noticed you came here all the way from Florida. How did you hear about us?" Or, upon saying thank you and good-bye, the host offers a business card and says, "I hope we'll get to see you again next time you visit New York. When you're ready to return, just let me know and I'll assist with your reservations."

When guests make reservations online using OpenTable.com, their two most frequent special requests are, "Quiet table, please" or "Romantic table." Over the years a number of people have called us in advance to let us know they're planning to propose over dinner. We definitely share that detail with the host and waitstaff. The kitchen can then be ready with a congratulatory dessert plate, and the manager with a bottle of champagne.

Providing exceptional hospitality depends on the alertness and instincts of empathetic staff members. We urge them to develop their own athletic style in actively looking for golden moments of opportunity to go above and beyond.

We truly value our guests' opinions, whether these opinions are expressed on comment cards or in face-to-face exchanges. But there are many businesses, restaurants included, that don't really want to learn from such feedback. Their strategy is "Don't ask, don't tell," and it sends a message that these businesses aren't looking for problems and aren't interested in you. No news is good news.

I'm not pleased when a waiter or host asks a perfunctory "How was everything?" as you're leaving. You'll probably say "Fine," which is exactly what the waiter or host wants to hear. In our restaurants, if the answer is "Fine," we've failed. If our overarching goal is to create a rave for each and every guest experience—"fine" falls short of the mark. Some variation of "thank you" and "I hope we'll see you again soon" is more to the point.

3. *Community*

One of the most significant benefits we offer our employees is the opportunity to work for a company that stands for something well beyond serving good food in a comfortable environment. I make it very clear to all new employees that they've joined a company that chooses to take an active interest in its community, and that we rely on members of our staff to step up and participate as citizens within that culture. We encourage employees to become involved in the community because doing so makes them even better at taking care of one another and our guests. And it's the most effective form of team-building I know. When our colleagues work, serve, and play together beyond the normal confines of work, they invariably return to work knowing each other better and working together more effectively. They become stronger leaders and tighter teammates.

At its best, investing in our community also creates wealth for the community, which in turn often leads to good luck for our own company— something any corporation needs in order to sustain its success. Our good luck spreads goodwill among our stakeholders, making them even prouder and more satisfied to be affiliated with us. By taking active leadership roles in working to revitalize two great city parks that anchor the neighborhoods in which we do business, we've demonstrated that a rising tide lifts all boats. This component of enlightened hospitality has beautified our neighborhood, and in turn has enhanced our business.

I am convinced that doing things that make sense for the community leads to doing well as a business. We would never undertake a project in the first place if we didn't believe it was the right thing to do, or a useful thing to do. But we also understand that doing good things well brings loads of potential ancillary benefits.

It is in any company's self-interest to take what it does best and apply that core strength to an appropriate form of outreach beyond its own four walls. For those of us who make a living by nourishing and nurturing guests in our restaurants, there's a logical connection to feeding people in our community who don't have enough. Over the years we have hosted or participated in hundreds of hunger-relief events that build on the natural synergy among our staff, other great chefs and restaurants, our guests, and the organizations—most notably Share Our Strength—that share our activist spirit. For years, City Harvest has made regular pickups of our leftover food. It's natural for us to want to support a rescue agency that annually delivers more than 20 million pounds of food to New York City's missions and shelters, but we don't dictate to our staff members what community programs they should or shouldn't be involved in. We do urge them to play leadership roles in causes that are personally important to them, and we invite them to seek our support. Our hospice dinner program at Beth Israel Hospital, in our neighborhood, was the brainchild of Blue Smoke's general manager, Mark Maynard-Parisi, who previously had managed at Union Square Cafe. Mark approached me, confident that his idea would fall on eager ears. I told him that conceiving a good idea was one thing and executing it was something else; and I encouraged him to grow as a leader by asking him to persuade all the other GMs and chefs to embrace the idea, which he did. (Mark is now managing partner of Blue Smoke.)

Every Tuesday and Wednesday night, one of our restaurants prepares about twenty dinners for the hospice unit, and volunteers from that restaurant's staff bring the food to Beth Israel, serving the meals to the hospice patients and their families as well as to the unit's nurses and attendants. Emotionally, it's a tough experience to confront people who are steps away from dying. But for our staff to be able to serve others this way, and possibly to put one of life's last smiles on the faces of the patients and comfort their anguished families, is actually a gift for us. It's impossible for anyone on our team to serve at the hospice program and not return to work with a far deeper understanding of the true meaning and impact of life and hospitality. (It's no coincidence that *hospice* and *hospitality* share etymological roots.)

Whenever our employees take a leadership role and collect pledges from colleagues in order to participate in an event like the Avon Breast Cancer Walk or the Northeast AIDS Ride, their restaurant matches the money they've collected from their colleagues. If an employee asks for our help with a more personal cause (for example, supporting a special school for someone related to an autistic child), we'll very often say yes. Our restaurants have also pulled together and organized events to raise funds for disaster relief. For example, the catastrophic floods of 1993 that ravaged vast stretches of the Midwest (where I'm from), and an earthquake in western India (where Tabla's executive chef Floyd Cardoz is from), led us to build instant constituencies and host dinners to raise funds for emergency relief. And in response to the devastation of Hurricane Katrina in 2005, each of our restaurants took a leadership role in a national "dine-out" evening sponsored by Share Our Strength called Restaurants for Relief. We donated a percentage of our revenues to Share Our Strength for its relief work in the Gulf. Additionally, we invited our employees to contribute a portion of their paychecks to relief. Together we raised $30,000. The program effectively allowed us to join forces with our staff and our guests to make a meaningful community contribution.

Our efforts to connect with and support our neighborhood through the years have paid off both in the community and for our business. Nowhere is this more apparent than in Union Square, now one of the busiest retail destinations in Manhattan. Way back in May 1986, before Union Square Cafe was even open for Saturday lunch, I agreed to host a brunch on behalf of the Union Square Park Community Coalition. The USPCC was a grassroots group seeking to improve quality of life in and around the park—which was then a dangerous place—and to protect the interests of the greenmarket and the historic neighborhood. We designed our menu around ingredients from the greenmarket (this was years before it became the practice of chefs all over New York to buy seasonal produce there), and raised close to $10,000—not a bad figure for those days.

It was a pivotal day for me because the brunch was the very first project that connected me as a citizen to Union Square. The event also proved to be a marketing coup for our restaurant. Attendees responded so favorably to our brunch that within weeks we launched a regular Saturday Greenmarket Brunch. Everything (appetizer, soup, entrée, dessert) was prepared using products from that morning's greenmarket items.

Union Square has long since become a magnet for the city's chefs—and for anyone who loves fresh food. To this day, between May and October our chefs and sous-chefs (from each of our restaurants as well as Hudson Yards Catering) buy between 80 percent and 90 percent of all of our fruit and vegetables at the greenmarket. For years we have conducted tours of the greenmarket for both adults and school-children, and we invite farmers to our morning "market meetings" to discuss their produce before we use it to demonstrate a recipe.

We also support the Union Square community by participating in the annual Harvest in the Square, an event I had a hand in creating. In the 1990s, Rob Walsh, who had been instrumental in first getting me involved in the redevelopment of Union Square Park, came to me with an idea to raise money for the Fourteenth Street–Union Square Business Improvement District and Local Development Corporation. (That name was an impossible mouthful, so Walsh, the organization's executive director, was commonly called the "mayor of Union Square." He went on to become New York City's very effective Deputy Com-missioner for Small Business.) The original idea was for a $1,000 sit-down dinner with chefs from the top four or five restaurants in the neighborhood, which at that point was filling up with three-star res-taurants. I told Rob, "Why not make it far less exclusive, make it af-fordable for a lot more people who love the park, and let's really brand Union Square as the best-tasting neighborhood in the city? And in-stead of charging $1,000 to a few, let's charge $75 to attract as many people from the community as possible. We should get a big tent and make it a walk-around party with a lot more restaurants involved. We can invite the farmers, too, and try to show the restaurants in the neighborhood how easy it is to buy from the greenmarket."

For an entire decade, the event has been a huge success. Forty-five neighborhood restaurants participate and nearly 1,500 guests attend, under a huge white tent. The party nets over $100,000 with proceeds used for park improvements and restoration projects. Just as the Amish perfected the barn raising, Harvest in the Square has become our local "park raising"—a community joining together to care for its own park. The annual party has raised funds that have been used for large capital projects like new park lighting and the addition of ornate iron fencing.

By the late 1980s, my community involvement was limited to serving on the boards of the Union Square Local Development Corporation and the New York Chapter of the American Institute of Wine and Food (AIWF). The AIWF was a not-for-profit organization founded by Robert Mondavi and Julia Child to educate the masses on the joys of gastronomy. We raised money from culinary events that brought consumers together with producers. I remember organizing a series of ethnic breakfasts—one morning each in Chinatown, in Little India, at a kosher deli, at a Mexican restaurant, and at a good old-fashioned American brunch—to experience and learn how different cultures approached breakfast. We also held microbrew beer tastings (in the days before most people had ever heard the term), wine-and-food dinners, artisanal cheese tastings, champagne dinners, and farmers' events.

For much of the food-loving public these were heady days of learning, and it was a thrill to be along for the exciting ride at the outset of New York's culinary revolution. And being there was good for business. The board of AIWF presented excellent networking opportunities among people—chefs, restaurateurs, consumers, wine makers, journalists, producers, and growers—who were passionate about food. By attending AIWF's national conference, I had the chance, very early in my career, to meet all kinds of industry luminaries and develop meaningful relationships that would serve me well in building our business. I have always believed that networking builds stronger relationships that can lead to good luck for a corporation. But I was putting a lot of my time into AIWF, and it dawned on me that I'd derive even more joy if I could do this for a group that was feeding people in need, and not just educating attendees.

My first chance to engage Union Square Cafe in a philanthropic leadership role came about through serendipity. "Taste of the Nation" was a pioneering benefit organized by Share Our Strength in cities across the United States and Canada. Charging people money to attend a big party where you could walk around to taste small plates

from big-name chefs was still a fresh concept in 1989, and when chef
Lidia Bastianich of Felidia ristorante invited Union Square Cafe to
contribute and serve our food at Taste of the Nation in March 1989,
I was flattered and quickly accepted the invitation, knowing it would
be a great opportunity to showcase our new chef, Michael Romano.

However, I didn't appreciate the experience. All of our pre-event
planning had been about logistics, with little said about the cause
we were supposed to be addressing. It occurred to me during the
course of the evening that I didn't even have any idea what Share
Our Strength actually was. *Bon Appétit* magazine was the chief sponsor of the event, at Lincoln Center, and, more than an event to raise
money to fight hunger, it seemed primarily to be an opportunity for
the magazine to throw a top-toque gourmet party to entertain their
advertisers. At one point, as I stood over a chafing dish, trying to keep
up with scooping food for a long line of guests along with Michael
and our sous-chef, Jamie Leeds, I began muttering under my breath,
"Who and what are we trying to raise money for here, anyway?"

At that moment, the guest holding her plate out in front of me
overheard my impolitic carping. She happened to be Debbie Shore,
who, along with her brother Billy, had founded Share Our Strength
in 1984. Debbie brought Billy over and they introduced themselves.
Turning over the rocks, in a matter of moments we began connecting dots and I learned that Billy Shore knew both my grandfather
Irving Harris and my uncle Bill Harris. Before founding Share Our
Strength Billy had worked for Senator Gary Hart of Colorado and
later Senator Bob Kerrey of Nebraska, both of whom supported investing in early childhood (zero to three) research and programs, a
cause my grandfather and uncle worked for with limitless passion
through an organization called KidsPac. My social gaffe—complain-
ing aloud about the event—was about to create one of my life's most
extraordinary learning and leading opportunities.

When I mentioned to Debbie and Billy that I felt their message
was not coming through clearly, Debbie said, "You're absolutely right.

More people do need to understand that this is an event to help fight hunger. We'd love to tell you more about it, and we could really use your leadership. Since you obviously want the event to be stronger, you need to be its leader. How about sharing your strength next year?"

For the next two years, I took on the responsibility of chairing New York's Taste of the Nation, and I loved it. I convinced the city's best chefs to participate by telling them, "I don't want you to do this unless you're fully committed to fighting hunger." Interestingly, the more chefs I asked not to participate unless they were doing so because they cared about the cause, the more chefs chose to commit themselves. We got World Yacht to contribute use of its largest yacht, the *New Yorker,* and to let us host a 1,400-person party onboard while cruising out to the Statue of Liberty. We raised ticket prices to $200 and got just about everything donated—food, wine, auction items, design, flowers, printing. Even the coat checkers contributed their tips to Share Our Strength. We got the right companies to support the cause and raised serious money in the process of getting them to become sponsors. The event turned into a brilliant confluence of gastronomy, commerce, philanthropy, and fun. Having raised $40,000 at the event at Lincoln Center in 1989, Taste of the Nation now raised $240,000 and then $360,000 in the next two years. It was a stroke of genius when my friend Jim Berrien, then the publisher of *Food and Wine* (owned by American Express Publishing), asked Schieffelin and Somerset (importers of Möet et Chandon) to sponsor Taste of the Nation. The beverage company agreed to donate $100,000 as well as several cases of Dom Perignon as an inducement for attendees to spend more money to arrive early and gain entrance to the "VIP Dom Perignon Lounge." Share Our Strength distributed every penny of our revenues to hunger-relief agencies like City Harvest, God's Love We Deliver, Oxfam International, and Food for Survival, which later became the Food Bank For New York City.

With the help of Jim Berrien and another visionary at American Express, Tom Ryder, I was able to bring Amex on board as a national sponsor, to the tune of $250,000 for each year I chaired the event. In that instance, creating community absolutely led to good luck for Union Square Cafe and me.

But first, the backstory: In the 1980s, Amex had been the dominant charge card for fine dining, especially among those who used it for business entertaining. But by the early 1990s, as a deep recession approached, the company was losing restaurant market share to other credit cards. In no small part, one factor was Amex's attitude: "You need us, so we'll charge what we like. Take it or leave it." American Express had always charged higher "merchant's commission" fees than other credit card companies, but now its arrogance was inciting a revolt. In Boston a large group of restaurateurs now threatened to boycott American Express cards in their establishments, dramatically planning to slice up Amex cards with scissors and dump the plastic pieces into Boston Harbor—a new twist on the Boston tea party.

I had my own reasons to feel miffed about American Express's attitude. The company had a new marketing program called Plus Business. Our local account manager told us that if we agreed to provide discount coupons to cardholders, Amex would drive "plus business" our way—customers who, they claimed, would subsequently spend more money in our restaurant than people using MasterCard or Visa. I couldn't abide the notion of issuing discount or giveaway coupons at Union Square Cafe. The company's arrogant approach was making me furious; it implied, "You need this, and if you don't do it you're stupid."

Around that time, I went home to St. Louis for one of my periodic visits to see my father, who was battling lung cancer. I told him I was angry with American Express and that I was considering joining the boycott. He shook his head. "I understand your frustration with their behavior," he said. "But American Express is a well-established, very successful company that's not going away for a long time. They've got a lot more muscle than you'll ever have. And you're going to lose if you try to fight them."

But I was young and feisty, my restaurant was packed for every lunch and dinner, and I was feeling my oats.

"But we could make a difference," I argued. "We'd be fighting alongside a lot of other restaurants."

"Why don't you figure out a way to embrace them instead ?" my dad urged me. "Maybe they'll listen to you if they feel like you're working with them, and not just one more restaurant owner like all the others."

I could see his point—and I sensed an opportunity to do one of my favorite things, and be a bit of a contrarian. Back in New York I met with Jim Berrien and Tom Ryder—the two friends I had grown to love and admire who ran the magazine publishing side of American Express. I once again told them that I had just attended Share Our Strength's Conference of Leaders—the annual gathering for its network of Taste of the Nation leaders from across the United States and Canada, many of whom were chefs and restaurateurs. I had been struck by our industry's passion for helping Share Our Strength fight hunger, and it was clear to me that more and more restaurants were realizing that participating in a Taste of the Nation event was a really smart way to do something good while also making a special connection with their customers. And everyone involved enjoyed it. This community-marketing model seemed the best of all possible worlds.

"The bulk of the American fine-dining industry is up in arms against your company," I told Jim and Tom. "An amazing way for American Express to re-earn their favor would be to champion a cause that so many chefs and restaurateurs have already shown is very important to them. Now you're seen only as the company that is charging us all more money and imposing your own marketing desires on us." I suggested that they find a way for American Express to put serious dollars on the table and become the national title sponsor for Taste of the Nation. The two men liked the idea, quickly ran it up the corporate flagpole, and succeeded at getting Amex to become the $250,000 title sponsor. At a time when Taste of the Nation had no other national sponsors, this was a trailblazing move for American Express. And by finding a way to embrace the huge company when it was down, and when so many others in our industry were reviling it, I became a friend. My father's advice had been sound. One by one, restaurants across the country took note of the role Amex was playing with SOS, and slowly, but surely, the company began to pick up momentum in rebuilding its relationship with establishments.

Soon thereafter, American Express invited me to do a test radio spot that would be broadcast in the Boston area. They hoped it would defuse the still explosive situation with Boston's merchants. They assured me that the spot would raise the profile of Union Square Cafe. But mainly they wanted me to tout the Amex card for bringing my restaurant "a higher quality, higher-spending customer than any of the credit cards."

I said, "No thanks." That message would sound offensive to those guests of ours who chose to use other charge cards. But I made a counteroffer. "What I *would* do, and do very proudly," I said, "is talk about American Express's incredible generosity in supporting Share Our Strength. For your company to be partnering with our industry for the purpose of fighting hunger is an extraordinary story, one you should be proud of, and I'd be delighted to tell it."

They looked at me as if I were crazy. A cause-related ad by a big corporation was all but unheard of then. Months went by without a response, and I had just about given up hope of hearing from them when an executive from Ogilvy and Mather called me saying that Amex had scrapped the test radio spot in Boston. Instead, they wanted to launch a *national television campaign*. It would tell the story of American Express's work for hunger relief, and they wanted me to appear in it. I thought about the invitation overnight and phoned in my enthusiastic "yes" the next morning.

The commercial was eventually filmed at Union Square Cafe using a big league production company. We staged a scene of people dining late at night. There was a jazz saxophonist playing in the background. The ad cut back and forth between scenes of people dining at Union Square Cafe and cutaway shots of hungry New Yorkers. I talked about hunger in New York and how Share Our Strength raises money so that leftovers could be delivered to shelters in New York City (there was a scene with a City Harvest truck picking up food). "Because American Express has provided the funding," I say, "their dollars are actually going to connect food with someone who needs it."

American Express spent huge amounts of money on the campaign. The commercial reached an enormous audience when it was broadcast during the first inauguration of President Bill Clinton on January 20, 1993, and again during that year's Super Bowl. Two-page print ads with my photo ran in the Sunday *New York Times Magazine* and the *Washington Post Sunday Magazine*. The campaign marked a pivotal moment for me in appreciating the intersection between business and philanthropy. It conclusively identified Union Square Cafe as doing business in a particular way; and because of the public awareness it created, it raised the stakes by encouraging my team and me to find other ways to do even more to support the community.

My ongoing active affiliation with Share Our Strength as a board member has allowed me to meet some extraordinary thinkers. Billy Shore has always recruited an exceptional roster of board members, staff members, and experts in hunger relief, whose ideas have helped shape how my company continues to work for community outreach. What helped me to understand Share Our Strength's work was viewing it as a mutual fund whose expertise was hunger relief. The organization has done all the homework, and has identified the most effective hunger-relief agencies in which to invest. I liked that. I also admired the way it knew how to blend entrepreneurial and not-for-profit cultures. Share Our Strength truly understands how to tap into corporations and encourage profitable, cause-related marketing.

The greatest gift I have received from Share our Strength
founder, Billy Shore—beyond his friendship—is his brilliant
notion that creating community wealth is the most effective way
to achieve lasting social change. Instead of relying exclusively on
individuals to make charitable donations or on governments to
make grants or subsidies (the two traditional—and self-limiting—
means of fund-raising), Share Our Strength has encouraged
the corporate community to create self-sustaining, for-profit
businesses and programs that in and of themselves add consumer
value, build business, and do the community some lasting good.
This creates a virtuous cycle that links the corporate interest in
earning profit to the consumers' desire to affiliate with brands
that embrace social causes they believe in.

I've often seen this model at work. For several years, Calphalon,
the cookware manufacturer, marketed a "Share Our Strength" pot
that was sold in department stores. The packaging prominently featured Share Our Strength's logo, and let the buyer know that $10 of
every purchase would go to fight hunger. For customers browsing
through the housewares section of a department store, this created a
reason to purchase Calphalon's pan rather than any of fifteen other
brands. If the buyer didn't already think the Calphalon pan was best,
here was another outstanding reason to buy it: "When I cook for
myself, I'm going to help feed somebody else. Why wouldn't I want
to support a brand that does that?" The promotion spurred lively
retail activity; Calphalon made more money on sales; and for its percentage, Share Our Strength received close to $250,000 annually.

In the late 1990s the organic yogurt producer Stonyfield Farm
used its plastic container lids to promote Share Our Strength. Stonyfield's founder, Gary Hirshberg, viewed each container lid as a minia-

ture billboard to be used for messages promoting causes he believed were important. Stonyfield's commitment to use its lids to promote the work of Share Our Strength led me to select its product as the main ingredient for our yogurt-based *raita* when we opened Tabla in 1998. We identified it on our menu ("Stonyfield Farm *raita*") and, in return, Tabla got a discount on purchases of the yogurt. It was good business and a satisfying affiliation for both companies.

As I learned with Union Square Park, it's essential to create programming that gives people good reasons to use a park. For that reason, we selected Madison Square Park as the site for our annual Big Apple Barbecue Block Party (BABBP), held over a weekend in mid-June just a couple of blocks from Blue Smoke. For this 'cue-lovers' event, we invite ten of the country's leading barbecue chefs to visit New York and cook their award-winning barbecue right in the middle of Manhattan. In 2006, nearly 110,000 barbecue fans attended BABBP during the two-day event, and devoured over 5,000 pounds of brisket, three dozen whole hogs, and close to 10,000 pounds of ribs. Beyond attracting so many people to enjoy two days of food and music in the park, BABBP makes a contribution from its revenues to the Madison Square Park Conservancy, and in its first three years it raised $140,000 for the organization, which in turn plowed the money into horticulture, and more programming (sculpture, music concerts, performances for kids, readings, and so on).

Because our company is committed to community outreach week after week, year after year, we've also been able to recruit a different kind of employee over time. Certain people are drawn to work for us because of this reputation. The person for whom this stuff is exciting tends also to be someone who intuitively cares about making other people happy. That is what hospitality is all about.

In the hours and days after 9/11, it was quite natural to question the significance of one's own life role or profession. I know I was asking myself, "After all this, who really cares about restaurants?" Quickly, though, I answered my own doubts. In their ability to nourish and nurture, and to provide a buoyant place for human beings to be with one another, and to smile, restaurants—as a healing agent—seemed more relevant than ever.

The collective experience of 9/11 caused the entire city to put down differences and pull together as never before. At that time I was the chairman of the Restaurant Committee for NYC and Company, the city's tourism marketing organization, and in the first weeks after 9/11 we met practically every day. At first, we tried to figure out what we could do for the rescue workers and for the bereaved families. Next, we tried to figure out what we could do for our community of restaurants, many of which were empty and in financial jeopardy. The downtown restaurant community especially was paralyzed. As far north as our Union Square–Gramercy Park–Madison Square neighborhood, one could smell the acrid, burning rubble for two months after the towers fell.

It was especially gratifying that in a crisis of this magnitude, the greatest strength of the hospitality industry expressed itself. By following their natural instincts, New York's chefs and restaurants, including the members of our own team, knew exactly how to play a special role in aiding and comforting other New Yorkers.

4. Suppliers

These days, more and more people want to do business with a company in whose business principles they believe, not just with a company whose roast chicken and creamy polenta they find delicious. We're the same way when choosing suppliers. At the outset, we make our own business values and goals very clear, and we try to understand theirs. We look for common ground, and we put a premium on integrity. We're looking for enlightened companies whose teams consist of "51 percenters" who are passionate about what they do. Just as we ask our employees to join us in community outreach programs, we admire suppliers who do so.

We express care for our fourth core group—our network of pur-

veyors and vendors—by building loyal, mutually respectful relationships and by seeking win-win transactions. The most fundamental
way we accomplish this is by doing what we say we're going to do. If
we strike a deal for certain payment terms, we honor it. Saying what
we will do implies an agreement to also say what we cannot do. If un-
foreseen circumstances arise—a compressor breaks, for instance, re-
quiring a large cash outlay for repairs—and we unexpectedly cannot
meet our obligations to a supplier, we need to be absolutely upfront
and ask the supplier's permission to work out an alternative solution.

Not long ago we made a shift in several of our restaurants from
Evian bottled water to Fiji. Primarily, this was because I had heard
from more and more of our chefs, staff members, and guests that they
preferred the taste of Fiji, which they said "seemed wetter," more
effectively quenched their thirst, and had a less "oily" texture than
Evian.

I had insisted on using Evian for years, out of loyalty as well as for
emotional reasons. The first time I had ever seen bottled water was
when my family took me on my inaugural trip to France when I was
seven years old. I kept a bottle of Evian next to my bed at night and
loved snapping its plastic cap on and off. I grew up associating Evian
with the adventure of traveling to France, as well as with memories
of dining in excellent restaurants there, and so we began serving it. In
fact, I'd credit Evian with playing an important supporting role in the
legitimization of fine dining in America in the late 1980s and early
1990s. Restaurants that wanted to be taken seriously carried Evian. It
was like having a French stamp of authenticity and approval.

Second, through Audrey's role in advertising sales for *Gourmet*
magazine, we became quite friendly with some terrific people at
Evian, one of her accounts. Evian's CEO, David Daniel, and his suc-
cessor, Mark Rodriguez, were both brilliant market-builders and ambassadors for their brand. I always felt intensely loyal to them. Through
those relationships, I helped persuade Evian to sponsor Share Our
Strength's Taste of the Nation events, using the same logic that had

earlier convinced American Express. For several years, Evian was spending approximately $500,000 each year to help Share Our Strength fight hunger and to reach their target fine-dining audience. If all things were equal in terms of product quality and pricing, Evian's commitment to Share Our Strength had given them an edge with me (and others in my industry) over any erstwhile competitor.

But in later years, Evian had undergone significant changes in management leadership and distribution; with direction from its French management, the company had started to retrench in its sponsorship of Share Our Strength, cutting back its financial contributions as well as its overall marketing commitment to the fine-dining community by eliminating a large part of its consumer advertising budget. It was no coincidence that now, for the first time, I was open to hearing the enthusiastic comments about Fiji's quality; and three of our restaurants made the change. Before doing so, however, I felt obliged to call a manager at Share Our Strength to help ascertain any potential conflicts. "I want to make sure that this move on our part will in no way cause Evian to further remove its support and undermine your fight against hunger."

"They've already been diminishing their financial support," the manager said. "You should do whatever you need to do for your business, but thanks for caring enough to ask."

When we interviewed Fiji, we asked: "Will you join us in supporting causes that are important to us and our community? We'll ask you only when we think it will actually help your business." Their answer was resoundingly positive.

Fiji came on board, and in 2004 we asked the company to become a sponsor of our annual Autumn Harvest dinner for SOS, an event Evian had cosponsored for years. Again, out of loyalty to our relationship, we asked ourselves if we should invite Evian one last time. We decided not to. But Fiji then asked if it could donate just product, not money. (Sponsors generally contribute both.) We were very honest: "Evian has sponsored us historically with both product *and* dollars. We made a conscious decision not to go back to them because it might be uncomfortable now that we have Fiji at Eleven Madison Park"— that was where the Autumn Harvest dinner was held. "But we can't ask you to do less than Evian did. That wouldn't be fair to Evian, or to Share Our Strength." Fiji, fortunately, found the cash.

This isn't business as usual; most businesses ordinarily just go with the best supplier that offers the best price. Of course pricing is an important calculation; but for us, excellence, hospitality, and shared values must also be prominent factors in the selection process. It's hard for me to imagine deriving so much pleasure from the restaurant business were it not for the important and enjoyable relationships we've had with our suppliers. And the range of those relationships is broad: greenmarket farmers, wine producers, meat suppliers, kitchen repair people, cheese mongers, printers, graphic designers. The enthusiasm with which we approach each day is infused with a deep respect for how well we represent those people who have supplied us with the tools to succeed.

5. *Investors*

It's not natural for a young child to be inclined to share. Until we were taught by parents and teachers about the importance of sharing, none of us wanted to do it. Sharing something important to us with someone else always meant that there would be less of it for us. With patience, maturity, and practice at the art of negotiating and compromise, most of us eventually learned that sharing a toy, a candy bar, or even a friend could actually enrich the experience of life. Less of something for us now could ultimately yield more.

That's the way it is when you choose to take on investors for your business. I suppose if I had all the money in the world, I might choose to own 100 percent of the risk and the financial returns. But I've learned over time that while the child in me may want the pie all to myself, the wisest thing I can do in my own self-interest is to share pieces of that pie with others. By selling or even giving away some pieces, I've never given up having control in preparing the recipe, but I have always ended up with a bigger, better-tasting pie.

For that reason, in each of my businesses I have chosen to share ownership with managing partners who can earn and purchase a slice of the pie through their hard work and their excellent, effective adherence to our business values. Ethics, loyalty, longevity, and the highest possible leadership skills also count for a lot. These are leaders who have helped make others on our team successful, whose judgment mirrors my own, and who, above all, are on my side. There's nothing original about my discovery that a business stands a better chance at thriving when an ownership point of view is present. Clearly, had I chosen not to share equity with leading managers, I would have diminished my own opportunities to expand our business, and shortchanged the potential of each of the restaurants within my company.

As our company has grown, it has done so with the benefit of funding from an array of sources. I've never done a deal without investing a sizable amount of my own funds. If I'm not willing to make a personal bet on the successful outcome of a project, why should I expect anyone else to do so? Additionally, I welcome and encourage investments from my managing partners. It gives comfort and confidence to an outside investor—whether it's a bank, an organization, or an individual—to know that those of us charged with running the business have our own "skin" in the game. Beginning with my first restaurant investment at Union Square Cafe, I invited a few close relatives to join me in taking on the financial risk of opening a new restaurant. I had no track record as an entrepreneur, and their faith in me was clearly an act of love and support more than a reasoned investment. Fortunately, the restaurant's performance exceeded our expectations, and 100 percent of those investors subsequently chose to come along for the ride at Gramercy Tavern.

It wasn't until the simultaneous openings of Eleven Madison Park and Tabla—at the collective cost of more than $11 million—that I actually needed to solicit significant additional outside funding just to get the places built and open. With some trepidation I went first to my grandfather, who was then eighty-eight years old and whom I hadn't invited to invest in either of my first two restaurants. His response was characteristically direct and tough: "I'm in a position where I could take on the entire piece of the investment you're talking about, but I'm not going to do it. You need to find other, nonfamily people to buy into your plans. You need to know whether this is actually a good investment. Family members alone won't tell you. When you find other support, come tell me and we'll discus it further."

I was deflated. Why was he making this so unnecessarily complicated? I turned to a very small group of friends whose combination of financial wherewithal, sharp business acumen, and longtime loyalty to me made them seem like excellent candidates. I explained that these would be long-term investments, and that the time until payback—assuming the restaurants were winners and survived—would be lengthy. We'd be spending quite a lot to build the restaurants, and would be further delaying any return on their investment by taking a necessary leadership role in the revitalization of the park and neighborhood right outside the front door of the restaurants. These restaurants were the kind that might one day become New York institutions. At that point, they'd also provide a solid financial return—we hoped. For any rational investor, from a purely financial standpoint the time frame for this investment was only mildly attractive lined up against any number of other possibilities.

Despite that, the funding flowed in. People trusted me and my management team, and were above all pleased with the opportunity to affiliate themselves with our new restaurants and with our existing approach to the restaurant business. They also believed in the investments as a solid long-term play.

I've repeated that model with each subsequent business and have accepted that my grandfather's advice was sage. By taking on the right kind of outside investors, we've not only given our business the fuel necessary to grow, but enlarged our spheres of information, advice, wisdom, contacts, and influence. The fiduciary responsibility I feel toward our investors (both managing partners and outside investors) has also sharpened my own discipline as a businessman to provide a healthy, sustainable return on their investment.

Investors are a crucial link in the virtuous cycle of enlightened hospitality. Without trusting, satisfied, confident investors we cannot continue to grow, and therefore cannot provide opportunities for those members of our staff who are ready to grow. Nor can we reinvest in and re-up the kind of operational excellence that made them want to be associated with our restaurants in the first place. Our investors understand—and believe—that by taking their place in line behind our other chief stakeholders, they stand an even better chance to reap sound, ongoing financial rewards. They are buying into a business whose employees, customers, community, and suppliers have been given good reason to support our success. From the moment I first went into business, I was far more focused on excellence and hospitality than on profitability. Today, earning a profit is still not the primary destination for my business, but I know that it is the fuel that drives everything else we do. Whether you call it enlightened hospitality or enlightened self-interest, it's the safest and surest business model I know.

CHAPTER 12

Context, Context, Context

I DRIVE MY COMPANY WITH an eye on the same kinds of destinations—excellence, growth and profitability—that most other leaders would have. No matter what the destination, my style as CEO is to steer Union Square Hospitality Group along a route that represents a balanced quest for safety, for thrills, and, mostly, for taking the road less traveled. I tend to view new business opportunities as chances to explore and learn, rather than as a license to expand the company without limits, at any cost. I'm not hell-bent on opening the greatest number of restaurants we are capable of operating. That would feel reckless and would make it nearly impossible for a company whose success is based on meaningful human interaction to retain its soul. I am not too interested in making deals just because we can make them. Since there will never be more than twenty-four hours in a day, the careful choices I make about how to spend that time determine the style with which my colleagues and I will spend it.

I have always believed that you can tell as much about a company by the deals it does not make as by those it does. Much of the success we have had has resulted from saying "no, thank you" to opportunities that, while initially compelling, would not have been wise to pursue. In fact, by avoiding some potential mistakes, I sometimes wonder whether we've made much more money by choosing the right things to say *no* to, than we have made from those things we've chosen to say yes to. I often try to measure the money we haven't lost and all the quality and soul we haven't squandered. There is much to learn by understanding what goes into a "no" decision, and there's an art to analyzing the deals you don't make.

Over the years, we've declined some amazingly generous offers to create restaurants in casinos, chic hotels, upscale shopping malls, train stations, sports stadiums, airports, and office buildings. Many decisions to decline have been primarily driven by our own sense that the framework within which we'd be doing business just didn't feel right. It's similar to a gallery owner who, having first selected a wonderful piece of art, must not only take exceptional care to frame, hang, and light it in the most careful, appropriate way, but also to ask the most important question: Does this piece of art even belong in this gallery? To make such decisions with confidence and clarity involves knowing who you are, and precisely what your product or brand represents for your stakeholders. Even when the context feels right, before entering into a deal I also make a very careful "gut check" of my own sense of personal balance, knowing that a new project will challenge me (and my colleagues) in every possible way.

Sometimes my senior team and I make as many as fifteen exploratory forays to learn about a new venture that we eventually don't undertake. Each step is a process of learning about the specifics of the deal and—even more—an opportunity to "try it on for size," to see how saying yes would feel. Too many people throw themselves into a deal without considering whether or not their business actually needs the deal or should be undertaking it in the first place. In the process of exploring a new venture, we make repeated visits to the prospective site; meet with the landlords, developers, or prospective partners (in their office as well as ours—since you can learn a lot by seeing and feeling how people conduct their own business in their own environment); get the flavor of the surrounding community (thinking ahead about what role we might one day play there); and assess our prospects and capacity for fielding a winning staff.

THE "YES" CRITERIA FOR NEW VENTURES

1. The opportunity fits and enhances our company's overall strategic goals and objectives.

2. The opportunity represents a chance to create a business venture that is perceived as groundbreaking, trailblazing, and fresh.

3. The timing is right for our company's capacity to grow with excellence, especially in terms of our having enough key employees who are themselves interested and ready to grow.

4. We believe we have the capacity to be category leaders within whatever niche we are pursuing.

5. We believe our existing businesses will benefit and improve by virtue of or notwithstanding our pursuing this new opportunity.

6. We feel excited and passionate about this idea. Pursuing it will be an opportunity to learn, grow, and have fun!

7. We are excited about doing business in this community.

8. The context is the right fit. Our restaurant and our style of doing business will be in harmony with its location.

9. An in-depth pro forma analysis convinces us that it is a wise and safe investment.

The greatest source of entrepreneurial inspiration for me has always been my rich storehouse of personal memories and interests, from which I draw ideas for new business ventures. For instance, I have always loved sports—and I continue to follow every game of my hometown team, the St. Louis Cardinals. It has occurred to me from time to time that there might be something to add to the quality and kinds of food available at sporting events, a category which has certainly improved since my youth, but which still has a long way to go. There must be an enormous number of people who love both sports *and* good food. Why should the two be mutually exclusive? And a little more hospitality at the ballpark certainly wouldn't diminish a fan's enjoyment of the game.

Now that our company has begun to gain experience in the kind of businesses—off-site catering, burgers, hot dogs, frozen custard, barbecue—that could easily be adapted to a sports stadium, I'd be willing to listen carefully if the right opportunity to do something distinctive in this niche presented itself at the right time. Sports are entertainment, and so is eating out. An excellent food experience can enhance the fun of watching your favorite team win, and even take some of the sting out of a defeat.

One of the more unusual business opportunities I've seen was actually presented to us by a house of worship, asking if we might be interested in opening a café on its premises. Manhattan has a number of beautiful old churches sitting on prime real estate. In recent years many have apparently gone underutilized, with fewer people attending church regularly. Churches often have a next-door auxiliary building that can be used as a community center or reception hall. The idea was to create a popular, well-run café in the adjoining space as a means to entice more people to come to worship and to realize some income for the congregation. The church was in the same neighborhood as our restaurants, and the proposal was definitely worth at least one meeting because it satisfied both our community and our "groundbreaking idea" criteria. But there was no need to go forward. Where would it lead? Which of our staff members would find this a satisfying move in their careers? Where was our passion for operating a church café?

We have considered very lucrative proposals whereby we would open a second unit of one of our existing restaurants in another city, such as Las Vegas, Miami, Atlantic City, or Tokyo. From a short-term financial standpoint it has been frustrating to turn down some of these proposals, but either the timing or the context discouraged a "yes." For instance, the underlying premise of Las Vegas—the world's most successful marketer of illusion and fantasy—makes it an improbable context for an authentic restaurant possessing soul. Since we have built our company's long-term success in New York on a foundation of a genuine sense of place, rather than by selling illusion, those options didn't feel like the proper context. This has been particularly true of our restaurants named and created explicitly for their locations. Union Square Cafe, Gramercy Tavern, and Eleven Madison Park are not concepts. They are restaurants of, by, and for their communities. It's important for me to understand that and act accordingly.

Of course, there may yet come a time when the context, timing, and value feel just right for us to open something in Las Vegas, or perhaps in Tokyo, whose restaurant-going public seems to adore all things "New York." For example, I would not rule out opening a Blue Smoke or Tabla in Las Vegas. For me, that context feels more appropriate for a restaurant with a strong theme. After all, opening a barbecue restaurant and an Indian fusion restaurant in New York required a certain culinary poetic license; doing so in Las Vegas would be no different. And the challenge could be thrilling. But I would have to be very careful before going forward. I would first have to believe that, say, Blue Smoke was on a very solid, steady course at home in New York. Next I'd need to feel confident that our organization had enough depth, and enough managerial and culinary capacity, so that I would not have to be the one traveling continually to Las Vegas or Tokyo or London or wherever. If I were to do that, I would be putting into jeopardy not only my sense of corporate balance, but also my sense of personal balance and my preference to spend as much time as possible with my family.

Another serious consideration is that wherever and whenever we open a new restaurant we must have the talent and capacity on all levels to meet our guests' expectations for high quality. And if our existing businesses are not constantly improving, then expansion loses all of its merit. Think of a balloon: it isn't really a balloon until it's inflated, but as soon as you blow too much air into it, it's going to pop. Having seen firsthand the consequences when my father expanded his business too rapidly, I am wary of blowing too much air into our balloon. Often, when businesses fail in our industry it's because of too much expansion; quality suffered and the organization couldn't handle it.

As my company's leader, I have certainly learned to be decisive with an appropriate sense of urgency, but I always prefer to make my decisions after first building consensus among various colleagues, whose unique vantage points give me further confidence to move forward. This process can be lengthy, but so long as the spirit of any decision is consistent with what I'd want, bringing others' views to the table allows us to move forward with a more fully realized plan supported by those who are responsible for its execution. Our decision-making about whether or not to pursue new deals is always sharpest when I call on members of my advisory board to advocate on behalf of their *primary role* in our company.

First I call on our senior vice president of strategic business development, David Swinghamer, as our "secretary of the future and forward movement." He is our minister of deals; and he is especially gifted at imagining, structuring, designing, and developing new projects. He also creates and analyzes financial models and pro formas. I rely on our senior vice president for people, Paul Bolles-Beaven, to tell me if we have the requisite depth of human capacity and essential training systems we'll need for more growth. Our senior vice president of operations, Richard Coraine, is my secret weapon for assessing whether we can actually execute a plan. He knows what it takes to make things work at the level of excellence expected from us. Our culinary senior vice president, Michael Romano, who excels at carefully figuring out the specifics of any recipe, helps to stop a half-baked plan, contributes essential know-how to kitchen design, and contributes his wise culinary counsel to ensure that what we end up with is delicious.

I meet with this "kitchen cabinet" for ninety minutes every Tuesday morning to discuss and debate the strategic direction of our company. We also include our chief adviser and "wisdom keeper," Richard Goldberg, a penetrating thinker and brilliant teacher who assumed that role for us after his retirement as a partner at the law firm Proskauer Rose.

Also at the table is Jenny Dirksen, our director of community investment, who's there to take minutes to assure that we follow through on agreements and do what we say we're going to do. She is our "agenda keeper." Each participant may initiate and "own" a weekly agenda item so long as he or she relays it to Jenny by the end of the previous week and provides the rest of us with any supporting collateral materials so we can prepare for the discussion in advance. As an experienced colleague whose views are valued, Jenny is free to express dissenting, supporting, or new perspectives on whatever it is we're discussing. These meetings give me a balanced input on decisions I'll need to make about our company, with the point of view of just about all of our stakeholders represented by a trusted associate.

Even after all the business aspects of a prospective new deal are discussed, dissected, and examined, I always call on Audrey, who, as my "secretary of life balance," generally has an opinion as to whether a presumably good business decision is or isn't a good thing for me and our family.

Audrey is the first to notice when I'm out of balance, and call me on it. She knows that I tend to approach a new opportunity the way mountain climbers assess another mountain. It's a tempting challenge that may look quite good from afar; but on closer scrutiny, many opportunities are far from good. I'm curious to see the view going up the mountain, and I'm curious to see it from on top of the mountain. One aspect of climbing I especially enjoy is the adventure and challenge of getting to know all the people with whom I'll collaborate along the way. Each business journey attracts a new and different group of players—chef, general manager, cooks, waiters, hosts, reservationists, managers, bookkeepers. The joy I derive from creating something new with a fresh ensemble is a major part of what I enjoy about growth. I also check in with a small group of longtime trusted friends and mentors before I make a decision. Many of them are acquaintances and even customers, and some have become investors in our new restaurants. Their business perspectives and expertise have often proved indispensable. They also know me well enough to call me on the carpet when that is warranted—always doing so out of a sense of support, and with respect. I've taken great care to surround myself with highly capable people of integrity, each of whom brings something different to the table, and often something I am lacking. "What are you *thinking?*" is neither an uncommon nor an unwelcome response to some of my unbridled dreaming.

It's David's role to explore and help create new business ventures that are true to our strategic vision and to further the dialogue with a prospective business partner. If things advance to a second conversation, David and I then discuss the project with our other partners, who most often shoot holes in it. Michael brings thoughtful balance to this group, being somewhat risk-averse and highly analytical. Richard Coraine is the ultimate realist. He knows what it takes to launch a new business, and he doesn't mince words. He also knows food and wine and lives for the tireless discovery of the best. He's actively involved in the selection of chefs and general managers. He'll most often stick to his guns whenever our growth seems to outpace our ability to execute at the highest levels of quality. After all, when something goes awry, he and his operations team will be the ones most responsible for fixing it. Paul keeps us focused on the quality and capacities of the people who work in our organization, knowing that they are our core strength. He's the adviser who best knows how much or how little "people depth" we have at any given time. And as the only one of my colleagues who's been with me since day one in 1985, Paul also has a deep knowledge of what makes me—and us—tick.

I actively seek and benefit from my partners' input, a process that often generates some healthy tension among us. The conversation is always candid, passionate, and constructive. I carefully weigh all of their views as well as my own gut as I study our options. Making a unilateral decision to grow is not my style, and I believe that such a decision won't lead to optimum success down the road. Being in agreement is important so that when we go into the new business, we'll be a more effective team and better able to excel.

I DON'T REGRET ANY of the "no" decisions we have made, but to this day I have occasional misgivings about passing up an opportunity to create a new restaurant in the Metropolis Cafe space next door to Union Square Cafe in the early 1990s. Even though I am entirely convinced that this was the right decision for our company at the time, it's about the only deal we passed up that I continue to think of, primarily because I walk by the space nearly every day.

Metropolis Cafe had opened just days before Union Square Cafe in 1985; and more than any other restaurant space overlooking the park, the Metropolis, on the northwest corner of East Sixteenth Street and Union Square West, benefited from the increased development and energy surrounding Union Square. Nowadays, the park is almost always filled with a diverse group of residents, businesspeople, students, shoppers, theatergoers, and tourists. The Metropolis space fronts directly on the square, and along its long East Sixteenth Street side, contiguous to Union Square Cafe, it has a narrow strip of a terrace that is a compelling place to sit and watch an endless parade of passersby, not unlike a café on the Via Veneto in Rome. Our two restaurants shared a landlord, and I had a neighborly relationship with the outgoing restaurateur, so I was given the opportunity to take a first look. The context and location were ideal; the issue was the timing, which was off by a couple of years. Intrigued though I was, I just did not have it in me then to open a second restaurant. I still wasn't ready emotionally; nor were we prepared as a business. In 1991 I was still struggling with whether or not I would or should ever expand my company.

Despite any second thoughts about having passed up that space and missing out on operating a bustling, highly profitable café with outdoor seating just off the park, I know I made the right decision at that time. Given our lack of managerial depth at all levels coupled with my own ambivalence, a restaurant in that space would likely have proved problematic. And had I said yes, Gramercy Tavern would never have been born three years later.

Metropolis Cafe was the last remaining great space adjacent to Union Square Park. That frontier had closed, but by 1996, and with Gramercy Tavern beginning to hit its stride, I thought the timing was right for us to begin thinking about the next project. I now knew that the gestation period for one of my restaurants was often three years from initial idea to opening day. I had become determined to be a restaurant pioneer on Madison Square Park, and to take a leading role in that park's restoration. I remember thinking that creating a restaurant overlooking Madison Square Park—desolate as it was back then—would be like flying to the moon and planting the first flag.

In order to do a gut check on how much I really want to take a space or do a deal, I always ask myself whether I would do this deal if it were given to me for free. That sounds simplistic, I know, but it works. Believe it or not, my answer to this question is most often "no."

When Tom Colicchio and I scoured the city in 1993 in search of a location for the new restaurant we were cooking up together (which would eventually become Gramercy Tavern), we went one day to the site of the recently shuttered Coach House Restaurant in Greenwich Village. We walked through the depressing space, which had once been a glorious American restaurant—it received four stars from Mimi Sheraton in the *New York Times* and was a favorite of James Beard's. Now it was musty and depressing: there are few things more putrid than the stench of a dead restaurant. After touring the place, we walked across the street, looked at the building, and reflected.

"I don't think I would want that even if it were free," I said. Tom wholeheartedly agreed, and we passed it up.

Not long thereafter, Mario Batali and Joe Bastianich opened the excellent and enormously popular Babbo in that very space, creating magic within those walls. Their guts told them that the space was right for their vision. It just wasn't right for ours.

Selecting a restaurant space is a lot like trying on a pair of new shoes. The style has to be right, the size has to fit, and they have to feel good, or I simply won't buy them. If I did buy them, I'd never wear them. I've declined a significant number of sweetheart deals from developers that were essentially offered for free. I understand how that resistance can frustrate my partners and investors. But the fact that something is free alone doesn't make it wise or compelling to proceed.

Also, there really is no such thing as a free lunch. We've learned that even when a landlord or developer is generous in offering to contribute some or all of the costs associated with building a new restaurant, there are proprietary expectations to consider that are real and very natural. For example, The Modern is our restaurant, but it must operate in harmony with the overall goals of the Museum of Modern Art. We are prohibited from using our restaurants there for weddings or fund-raisers—two typical sources of profitable business. Eleven Madison Park and Tabla are also our restaurants, but they operate with sensitivity to the business goals of the mammoth office building (headquarters of Credit Suisse) in which they are housed. We must keep the building informed of every new initiative we undertake, and sometimes our business is affected by its needs. For example, after 9/11 the building increased its security, and we had to decrease the serving area of Tabla's outdoor patio to accommodate a huge concrete planter constructed to prevent a wayward vehicle from penetrating the building.

I don't take a "rearview mirror" approach to life. Generally, I drive looking straight ahead. But I do try to spend time analyzing the wisdom of choices I've made not to go forward with new ventures; and that analysis requires abundant self-awareness and some hindsight. There are a handful of difficult "nos"—projects that I thought would have been the right fit for our company but that presented themselves at the wrong time. Other assessments have led me to conclude it was the right time for a project, but the wrong fit. A yes decision has to meet both of those criteria. My regret isn't that I came to the wrong conclusion, but that I made a difficult, though correct, decision about what our company needed at a precise moment in time.

I remember the difficult decisions my colleagues and I made to decline opportunities to open restaurants at the W Hotel and the Gramercy Park Hotel in Manhattan. In 1997, just as Starwood Hotels was planning to launch its new "W" brand, senior executives reached out to us to discuss creating the restaurant for their first W Hotel in New York, on Lexington Avenue and Fiftieth Street. I had three core concerns. First, the timing was definitely wrong. These discussions took place while we were in the process of conceiving and designing Eleven Madison Park and Tabla. That double project alone had forced me to question whether or not I could maintain excellence at my two existing restaurants while simultaneously opening and operating two new restaurants at 11 Madison Avenue. Some people already thought we were crazy to be opening two ambitious fine-dining places at once, so adding another new project—no matter how exciting—would have been mad. It would take attention, focus, and time to develop the kind of soul necessary to make the two new restaurants into great restaurants. I didn't feel we needed another project.

The second issue was location: I was still insisting that I needed to be able to walk to each of my restaurants from home within five minutes. (The first exception I made, and only after nineteen years, was for the opportunity to create a restaurant and cafés for MoMA.)

The third issue was context. Here I was thinking of the W Hotels brand itself. The Starwood executives I met were extremely effective at communicating how they would position their new brand. What they described was a trendy, hip, sexy, more youthful version of a Four Seasons hotel. They were out to attract high-end, experienced travelers looking for a bit of nightclub in their hotel experience. But anytime I hear or sense "trendy" (as opposed to "enduring") as an important aspect of what's going on, my antennae go up. It all comes down to knowing what you stand for and putting your product in the proper context. None of that description sounded like any of the restaurants I had opened to date, and so we passed up the offer. Neither the timing nor location nor the context fit.

In 1999, not long after we'd opened Eleven Madison Park and Tabla, Starwood's developers approached us again, this time about creating a restaurant for their next big W Hotel, to be situated in the renovated landmark Guardian Life Building, just off Union Square. The timing now felt right, the location was perfect, and the W had successfully realized the initial, very hip vision of its brand; but the context still didn't pass my gut check. Tabla, whose sensuous flavors and décor were attracting a dynamic clientele, might have been an apt concept, but we had just opened it eight blocks to the north. Once again, we passed up the offer.

In 2004 we were invited by the hotelier Ian Schrager (then the owner of the Royalton and the Hudson Hotel in New York and the Delano in Miami) to open a restaurant as part of his very upscale renovation of the Gramercy Park Hotel. It overlooked another gorgeous park in New York, and it was a tempting opportunity. David Swinghamer and I knew we should closely examine its context, timing, and value for our company. The hotel was about as centrally and perfectly located as anything could possibly be, directly across the street from Gramercy Park, just blocks from our office and five of our restaurants, and a stone's throw away from my home. Given our history of wanting to connect restaurants with parks and to be on parks, we met twice with Schrager. He lavished praise on our restaurants and discussed the generous business terms he had in mind, which were impossible to ignore. I sat there thinking, *This will be a huge, lucrative business for someone. How can we not do it?*

Schrager, famous for having founded Studio 54 in 1977 with the late Steve Rubell, described his vision for his new hotel as a "downtown version of the Pierre," a classy grande dame of a hotel that overlooks Central Park, and said he was ready to create his own enduring legacy—one that would be a perfect context for the kind of "New York institution" we were known to create.

Still, I was wary. "I want to make sure that we're not putting a trendy frame on a traditional painting here," I told him. "You may say you want nothing more than to have our painting hanging in your hotel, but as much as I admire your style, it's quite different from ours."

"You've got to trust me," he said. "I've changed. No more Page Six. We're going for a low profile. For quality. This is going to be my masterpiece. I'll even share the bar business and give you the banquet opportunities for your new catering company. Trust me. You are perfect for this." He was beginning to be convincing.

By our ballpark calculations, he was handing us a potential $12 million business. I was almost willing to ignore my gut and take a leap of faith on the context, considering how effectively he had addressed all our concerns.

Against that temptation, I spent a week arguing with myself: *This is a born-again Ian Schrager. He's no longer interested in hot places, not interested in the* New York Post's *Page Six. Not interested in paparazzi and gossip. His company has upscale hotels all over the world. He says he wants to do something of substance that will stand the test of time. That's precisely why he's calling us. If he merely wanted to create a hot new restaurant, he could have called any number of other restaurateurs all over the world with whom he has relationships. They would say yes in a heartbeat.*

The deal was favorable. David wanted us to explore the strategic fit: would there be abundant banquet space that could be served by our forthcoming new company, Hudson Yards Catering? Paul wondered if the new restaurant would provide growth opportunities for any of our top staff members, and, as importantly, whether or not we had enough of them to go around. Was anyone on our team ready to be promoted to chef or general manager? Looking ahead, would anyone be prepared in thirty months, when the hotel was to open? Audrey had another wise question. Perhaps this restaurant was *too* well located: "Do you really want to walk right by your restaurant every morning and night as you walk the dog and take the kids to school? You'll never get away from it." Also, Schrager's restaurant would butt up against the enormous project we had just undertaken at the Museum of Modern Art. Even though the hotel opening would be nearly three years away, we were so involved with the launch of our MoMA restaurants that there wasn't even enough time or mind space to dream. Saved by timing! It kept me from soul-searching over whether the context was truly right. Tempting as this offer was, we passed it up.

There's another kind of "road not taken"—a decision that falls between a definitive no and an unequivocal yes. A potentially excellent venture may not be something we should pursue at the time of the offer, but might very well become right in due time. For example, JetBlue Airways approached us to get into the business of airport food kiosks. It was worth listening just for the opportunity to learn more about an engaging company whose culture of excellence and employees-first hospitality seemed so closely aligned with ours. The JetBlue officials explained that the opportunity had enormous growth potential, given the significant amount of "dwell time" travelers now spend in airports because of the increased security after 9/11, and because the airline does not serve passenger meals. The sales potential appeared quite large. "We love your restaurants," their people told us. "We love the way you do business. It feels consistent with our culture. We want to be on the cutting edge of this business and we'd like to talk to you about it."

We were delighted to meet them at their hub, John F. Kennedy International Airport, and take a good look at their blueprints and plans for their terminal. But once again, the timing wasn't right for us. With a year to go before opening at MoMA, we were entirely focused on that project and lacked the additional organizational capacity we'd need to succeed at this new opportunity. But by exploring it, we did realize that the time might come someday for us to venture into the airport food business. The risk in saying "not yet" is that an opportunity could be taken by some other, more prepared company. Still, our hope was that if we built a solid relationship with JetBlue and did not put our reputation for (and ability to deliver) quality in jeopardy, some aspect of the opportunity might one day jibe with our own timing. I trusted that there could come a time when we would have the operational, tactical, and human capacity to pull it off, especially since we were just about to build a large off-site kitchen facility for our Hudson Yards Catering venture. (Hudson Yards was a logical outgrowth of our deal with the Museum of Modern Art, for which we were to become the "preferred caterer." It also made sense to launch an off-premises catering business as an effective and profitable way to extend our brand of culinary excellence and enlightened hospitality into the off-premises event niche.)

Moreover, we were developing businesses—Blue Smoke, Shake Shack, and Cafe 2—that could be adapted smoothly for airport terminals. There might even one day be a way to open a Bread Bar concession stand for Indian "street" food, or to create something new from scratch that would effectively add to the dialogue on how food is viewed and enjoyed in airports.

Timing is everything. There is an important art not only to determining whether one should or should not go into a deal, but to knowing whether one *might* want to go into such a deal somewhere down the road. Especially in cases where timing was the decisive factor in *not* making a deal, there is value in remaining in close contact with the potential future partner. While it's true that today's potential business deal may later evaporate, it also may one day evolve into something bigger, better, and more richly textured. Patience has its rewards.

I want to expand our company on my own terms. My unwavering, long-term vision of our company is that everything else is subsidiary to *context*—no matter how seductive a prospective deal may appear. In the early 2000s, we were shown plans for, and briefly flirted with opening, a restaurant in Manhattan's enormous Time Warner Center at Columbus Circle. One fundamental issue was that a number of other elite dining establishments would also be opening there. That clustering of excellent eateries was the reason developers felt the complex would be so successful—they believed the restaurants would constitute a critical mass. But I didn't feel especially comfortable joining a collection of great restaurants in a Manhattan shopping mall, no matter how beautiful it was supposed to be.

In almost every way, the opportunity at Time Warner didn't feel ideal for us. First, beyond my own personal preferences, I believe that other New Yorkers also prefer to dine out at street-level restaurants that are themselves destinations, rather than being ensconced in higher floors of a shopping center. Second, the mall itself, and peoples' experience of going to the mall, was not a frame that seemed right or would add any value for any restaurant that we might open there. Third, opening in the Time Warner Center would not have marked any kind of growth or evolution in the kind of company we are: There was no true community to engage (with the possible exception of Jazz at Lincoln Center), and there was no niche we could creatively fill. It was a deal I knew we didn't need.

I became convinced that I was making the right decision the day I drove my daughter Hallie, who was then eight years old, home from a weekend soccer game. In slow traffic, we inched by the Columbus Circle site, which was then just a deep construction pit. "What would you think," I asked Hallie, "if Daddy opened a restaurant there?" She stared over at the hole in the ground. "Why would you open a restaurant in there?" she asked.

"Oh, it's going to be a beautiful new building," I explained, there's going to be a fancy hotel (the Mandarin Oriental), a beautiful jazz hall (Jazz at Lincoln Center), and a big TV station (CNN) is going to be there too. A lot of people who like restaurants will live at the top, in a really tall apartment building. There are going to be all kinds of nice shops, a grocery store, a gym, and they're going to have four or five other great restaurants there."

With that, Hallie burst into tears. "I never want you to have a restaurant where people are going there for some other reason than to go to your restaurant. People go to your restaurants because they want to be at *your* restaurant," she said.

That day, I added Hallie to my list of unofficial advisers. I knew she was right. It was her wise way of telling me that the context would not have been right for our company.

Context, context, context! For years I had heard the business mantra, "Location, location, location"—an ironclad principle that the key to the success for any retail establishment was picking the right address to set up shop. My own experience indicates that a far more significant contributor to success is context. A powerful example is Tiffany's famous blue box. The box is the context that provides a strong indication of what you can expect to find inside. Whatever is in that box may not be the exact gift you were anticipating, but it must be entirely consistent with your expectations of something that belongs in a Tiffany box. The box enhances the value of the object inside; and conversely, the object inside supports and further defines the meaning of the blue box. That's not location. That's context!

I had a chance not long afterward to tell Hallie about yet another venture—again, at a site where thousands of people would be gathering for purposes other than for dining. But this time, there would be no restaurants other than ours at the site. We would have our own entrance for our guests, and we would have a chance to add something to the dialogue on dining for people who would be visiting the site anyway.

In many ways, opening The Modern and two visitor cafés at the Museum of Modern Art was the biggest gamble that I'd ever undertaken, and a test of my organization's core business values and competence. But if ever there was a case to be made for growing and stretching, this was it. We'd be in very new territory in terms of concept, context, and complexity. If we could pull this venture off, it would open unimaginable new doors of opportunity for our business.

CHAPTER 13

The Art of Hospitality

NOVEMBER 20, 2004, WAS a day I'll never forget. New York's Museum of Modern Art, which to my art-loving family's way of thinking vied for interest with the seven wonders of the world, had closed for major renovations in 2001. Now, on this red-letter day three years later, it was reopening after a stunning new expansion as the art world looked on in anticipation. And Union Square Hospitality Group was part of all this, opening not just one but four eating establishments within the museum's complex. For us this was not just a matter of conceiving and operating all of the food service at MoMA; it was about doing so during the high-profile relaunch of an internationally renowned institution. The degree of pressure and scrutiny I felt numbed me into a surreal sense of calm.

As a businessman, I listen to two internal voices. First, there is one urging me to succeed, expand, and grow. The other is a persistent ambivalent voice whispering, "Caution: go deeper, go slower." Sometimes I have to get smacked in the face a few times before my competitive juices start flowing and I say, "OK, I'm ready for it." I'd really wanted our company to win the high-stakes competition for the MoMA contract, but now that we had it, I wondered if we'd bitten off more than we could chew.

The museum had been doing everything possible to overcome all kinds of complicated last-minute construction obstacles and delays so that it could be ready for its announced reopening on November 20, and it mandated that we be open that day too. Making matters even more challenging for us, MoMA had decided to offer free admission to the public on November 20—there would be 20,000 people descending on the museum that day. There was no way to tell them they couldn't come to the restaurant; ready or not, we just had to serve them. Despite having only four days to train our staff, we managed to get Cafe 2, our fresh take on the traditional museum cafeteria, open that day, and we served around 1,500 people there. We served another 500 hungry visitors at Terrace 5, our café for desserts and light fare; and 250 more guests in the Bar Room portion of The Modern, the only part of that restaurant which we were even remotely prepared to open on November 20. (For several nights leading up to the opening, I had uncomfortable visions of museum trustees and executives peering at us with disapproval, wondering why they had selected us, and why we weren't yet on top of our game. And that was in addition to even sharper concerns about what the critics would have to say.) Because the museum prohibits open-flame cooking at Cafe 2 and Terrace 5 (the kitchen is in the basement, and with no service-elevator access to the fifth floor), our inexperienced staff members were pushing white carts full of meals and dishes up and down the public elevators, riding cheek to jowl with the throngs of visitors.

Our new staff members brought a bright attitude to work that day, but I was concerned about whether we had done enough to prepare them for the onslaught I knew they were about to face. In just over three months, we'd enlarged our overall USHG staff by nearly 50 percent, from 650 to more than 1,000 employees. And we'd engineered that buildup under substandard circumstances: We'd had insufficient time for careful interviewing, hiring, and training them. In fact we had no place to train them. Because construction delays meant there was no certificate of occupancy for the restaurants, it wasn't until October that these spaces were even habitable. And even had we hired the staff, there was no locker room available—there was not even a staff bathroom. At one point on opening day, as I watched the snaking line of people waiting to get into Terrace 5 brush up against Henri Rousseau's *The Dream,* I had two distinct reactions that encapsulated my ecstatic anguish at achieving this day at MoMA.

First: *Oh, my God. We've just opened a restaurant with one of the art world's greatest masterpieces hanging outside the front door!*

Second: *Oh, my God. The people waiting in line to eat at my restaurant are going to ruin the masterpiece, and I'll be responsible!*

The courage to grow demands the courage to let go. Whenever you expand in business—not just the restaurant business—the process is incredibly challenging, especially for leaders who first rose to the top because of their tendency to want to control all the details. You have to let go. You have to surround yourself with ambassadors—people who know how to accomplish goals and make decisions, while treating people the way you would. They're comfortable expressing themselves within the boundaries of your business culture, and content with the role they play in helping a larger team achieve its greatest potential success.

Opening a new restaurant can make some of your existing customers irate. Each time we've undertaken a new venture, a certain percentage of our existing customer base opts not to come along with us. Some people won't even try the new place; some others go just once out of politeness. My first awareness of that reality was a crushing blow for me. *You mean not everything we do is necessarily lovable to those who love us?*

But this has happened so regularly that I've had the chance to analyze what's going on. Sometimes our loyalists are unable to embrace a new restaurant, just as an older child may not fully celebrate the arrival of a newborn sibling. Customers have a natural fear that we might forget them. You can almost hear some of them saying, "Why the hell is he going into Indian food? Now he's going into the barbecue business? Is he off his rocker? What? Another one? Frozen custard? This is the end. I'm done. He doesn't love me anymore."

One of the first people to express that concern to me was Paul Gottlieb, then publisher at Harry N. Abrams. Paul began eating lunch at table 24 at Union Square Cafe in 1985 and continued to do so on more days than not for the next eighteen years. He became a great friend—always providing caring feedback—and we talked frequently. His reactions were typically paternal and direct, starting with the first time I told him about my plans to open Gramercy Tavern in 1994. "You're not going to open a second restaurant!" he said. "We'll never see you here again. It won't be the same."

Paul, who was also a trustee of the Museum of Modern Art, expressed the same concern about my expanding four years later, with the opening of Tabla and Eleven Madison Park. Yet, ironically, it was he who in the early 1990s, even before Gramercy Tavern existed, had first tried to persuade me to open a restaurant at MoMA. We met at his office, and Paul spoke on behalf of the board of trustees. The museum then had a restaurant on its second floor called the Members' Dining Room. I had been fascinated with MoMA since I was a child: people on both sides of my family were serious collectors of modern art, and my mother had run an art gallery and was a trustee of the St. Louis Art Museum. Our kitchen calendar was always from MoMA, and our home was furnished with all kinds of products from the museum's design collection. In fact, for the twenty-five years my parents were married, the bond they most consistently shared, beyond their children, seemed to be their mutual affection for contemporary art.

Paul's entreaty was compelling, but after two or three enticing meetings and lots of careful thought, I told him that I simply wasn't ready to open a second restaurant, and that if I ever did, I couldn't imagine opening one in midtown. I lived downtown and understood how important being able to walk to all my restaurants had been as a factor in our success. Nor did it seem to make economic sense to operate a restaurant in which people could eat only during museum hours. This would essentially be a lunch restaurant—and one that didn't have its own separate sidewalk entrance.

Paul remained a close friend and source of sage advice through the years. One day in mid-2001 he called and said he had something very exciting to tell me. "We're closing the museum," he confided when we met. "There's going to be a fantastic expansion and renovation unlike anything in our history." He added, "We want to put a restaurant in the new MoMA, and this time we're serious about the food. The museum is ready to discuss a stand-alone restaurant with its own street entrance."

Recalling our discussion a decade earlier, he said, "This time around, you need to take it seriously. What you and your team could do with dining at the Museum of Modern Art could be amazing. There will definitely be others competing for this, but you *must* submit a proposal."

That meeting was one of the last times we ever spoke. Paul died suddenly a few weeks later at the age of sixty-seven, long before those who had the honor of knowing him were prepared to say good-bye. His revelation about MoMA's historic expansion—and his insistence that we be a part of it—started me on a passionate pursuit whose outcome ultimately became a legacy of our long friendship.

In November 2001, David Swinghamer and I had our first introductory meeting with the two senior executives at MoMA: James

Gara and Mike Margitich. We learned that the museum would reopen not just with a restaurant but also with three cafés—two for museum visitors and another for its staff. The restaurant organization selected for this opportunity would also become the "preferred" (but not exclusive) caterer for museum events. The museum executives urged us to consider opening a concession stand at MoMA QNS, the museum's temporary quarters in Long Island City, Queens, during its three-year absence from Manhattan. They enthusiastically told us about the throngs of people who would be attending the forthcoming block-buster Matisse-Picasso show at MoMA QNS. From our conversation, it seemed implicit that whoever ran the temporary concession would earn their favor and enjoy a competitive edge in landing the big deal when MoMA eventually reopened on West Fifty-third Street.

A t about this time, my assistant, Jenny Dirksen (now our director of community investment), shared a priceless expression her grandmother had taught her: One tuchas can't dance at two weddings. It's nice to be invited to a lot of parties. But as much as you may want to attend them all, it's important to acknowledge that you can be in only one place at a time, and do one thing well. My own grandfather used to express similar wisdom: Doing two things like a half-wit never equals doing one thing like a whole wit.

Regrettably, the timing for the concession in Queens could hardly have been worse. We were still in the throes of preopening construction at Blue Smoke, and it didn't take long to determine that we did not have the wherewithal to do both projects well. It was extremely difficult to turn MoMA down again, but that was the right decision.

Still, we assured the museum that we would be very interested in discussing the larger project down the road; and to keep our relationship with MoMA alive, we conducted several more meetings with executives, curators, and trustees over the next year. One opportunity presented itself when the museum temporarily shifted its basement film center to the Gramercy Theater on East Twenty-third Street off Lexington Avenue—a short walk from three of our restaurants. We created a co-marketing deal: museum members who came to see a MoMA film received a certificate good for dessert at Eleven Madison Park, Tabla, or Blue Smoke. We kept our irons in the fire until late 2002, when the museum set the deadline for receiving proposals.

Serving food in MoMA seemed like a remarkable opportunity, and yet we weren't entirely sure we really wanted to win this thing. Having received countless pitches from real estate developers over the years, we had always had the luxury of being selective about which ones to weigh seriously. Having the tables turned and being judged by others was uncomfortable. I also had my usual nagging mixed feelings about the pace at which we were now growing and at which we would continue to grow if we were to prevail. The MoMA project would transform our business by bringing us into the world of institutional dining, quick-service cafés, and catering. And all the new employees it would require to staff four new dining establishments and an off-premises catering facility would make the company balloon in size. Wasn't this the kind of expansionist dreaming that my more sober-minded colleagues and relatives had always counseled against?

But something unusual happened. The people in my life whom I had always counted on to ask, "What are you *thinking,* Danny?" were actually encouraging me. Right up until he died, Paul Gottlieb, who had groaned with dismay every time I opened another restaurant, was relentless in urging me to submit a proposal to MoMA. My mother, whose skeptical view of business growth had been colored by my father's failed expansions, was now a member of MoMA's Prints and Illustrated Books committee and was tickled by the idea of our opening a restaurant there. My grandfather Irving Harris had been a generous supporter of MoMA. He was now in the sunset of his life, but he urged me on. And then there was my own voice. I was increasingly confident in the capacity of the leadership team I had surrounded myself with. Most important, I trusted myself and my own motives.

So, the chance to create something for the Museum of Modern Art excited me. This was one venture I viewed not just as a business opportunity but also as a tremendous privilege. Then Audrey, who knew how consuming this project would be for me—and for our family—said, "Of course you've got to go for this!" That settled it.

I didn't know (and still have no idea) whom we were competing with in the selection process, but I did know that the thorough, painstaking evaluations (conducted for the museum by PriceWaterhouseCoopers) would be focused on three broad categories:

- Our overall creative vision—how we would conceive of the restaurant, the cafés, and the catering for museum events.

- The value of our financial package to the museum (what kind of capital investment we'd propose making along with the museum to build the restaurants, and how much we'd propose paying in rent).

- What we brought to the table in the way of relevant experience and organizational capacity to indicate that we'd actually be able to pull all this off.

Conceiving the restaurant itself, would no doubt be challenging, but it seemed relatively straightforward in terms of our prior experience. Tackling the two very different visitor cafés within the museum as well as the cafeteria for MoMA's staff would be a fresh challenge. And the blueprints for the museum didn't indicate enough space had been allocated for a catering kitchen, so it was clear we'd have to lease space and build an additional kitchen elsewhere. Funding all this would present its own steep hurdles, but the biggest question was whether we could actually juggle all those plates at the same time.

If ever we were to launch a restaurant outside the familiar precinct in which we had done business for twenty years, MoMA felt like the ideal place. The museum is viewed in the world of art precisely as I dreamed our restaurants might be in the world of fine dining: an institution that endures and is at once forward-looking, sensibly grounded in tradition, and relevant today.

I asked David Swinghamer to do much of the legwork for the proposal. We didn't go nuts trying to create the sexiest-looking presentation of all time, although we did enlist the professional support of Eric Baker, the imaginative graphic designer we had worked with on the logo for Blue Smoke, as well as many other projects. The proposal was a simple eleven-page document, describing our identity and why we saw ourselves as being a good fit for MoMA. Our financial offer assured MoMA that we'd have plenty of skin in the game (in terms of how much of our own money we'd be investing in the build-outs, as well as what percentage of sales we'd be paying to the museum as rent); our ideas for the restaurant and cafés were creative, reasoned, and sound; and as for relevant experience, that would be entirely up to MoMA to judge.

During the selection process, we chose not to lobby anyone connected to MoMA, even though I was well aware that a number of regular guests at our restaurants were trustees who might be involved in the selection. If we were chosen, I wanted the choice to be based on merit. Later, there would be plenty of opportunity to compete with passion at making the restaurant, cafés, and catering operations the best they could be. We were asked to participate in a few intensive interviews with members of the museum's senior executive team. I felt fully prepared to field their questions, and the experience was exhilarating.

About ninety days after we had submitted the proposal, we received a call from MoMA's chief operating officer, James Gara: we had been chosen. Within moments, another call arrived, this one from a trustee, Bob Menschel, who was warm in his congratulations and generous in his praise. At first the news was numbing; in a flash I began to imagine the extraordinary amount of work that lay ahead of us. And being MoMA's choice didn't mean that we had a deal. As it turned out, eight months of detailed work and negotiations still remained before we would actually sign our deal in November 2003. During those eight months we were not permitted to announce or discuss our selection with anyone.

We batted around different rent structures for our various food businesses and established that MoMA would have control over what kinds of art could and would be displayed in our dining rooms. We determined that the museum would have approval rights over our design of the restaurants, as well as in our choice of chef and general manager. (The museum's reasoning was that our dining facilities would be a representative extension of the museum experience, and that this high level of control would insure the institution against inappropriate or poor hiring decisions on our part.) We went back and forth over real-estate issues, debated design layouts down to the inch, struggled to find adequate space for our back-of-the-house offices, debated whose phone system we would use, and agreed about which museum restrooms were available to or off-limit for our staff.

Not long after signing our deal, I came up with the name for our fine-dining restaurant. I remembered what my dad had taught me during the naming of Union Square Cafe. "Just name it what it is." "The Modern" answered that challenge. I bounced the idea off trustee Ronald Lauder, who had taken a generously supportive and nearly proprietary interest in the restaurant project, and when he later expressed the board's enthusiasm, the decision was made.

AS MY TEAM AND I began to think about what we might add to the dialogue on museum dining, I asked myself: "Who ever wrote the rule that you can't enjoy an elegant, intimate fine-dining experience in a warm, hospitable ambience within the traditionally institutional context of a museum? And who ever wrote the rule that you can't get a warm welcome and have excellent food, hospitably delivered to tables in what is traditionally a tray-service museum cafeteria?" In both cases the challenge was to take what has historically been an institutional, captive audience experience and make it feel warm, personal, and worthy of becoming a dining destination on its own.

What was there to add to the dialogue on museum cafeterias? To begin with, we acknowledged the basic reasons museum visitors patronize a cafeteria: it gets you off your feet, feeds you quickly, and charges a reasonable price. Museum cafeterias are typically designed to appeal to a very broad swath of customers: older people, younger people, Americans, foreigners, locals, tourists, students. Not being permitted to cook in the cafés due to their proximity to the art galleries would add an element of challenge. We would have to come up with a delicious menu that could be prepared in our basement kitchen, delivered to the cafeterias, and still taste fresh and delicious.

We identified two aspects of museum cafeterias we thought we could improve upon. First, most people don't really like having to carry a tray and look for a cafeteria table, especially with young kids hanging on them, or while they're trying to assist an aging parent or grandparent. Second, cafeteria food—no matter how fresh it may once have been—has already been prepared and plated and has invariably been sitting out for some time in a steam table or wrapped in plastic.

We realized that if we could quickly assemble fresh ingredients to order and eliminate trays and prepackaged, preplated, prewrapped foods, we would have something special. I remember scratching my head, thinking about all the world cuisines that actually benefit from having been cooked in advance. What came to my mind most conclusively was the Roman *rosticceria,* one of the world's original quick service concepts, and one I had always enjoyed when I was a student in Rome. These places serve seasonal foods that have already been braised or roasted, as well as cured meats or cheeses, plated to order.

This kind of cooking has been done for ages in Rome, but it was a fresh approach for a museum eatery. It was a solution that suited our model perfectly: a classic culinary concept within a new framework.

In the style of service that we had in mind, you would order your food from a cashier, who would give you a number; then you'd go find your own seat; and soon we'd come find you with your food. Other restaurants had successfully done it in the past. In fact, David Swinghamer first brought the idea to us, having seen it used by his former colleagues at the Corner Bakery, and then I saw it again at Culver's (a frozen custard and burger specialist) in St. Joseph, Michigan. I was skeptical at first, but on seeing the system work in Washington, D.C., at a Corner Bakery, I was sold. As with almost everything else we've ever done, we were rearranging familiar, existing notes to play a fresh-sounding chord.

We looked at the respective roles of the three MoMA dining experiences we were creating as *replenish, refresh,* and *restore.* Cafe 2 would be for *replenishing,* filling your body with fuel. Terrace 5 is situated opposite the gallery in which are hung masterpieces from the museum's permanent collection—Cézanne, Seurat, van Gogh, Picasso, Matisse, and more. Not a bad address for a restaurant! We imagined Terrace 5 as a place to *refresh* visitors after the fatigue that can set in after seeing so much good art. We would serve lots of things that featured the stimulating triumvirate of sugar, alcohol, and caffeine. The very location of Terrace 5 added significantly, in our view, to the dialogue on museum dining (and, in fact, the whole museum experience). Being able to view *Starry Night* or *Les Desmoiselles d'Avignon* after enjoying a martini, a glass of wine, or an ice cream sundae and a cappuccino could allow you to see it as you'd never seen it before. The Modern would be for *restoring.* It would serve as a restaurant both for New Yorkers and for museumgoers whose choice was to sit down, eat well, and also be taken care of. The Modern was conceived to nurture food lovers as well as to nourish them.

WE WERE RELIEVED WHEN the museum agreed to select our long-time architects, Bentel and Bentel, as designers for the restaurant. Their family's deep modernist roots made them perfectly suited for the complex task, and our experience collaborating on four previous restaurants would be an important advantage in order to tackle MoMA's challenging project under a very tight timeline.

Another crucially important artistic decision for this project was selecting the chef for The Modern. I wanted The Modern to become a critically acclaimed destination restaurant—not just an excellent version of a museum restaurant. My initial thought was to find one chef for the restaurant and another to oversee the cafés and catering. By dividing these duties, I believed we'd have a better chance at excelling in all areas. I ran through my own mental Rolodex of many prospective chefs, most of whom, on reflection, would have been completely wrong. When I thought about someone who was cooking primarily Italian, it didn't make sense. If I thought about someone who was cooking with southwestern flavors, it felt odd (this was not the Georgia O'Keeffe Museum). So did anything else ethnic, such as Indian, Asian, Chinese, or Japanese.

The modernist art movement was rooted primarily in Austria, Switzerland, Germany, and France. Not only would the new restaurant be taking its design cues from the museum's existing architecture and from modernism; it would also be looking out onto the Abby Aldrich Rockefeller sculpture garden, with famous works by the artists Joan Miró, Henry Moore, Pablo Picasso, Ellsworth Kelly, Joel Shapiro, Gaston LaChaise, and Alberto Giacometti. If that was going to be the elegant backdrop for our restaurant, then our cooking had better present an entirely consistent foreground.

At one point I had made a list of thirty prospective chefs, and others called me to throw their toques into the ring. One leading contender took himself out of the running when the very complicatted scope of the project became apparent to him. Indeed, the reality of this complexity was catching up with me. The clock was suddenly ticking down to 365 days for an opening in November 2004, and we needed to hire a chef to get up and running by then, as well as to overcome major issues of design and construction that were suddenly no longer a matter of "what if"—they had become real. On New Year's Day 2004 I was at a party in the home of Dorothy and Doug Hamilton, founders of the French Culinary Institute, the most prominent culinary trade school in New York, when I ran into the school's dean, the esteemed French chef Alain Saillhac. I described my vision for The Modern and asked chef Sailhac whom he thought I should hire. Immediately he suggested a dynamic young chef named Gabriel Kreuther.

Why hadn't I thought of that? I had enjoyed Gabriel's cooking at Atelier, a French restaurant at the Ritz-Carlton Hotel in Manhattan, where he had served as executive chef following several years at Jean Georges. Gabriel was from the province of Alsace, in the northeast corner of France; and what I knew of his cooking style (forward, personal, classic, spare, and soulful) seemed completely compatible with a modernist setting. Gabriel was still in his midthirties but had already cooked at some of the best restaurants in New York. That year *Food and Wine* had named him one of the top ten best new chefs in America. The fit felt very right. Over the course of several months Gabriel and I proceeded to discuss the project and visit the construction site. We got to know one another before I made an offer, which Gabriel accepted.

In hiring chefs, my goal is to do three things: develop a close, mutually trusting and respectful relationship; establish a shared vision of what the food should be; and encourage them to search their own heart and soul for inspiration, urging them to go further than they've ever gone before. I am especially proud of the enduring bonds of shared success and loyalty that I have enjoyed with our chefs over the years.

I've learned that an effective way to achieve all those goals with a new chef (and to get to know the essence of the person) is to return with him to his roots. It was a moving experience to travel with

Gabriel in Alsace and to see his homeland through his eyes and his palate. Of course the region holds special meaning for me too; my parents had lived in the neighboring Lorraine for the first two years of their marriage. Alsace-Lorraine has historically been a melting pot, with French, German, Protestant, Catholic, and Jewish cultures living together through war and hardship, producing a resilient people and excellent, soul-satisfying food.

Gabriel devised our ambitious itinerary and chose the restaurants, which ranged from a Michelin three-star in Strasbourg (Buerehiesel) and another in the middle of the forest well to the north (L'Arnsbourg) to quaint, out-of-the way *winstubs*—the traditional "wine bistros" of Alsace. He took me to the village of Niederschaffolsheim (population 1,246), where he grew up, and told me how he began helping his mother and grandmother with kitchen chores by the time he was six. Before he was a teenager, he was cooking for real. Gabriel was fascinated by his family's cooking, or, as he put it, "our everyday home cooking." (Also, he confided that by making himself more and more useful in the kitchen he avoided more grueling farm chores outside!) He learned from his mother and grandmother everything he needed to know about selecting the best fresh ingredients. We visited his boyhood home, where his proud mother served us a hunk of perfectly ripened Muenster cheese (the local favorite) that she had procured at the nearby farmers' market; this Muenster was superior to the one we'd had the night before at the three-star restaurant. And even though she knew we were heading off for a three-star lunch, she insisted that we first try her homemade quiche lorraine with salad and cheese. Gabriel showed me his grade school; but he saved his greatest enthusiasm for our trip to the musty wine cellar in his mother's chilly basement where he had been collecting and storing bottles since the age of fourteen. He showed me where he lovingly made eau-de-vie—or schnapps, as he called it in German—and presented me with a Campari bottle filled with homemade *mirabelle* to take home to New York. It was an engrossing three days.

A pattern I've noticed in chefs is that many spend tremendous energy when they're young working to build a life away from where and how they grew up, in order to free themselves and define who they are on their own terms. It takes a lot of confidence and emotional security for people—and especially chefs, whose cooking can so clearly reveal their roots—to feel they have accomplished enough in the outside world to "come home" in a culinary or an actual sense. My "getting to know you" trips to Italy with Michael Romano and (before Gramercy Tavern opened) with Tom Colicchio were in part meant to encourage them to rediscover their culinary roots. It struck me that Michael had proved himself as an extraordinary French chef before he permitted himself to cook Italian from his heart and remember the joy that he got from his mother's or his grandmother's *cucina*. There had been little on Tom's excellent menus at his former restaurant, Mondrian, that revealed much exploration of his family's Italian heritage. Similarly, Tabla's executive chef, Floyd Cardoz, who was born in Bombay and grew up in Goa, a former Portuguese colony on India's west coast, had begun his stellar career as sous-chef to Gray Kunz and his French-based cooking at Lespinasse. Just as it took Michael some time to willingly express his Italian roots at Union Square Cafe, it took Floyd a couple of years to fully embrace his Indian identity and create not just Tabla's elegant fusion fare but the bolder, more ethnic Indian "soul food" we serve downstairs at Bread Bar.

I wanted Gabriel to be able to hasten that journey to his culinary home. Given the high-profile scrutiny I expected at The Modern, he wouldn't have the luxury of waiting years to learn and grow on the job. It's not that I was interested in seeing Gabriel faithfully replicate an Alsatian *winstub*. Some elements of that rustic cuisine would translate and others would not, if we imported them to the Museum of Modern Art in Manhattan. What was crucial was for him to cook for New Yorkers from his Alsatian heart.

We spent our time driving through farmland, strolling around small towns and villages, and studying dozens of menus—their shape, size, categories, formats, and even font styles. We talked about what kind of uniforms we'd want our staff to wear. We checked out pottery and furniture shops and discussed décor. We visited dozens of pastry, cheese, and butcher shops. It was easy to see how Gabriel's very personal style of cooking had been nurtured in and around the farmhouses of his extended family. He told me, for instance, all about the classic Alsatian *baeckoffe,* a pork, veal, or beef stew made by marinating the meat in local white wines (Riesling, Edelzwicker, and Sylvaner), and then baking it with layers of potatoes (sliced an eighth of an inch thin), carrots, leeks, onions, parsley, pepper, and tomatoes on top. Each family's recipe was just a little different. *Baeckoffe* means "baker's oven," and is so named because homemakers hauled their own huge pots to the village baker before church and would later pick them up, bring them home, and then serve the one-pot meal for Sunday dinner.

The idea of creating a new hybrid by blending classic Alsatian elements with dishes more familiar to Americans thrilled me. As we ate together I would look at a menu item—*baeckoffe, tarte à l'oignon, choucroute,* foie gras, *quiche lorraine*—and ask Gabriel: "What does that dish mean to you? Can you remember the best version you ever ate?" He'd say, "Sure. My grandmother made the best one I've ever had." "Well, then, tell me about that," I'd ask. "Can you imagine any application for The Modern?"

Together we saw how many wonderful things butchers did with livers and sausage and discussed how meats are butchered differently in Alsace, and throughout Europe for that matter. (Many familiar American cuts for steaks and chops are virtually nonexistent there. Instead one finds an abundance of lengthwise cuts and roasts.) We saw how many types of sausage are made from so many different parts of so many different animals. At one butcher shop I pointed to something that looked just like liverwurst and said, "Gabriel, there it is. We should be able to make the best liverwurst sandwich New York has ever had."

"Ah, that's *saucisse de foie!*" he said. "I remember when I was growing up we would stud it with black truffles."

"If you take something traditional, like *saucisse de foie,* that's done exquisitely well in Alsace," I said, "and then make it the best version of liverwurst that New Yorkers have ever had, then you've added something exciting to the dialogue."

I urged Gabriel to view his work at Atelier—excellent as it was—as a launching pad for what he would do next at The Modern. I told him that I was absolutely convinced that he had yet to do his greatest work. And where better to frame that work than inside the Museum of Modern Art!

Our gastronomic adventure was my version of an off-site management meeting designed to help me get to know, motivate, and build bonds with a new colleague. I love to encourage a pastry chef or a cook or an executive chef to remember the first time he or she ever successfully cooked chocolate chip cookies or brownies (or, in Gabriel's case, *tarte flambée*). If I can get people to relive the pride of such an accomplishment—the joy of having solved a problem, of tasting something delicious, and most important, the pleasure of presenting a gift to their parents—I know we'll be in good shape.

I also encountered more fortune when I met Ana Marie Mormando. In mid-2003, I'd heard that Ana Marie, the longtime director of operations for Jean-Georges Vongerichten's restaurants, was considering a career change. I'd agreed to interview her even though we didn't have any specific job opening for her.

We hadn't yet gotten the go-ahead from MoMA, and it hadn't dawned on me whom we'd put in charge of our museum operations if we were to take on the project. In our first meeting, I learned that Ana Marie had run an earlier incarnation of the Members' Dining Room at MoMA, and that she had experience operating restaurants at Lincoln Center. The lights went on. We brought her aboard for a full year before opening at MoMA, during which time she was responsible for our construction and opening timeline. We also wanted her to get a flavor for and become an established part of our Union Square Hospitality Group culture.

Ana Marie led a talented team of over 300 staff members to open our dining facilities at MoMA with little time, scant practice, and unrelenting pressure. And this was all without a general manager for The Modern, since the GM we hired at the outset had resigned about a week before the restaurant opened—acknowledging a mutual mistake. He was someone about whom we had heard wonderful things, but who unfortunately was just not the right fit to open this restaurant in this setting, and under this amount of pressure.

IN THE FINAL DAYS leading up to our opening, as it became clear that we were on a collision course with November 20, I remember saying something to the museum executives that was not especially appreciated: "Unlike a piece of art, restaurants are not inanimate objects. You can't simply hang them on a wall by a set date and expect them to work or even look good. They need to be trained, fine-tuned, focused, recalibrated." It was my emotional way of trying to bring reality to bear on the near impossibility of our mandate to hire and train so many people in a rushed, high-pressure situation. Reluctantly, the museum agreed to allow us to push back the opening of the Bar Room to the general public until January 2005. On February 7 we at last opened our doors to the public for dinner in the dining room of The Modern. And just one night later, on February 8, the *New York Times*'s restaurant critic Frank Bruni paid the restaurant a visit.

Unbeknownst to us, Mr. Bruni was also dining at Eleven Madison Park. His two-star review of the restaurant on February 23 caught the staff by surprise, and resulted in a demoralized team. We had never known what he looked like (the custom for food critics is to be anonymous whenever that is possible, even if it means dining in disguise), but the first time he came to The Modern, a champagne salesman who happened to be at the bar pointed to a dark-haired man at a table and said to one of our bartenders, "That's Frank Bruni over there." By our best count, the reviewer paid us eleven separate visits in total before he had at last gathered enough information to write his review. At the very least, his visits alone had generated significant revenue for the restaurants.

I have never opened a restaurant where the members of the staff were as keyed up and uptight about a review as everyone at The Modern was in anticipation of this one. Managers, cooks, and servers were so concerned about how well or poorly we would fare that many of them stopped acting naturally. The morning after one of Bruni's visits, at the end of March 2005, I was on a spring vacation with my family at the Colony Beach & Tennis Resort in Longboat Key, Florida, when I got a call just as I was leaving the tennis court. It was Ana Marie phoning to say that something terrible had happened the previous night. One of our wine captains had gone up to the critic as he was retrieving his coat at the end of the meal and told him how grateful she was that he had just given a glowing two-star review to her friend's restaurant, Stone Park Cafe, a small place in Brooklyn.

Some members of the staff were beside themselves because our wine captain had broken a ludicrous cardinal rule: even if you know who a critic is, you must play the game of pretending that you don't know. This wine captain, therefore, had acted unprofessionally, Ana Marie said. What should we do? I had to laugh.

It would be unnatural behavior *not* to extend especially warm hospitality to someone who has returned to the restaurant even three or four times, never mind *eleven*. That wine captain had been expressing "hospitalitarian" soul! And soul was what seemed to me to be missing from The Modern. We were quickly becoming technically proficient. In fact, knowing that we were on such a big, brightly lit stage (with all those trustees, foodies, journalists, regulars from our other restaurants, and museum visitors watching us at close range), I'd reversed my usual strategy and focused on hiring more "49 percenters," with their seasoned technical skills. But the staff was stiff and so psyched out by the perceived pressure to be perfect that our service wasn't nearly as warm and hospitable as our standards required, or as our guests expected it to be. The fact that incidents like this one were being blown out of proportion made me realize just how uptight everyone was. Did anyone truly believe that a genuine expression of gratitude would have any downward influence on the number of stars we would receive from the *New York Times*? Would a restaurant critic lower his judgment of the restaurant or its food because someone had actually spoken to him?

Eleven visits were a lot of experiences to arrive at the conclusion that The Modern was a two-star restaurant, as Bruni did in May 2005. I've always wished that restaurant critics would be more like wine critics. They taste wines that are very young and predict the future: "This is where the wine is going. It will be a classic someday." I don't think Bruni would have betrayed his readers or damaged his reputation if he'd written, "This restaurant is on a fast trajectory to become a three-star restaurant." We didn't conceive or design The Modern to be "very good." It was born to be excellent, and in its first year the restaurant was judged so by the *Financial Times,* the *International Herald Tribune, Newsweek, Esquire* ("Best New Restaurant in the United States"), *Wallpaper* ("Best New Restaurant in the World"), *Time Out New York* ("Best New Restaurant in New York"), The James Beard Foundation (Best New Restaurant in America), and even the 2006 Michelin Guide to New York City, which gave The Modern one star just months after its opening.

In some ways, Bruni's review was a turning point for the restaurant. It at last liberated the senior management team from the stress of waiting and wondering, and encouraged them to roll up their sleeves and begin to have some fun. It took the hot lid off a highly pressurized boiler. I even think the food improved soon after the review because Gabriel had been playing it safe in anticipation of the piece. The waiters loosened up and began smiling and looking people in the eye, and they too improved. Everyone had been playing not to lose, as opposed to playing to win. Now the staff was finding it enjoyable, for the first time, to exceed expectations. "You mean to tell me this is only a two-star restaurant? You guys are good!"

In fact, I too felt free. I was, for the first time in my career of opening restaurants, feeling relaxed. This project was so huge and so far beyond any fantasies I may have had about actually being in control that it forced me to let go. It made me do what I'd always known I needed to do—surround myself with very talented people; give them clear direction, goals, and feedback; and not try to be everywhere at once. Well, except for the first three or four months, when I made two trips each day to the museum to go on my rounds, collect and connect the new dots, turn over all the rocks, and check in on everything.

BEFORE WE OPENED THE Modern, I'm not sure there had ever been a museum restaurant in America that was a destination in and of itself. The museum restaurants I knew of had been designed primarily as amenities for attendees. They were meant more to serve a captive audience than to be competitive, stand-alone eateries. We were determined to create a restaurant that you'd want to go to even if it did *not* overlook one of the world's most spectacular sculpture gardens.

YOU CAN SPEND MANY years in the restaurant business trying to attract and earn the loyalty of a regular, core clientele. At The Modern we basically had a built-in club—the museum, its trustees, its curators, and its executives. That is both a wonderful privilege and a high-class challenge as we worked to build a new community of friends.

Since The Modern is the first restaurant at MoMA that has also been open to the non-museumgoing public, we'd presented ourselves with another new challenge: how do we operate, on one hand, as an exclusive club and, on the other hand, as a public restaurant? Learning to do this was quite tricky at the outset. People who were used to hearing "yes" were instead getting incessant busy signals, only to finally get through and hear, "I'm sorry, we're booked." We were trying hard to balance the needs of several constituencies, each entitled to the utmost in hospitality: the MoMA community, the legion of loyalists from our existing restaurants, our investors, and of course the thousands of curious New Yorkers who line up to be among the first to visit a new restaurant.

One day I stood in The Modern and observed a trustee of the museum sitting next to a high-powered financier. A couple of tables away were some art-loving tourists from Minneapolis; dining not too far from their table was the alternative singer Björk, who was sitting next to a well-known book editor. It's a richly diverse clientele, and one that is unpredictable—in the most positive way—each day. Making my dining room rounds is every bit as exciting at The Modern as it was when I began doing it at Union Square Cafe in 1985. I cannot wait to go there. Like all of our restaurants, The Modern will take time to fulfill its greatest potential, but I am confident it will become a great and enduring New York restaurant. That will have happened when it develops its own soul through the same process of conducting a dialogue with its guests that each of the other restaurants has gone through for a sustained period of time.

MoMA provides the perfect frame for The Modern: it's a peak career opportunity for my company and me. When the Museum of Modern Art buys a piece of art to hang on its walls, the artist's career is instantly affirmed. When MoMA selects a chair or a watch for its design collection, the esteem in which that product is held grows instantly and dramatically. I have to hope that the same has happened for us. The Museum of Modern Art is an established arbiter of taste, design, and art, and creating a living product for such an institution is something I could hardly have dreamed of as a restaurateur.

Soon after we embarked on our deal with MoMA, Glenn Lowry, who is the museum's director and a highly effective CEO, offered me some heartfelt advice. "Please don't get caught up in the aura of the museum," he said. "We selected you because of what we know of you. Too often, people try too hard with us and end up not doing their best work." I heard his advice, but for me it was impossible not to try hard, when I was part of creating a restaurant whose thirty-five foot windows overlook the Abby Aldrich Rockefeller sculpture garden.

WHY DO I KEEP climbing mountains? Because with a few exceptions there's always a higher, steeper mountain to scale, and I'm willing to confront all sorts of treacherous conditions, especially when I'm convinced that they'll lead to exhilarating views from the top. It's the same with opening new restaurants, and with any new business initiative. The MoMA project was a massive challenge for our organization. I wish I could think of an even bigger word to describe it. As with each new business I've ever opened, I am profoundly confident that this story will have a happy ending. Lacking a crystal ball, I have no idea how many or what kind of episodes and temporary setbacks there will be along the way, or what shape they'll take. However, we'll have no choice but to improve and persevere with each step we take up the mountain.

I am now growing excited about seeing our organization take on another new challenge: to expand one of our existing businesses. Replicating something that we're already doing will demand a new set of skills and will represent a wonderful opportunity for me to stretch as a professional and for the organization to stretch as well. Whenever we do it, our challenge will be to do so in a way that conveys excellence, hospitality, and soul. And of course, wherever we do it, the timing and context must be a neat fit.

That is precisely how we're addressing the challenge of off-premises catering. We launched Hudson Yards Catering in late 2005, and named it (as we like to do) for the emerging neighborhood in which the commissary is located. Through a persistant search, our team found a spot that was affordable and in Manhattan—overlooking the Hudson River, in the West Twenties. Just as we have done with our other businesses, connecting our catering company with its community reflects our broader, long-range interest in becoming an active stakeholder in the revitalization of an emerging part of the city.

We will also take the same approach to the catering business that has worked so well for every other business we've tackled: we'll apply the strategy of enlightened hospitality while challenging ourselves to find a way to add something fresh to the experience of off-premises catering. And we'll always look for unique ways and places for Hudson Yards Catering to serve its food.

On a Monday afternoon in May 2005, I came home unusually early, around four-thirty, to don my tuxedo and get ready for the evening's event: the James Beard Foundation awards. Getting home that early was so unusual that my five-year-old son, Peyton, tore himself away from his play date and ran down the hall to bear witness: "Daddy's home before dinner!" We hung out while I struggled—as I always do—with my tuxedo.

"You look like Mr. Davison," he said, pointing to my bow tie. That's the headmaster at his school. "Are you going to school tonight?"

"No," I said, "I'm actually going to an awards event."

"What's an award?"

"That's a kind of prize you can get if people think you did something really well."

"Well, Daddy, are you going to get one of those tonight?"

"I don't know. They're giving out prizes for people who do a good job at being in the restaurant business."

"Well," he said, "I think you should get that prize. I think Shake Shack is the best restaurant in the world. I love their frozen custard."

That joyous moment with my son was the most meaningful thing that happened to me all night. The second most meaningful was winning the first-ever James Beard award for Outstanding Restaurateur, in a national field of impressive colleagues. I proudly accepted it on behalf of our entire organization.

It was clear to me that we weren't really winning for being the best at any one specific cuisine or concept. The reason had more to do with our stretching the contours and the applicability of our hospitality-driven business model, from Union Square to Gramercy Park to Madison Square Park to Twenty-seventh Street, and up Fifth Avenue to the Museum of Modern Art. We won it because, whether you order a Shack Burger and a frozen custard at Shake Shack, or a lamb tenderloin carpaccio with black truffles at The Modern, whether you're eating on paper plates or dining on Limoges china, there's plenty on the table we've set to nourish and nurture you. Our job—and our joy—is to create restaurants you'd want to return to, and to build businesses that ultimately contribute at least as much to their communities as they reap from them.

For over two decades we've worked hard to create a broad community of people who have a real stake in our restaurants' success. And because we have first committed our loyalty to them, they have paid us back abundantly. When people choose to become regulars at Union Square Cafe or Gramercy Tavern or Eleven Madison Park or Tabla or Blue Smoke or Jazz Standard or The Modern, or our museum cafés, or at Shake Shack, or Hudson Yards Catering, they're telling us, "*This* is the place that most makes me feel I've come home."

ACKNOWLEDGMENTS

I've CHOSEN TO ACKNOWLEDGE by name only those people who played a direct role in the publication of this book. Yet I am also acutely aware of how privileged I have been throughout my years to have known and learned from so many more remarkable family members, teachers, trainers, colleagues, mentors, and friends. It's hard for me to fathom how I could have flourished in restaurants, business, or life without the benefit of their vision and guidance, as well as their faithfulness in standing by me while holding my feet to the fire. As my unofficial team, their collective role has been essential in shaping what lies within these pages.

Restaurants are a fascinating laboratory for life. It is hard work to master one's emotions, day after day, in the pursuit of providing service, excellence, and hospitality for others. As human beings with human emotions, some days are easier than others. But it's often the tough days that supply the most lasting lessons. I am deeply indebted to the thousands of staff members—past and present—who have shared a period of their lives with our restaurants and guests while making a living in the hospitality business. Thanks to them, there was no shortage of rich material that came to mind as I wrote this book.

Together with those colleagues, I have been engaged in an animated dialogue for over two decades with an army of devoted guests who have rewarded our restaurants with their loyal patronage and unflinching feedback in exchange for being listened to and feeling heard. Sometimes our performance as a business has measured up to and even exceeded their expectations; in other cases it hasn't. But because we've always taken a genuine, active interest in those guests, they have always stuck by our side no matter how the chips have fallen. I'm convinced that a business cannot be more successful than the sum of the human relationships it has fostered and nurtured. By that measure, we are triumphant. It is in that spirit that I thank the thousands of guests who have not only patronized our restaurants over these many years, but who have become part of our restaurant family.

Specific thanks for this book begin with Susan Friedland, my cookbook editor, whose solid conviction that people might be interested in lasting recipes for business—not just food—convinced me this was a project worth undertaking in the first place.

I am appreciative to Susan Lescher and Bob Lescher, who from the outset advocated for this book with heartfelt optimism and support. I am grateful to Jim Jerome, who spent dozens of hours hurling challenging questions my way, recording, transcribing, and chiseling away at my exterior until I could reveal what I really wanted to say.

Thank you to my editor, Daniel Halpern, who urged me to write this book long before he became its editor, and who managed to overcome the familiarity that comes with our having been close friends for many years to guide me with objectivity and excellence. I'm proud of the work we've done together.

I am humbly grateful to editors Lisa Chase and Susan Gamer,

who each helped me to apply just the right grades of sandpaper when I most needed them.

I am deeply thankful to my colleague Jenny Dirksen, who knows me well, and who got me off the mark in the first place by keeping me on schedule and providing the kind of frank feedback that assured I would say what I meant, in my voice.

To Haley Carroll, who contended with gallons of black print and red ink through a multitude of drafts and revisions with precision, persistence, and above all, poise. I owe her a lifetime supply of reading glasses, not to mention my immense appreciation. If she reads the book again, Haley will see that her comments made this a far better book.

To my partners, chefs, general managers, managers, and staff: thank you for the gift of operating such excellent restaurants and allowing me the time and space I needed to write this book over many challenging months. I hope you'll find that I was accurate, fair, and able to capture the indispensable role you have each played in the success of our restaurants. Mostly I hope you will feel proud of the way I've told our story.

Particular gratitude is due to my partner, Paul Bolles-Beaven, who twice pored over the manuscript to assure its accuracy. Paul has worked at my side since the day Union Square Cafe opened in 1985, and if anyone understands the step-by-step history of how and why we've gotten from there to here, it is he.

And I don't know how to properly thank my friend David Black, who expressed his care for me by pushing, questioning, challenging, encouraging, and pushing some more, always urging me to write a better book. I'm glad I listened to every word he uttered.

Which brings me to my family. To my beautiful children, Hallie, Charles, Gretchen, and Peyton: thank you all for being so curious and patient throughout every rewrite of every draft. You probably thought I would never finish! I tried my best to write the book on my time—not on yours—but I am aware that there must have been many moments you had wished I was doing something with you rather than engaged in the next round of editing. And I will never forget the pride you expressed when you first learned your dad was writing a book. That alone further fueled my interest in giving it my best shot.

Finally, I am deeply grateful to my wife, Audrey, with whom I have been fortunate to share my life and love for over twenty years. Her profound influence on me is obvious, but suffice it to say that her greatest gift has been to show me the way to my genuine center and always strive to be my most authentic self. Audrey is at least half again more successful than I when it comes to the career that matters most to both of us: parenting. I admire her for doing so with an uncommon wisdom and grace from which I learn volumes every day.

About the Author

DANNY MEYER is the co-author with executive chef/partner Michael Romano of *The Union Square Cafe Cookbook* and *Second Helpings from Union Square Cafe*, and the founder and co-owner of eleven New York establishments: Union Square Cafe, Gramercy Tavern, Eleven Madison Park, Tabla, Blue Smoke, Jazz Standard, Shake Shack, The Modern, Cafe 2, Terrace 5, and Hudson Yards Catering. He lives in New York City with his wife, Audrey, and their children, Hallie, Charles, Gretchen, and Peyton.